I0605789

Caribbean Crisis

By the same author

The Colonel's Table
Reveille & Retribution (as Sustainer)
Spit & Polish (as Sustainer)
Friend & Foe (as Sustainer)
On Laffan's Plain
K-Boat Catastrophe
Chitrál Charlie
Valour in the Trenches
Strafer: Desert General
Where Tom Long Roamed
Betrayal of an Army: Mesopotamia 1914–1916
The Logistics of the Vietnam Wars, 1945–1975
The Siege that Changed the World: Paris, 1870–1871
In the Service of the Emperor: The Rise and Fall of the Japanese Empire 1931–1945
Hunger: Food Denial as a Military Weapon

Caribbean Crisis

The Invasion of Grenada, 1983

N.S. Nash

Pen & Sword
MILITARY

First published in Great Britain in 2025 by
Pen & Sword Military
An imprint of Pen & Sword Books Limited
Yorkshire – Philadelphia

ISBN 978 1 03610 408 5

A CIP catalogue record for this book is available from the British Library.

Typeset by Mac Style
Printed in the UK by CPI Group (UK) Ltd, Croydon, CR0 4YY.

The Publisher's authorised representative in the EU for product safety is Authorised Rep Compliance Ltd., Ground Floor, 71 Lower Baggot Street, Dublin D02 P593, Ireland.
www.arccompliance.com

For a complete list of Pen & Sword titles please contact

PEN & SWORD BOOKS LIMITED
47 Church Street, Barnsley, South Yorkshire, S70 2AS, England
E-mail: enquiries@pen-and-sword.co.uk
Website: www.pen-and-sword.co.uk
or
PEN AND SWORD BOOKS
1950 Lawrence Road, Havertown, PA 19083, USA
E-mail: uspen-and-sword@casematepublishers.com
Website: www.penandswordbooks.com

Contents

Maps

Illustrations

12. USS *Guam*, in which Vice Admiral Metcalf flew his flag during Operation URGENT FURY.
13. Major Mark Adkin, BDF, a witness to URGENT FURY.
14. Bernard Coard – instigator of the overthrow and murder of Bishop and seven others.
15. General Hudson Austin (1938–2022).
16. Major General Richard A. Scholtes, USA (1934–), Commander of US Special Forces in Grenada. (*US Army photograph*)
17. Vice Admiral Joseph R. Metcalf III (1927–2007), Commander of Joint Force 20 and Operation URGENT FURY. (*USN photograph*)
18. General H. Norman Schwarzkopf Jr. (1934–2012). (*US Army photograph*)
19. President Reagan, conferring with George Schultz and Robert McFarlane early on 22 October 1983. (*Ronald Reagan Library*)
20. UK Prime Minister Margaret Thatcher, LG, OM, DSt.J, PC, FRS, Hon FRSC (1925–2013) and Sir Geoffrey Howe, CH, PC, QC (1926–2015), Secretary of State for Foreign and Commonwealth Affairs.
21. Outside Bishop's house on the morning of 19 October 1983, with the crowd pushing past to rescue Bishop from house arrest. (Nation, *newspaper of Barbados*)
22. The airport at Pearls, 28 October 1983, with a USAF C-130 on the runway and two Marine CH-46 helicopters in front of the terminal. (*US National Archives*)
23. The incomplete airport at Point Salines, looking from west to east. (*US National Archives*)
24. Black Hawks of 160th Special Operations Aviation Regiment over Point Salines. (*US National Archives*)
25. Lord Palmerston (1784–1865).
26. Richmond Hill Prison. The scene of some of Bishop's ill-treatment of his political prisoners, and in 1983, an American objective. (*US National Archives*)
27. The Radio Free Grenada station and transmitter building. (*US National Archives*)

28a & 28b A Russian ZU-23 23mm AA gun, manned by a crew of five, and a Russian DShKM-4 12.7mm AA gun. (*US National Archives*)

29. Captain Keith Lucas (1957–83). Black Hawk pilot killed in action.
30. Major General Edward L. Trobaugh (1932–2024), Commander 82nd Airborne Division. (*US Army photograph*)
31. CW3 Bill Flannery's Black Hawk, carrying the wounded Major Boykin after it crashed onto USS *Guam*. (*US National Archives*)
32. The barracks housing the Cuban labour force, commandeered by Brigadier Lewis and the CPKF on 25 October. (*US National Archives*)

Preface

I can recall the shock, in October 1983, when the news broke that the USA had invaded a Commonwealth country. I was not alone in my bemusement. Nor was I alone in not having the remotest idea why the USA, allegedly the United Kingdom's firmest ally, had acted as it had.

The sequence of events that led to the invasion was complex and influenced by broader political issues unrelated to domestic Grenadian governance. The role of the Governor General then raised issues generated by the intervention that were, and are, central to the constitutional governance of the island state.

Any military action, anywhere, and at any time, is *always* initiated by the need to satisfy a political requirement. Soldiers do not start wars; it is politicians who do so. In this case, the political requirement was determined by President Ronald Reagan of the United States. This book considers his motivation for the invasion he ordered, and the consequences of his decision.

As a historian, I am now equipped with the facts, which are immutable. They are the material that provides an objective view of those events of more than forty years ago. I have drawn on the research of Mark Adkin and Hugh O'Shaughnessy, who wrote contemporary accounts, and of Philip Kukielski, the American historian, writing decades after the event. The latter uncovered the dishonest way Operation URGENT FURY had been presented to the public and he, among others, throws into doubt the very legality of the American incursion. Some of the most vociferous critics of this American incursion and its conduct are American. Not the least of these was Ronald Cole, to whom fell the task of writing the official history in 1997. General Norman Schwarzkopf and Admiral Joseph Metcalf were both participants and I have incorporated their views into my text among the views of many others.

I served as a British Exchange Officer with the US Army for two years (1975–7). Thereafter, I have been a self-appointed, unpaid, informal advocate of the USA. Although I have an affection for the country, that is secondary to my role as a historian, in which I have sought to be objective.

Over the passage of forty years, Operation URGENT FURY has been subject to detailed analysis. The consensus is that it was politically ill-judged and ineptly executed. The consequences were worldwide, and the American incursion was roundly condemned by the United Nations.

All of those named above directed me to myriad other sources, duly listed in the bibliography and from which I have drawn my own conclusions. Others may well view those same facts from a different perspective. Nevertheless, I have aimed to produce a book that is even-handed but, where necessary, judgemental – it is what historians do, and it is perhaps the reason you bought this opus.

In October 1983, Grenada was wallowing in chaos and criminality. Rational government had fled and someone, somewhere, had to do something. This book seeks to explain the plunge into chaos and to chronicle the remedial action taken by the United States. It then tracks the longer-term political and military effects in the USA and the wider world.

Acknowledgements

This is my tenth book for Pen & Sword. When I first started to tap out this text, I knew that the final product would be managed by the same excellent team in Barnsley. Matt Jones and his team have demonstrated before that they have the abundant skills to turn my modest work into an attractive, professional-looking product. I am, as always, grateful to them.

My text editor was, again, the formidable Linne Matthews. She nit-picks for England and her awesome eye for detail has, over many years, excised errors in my work. Linne does far more than challenge my placing of commas. She identifies replications, inconsistencies and weak judgements. She is both my sternest critic and greatest supporter. I am once again very grateful for her willing and highly professional contribution.

In this text, and where it is appropriate, the Americanised version of spelling is used.

I am running to the end of my writing career, and I acknowledge, with much gratitude, the consistent support of my publisher, who has backed my work over many years.

Any residual errors in this tome are entirely mine.

Tank Nash
April 2025
Tetbury, Gloucestershire

Abbreviations Used in the Text

AFB	Air Force Base (USA)
APC	Armoured Personnel Carrier
CARD	Campaign Against Racial Discrimination
CARICOM	Caribbean Community
CCC	Caribbean Council of Churches
CIA	Central Intelligence Agency (USA)
CINCLANT	Commander-in-Chief, Atlantic Command (USN)
CPKF	Caribbean Peacekeeping Force
CSIS	Center for Strategic and International Studies (USA)
DZ	Drop zone
EC$	Eastern Caribbean dollar
EEC	European Economic Community
GCMG	Knight Grand Cross of The Order of St Michael and St George (UK)
GCVO	Knight, Grand Cross of the Royal Victorian Order (UK)
GULP	Grenada United Labour Party
HMG	Her Majesty's Government
IMF	International Monetary Fund
JCPC	Judicial Committee of the Privy Council (UK)
JCS	Joint Chiefs of Staff (USA)
JEWEL	Joint Endeavour for Welfare, Education and Liberation
JSOC	Joint Special Operations Command (USA)
KGB	Russian Committee for State Security
LZ	Landing zone
MAC	Military Aircraft Command (USA)
MAP	Movement for the Assemblies of the People
MAU	US Marine Amphibious Unit
NJM	New Jewel Movement
NSDD	National Security Decision Directive (USA)
OAS	Organisation of American States
OBE	Officer of the Most Excellent Order of the British Empire (UK)

OECS	Organisation for Eastern Caribbean States
OREL	Organisation for Education and Liberation.
PRA	People's Revolutionary Army
PRAF	People's Revolutionary Armed Forces
PRG	People's Revolutionary Government
PRM	People's Revolutionary Militia
PTSD	Post-traumatic stress disorder
RMC	Revolutionary Military Council
SEAL	SeaAirLand USN
SI	Socialist International
SOAR	Special Operations Aviation Regiment (USA)
TOW	Tube-launched, optically tracked, wire-guided
UFO	Unidentified Flying Objects
USAF	United States Air Force
USCINCLANT	United States Atlantic Command
USN	United States Navy
WISC	West Indian Standing Conference

Where is Grenada?

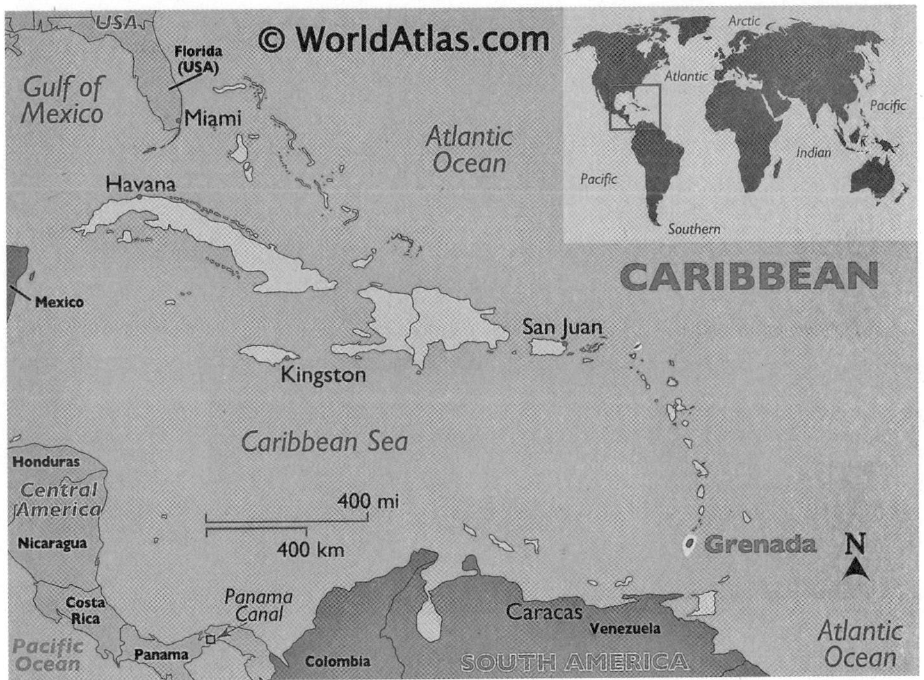

Chapter 1

An Inauspicious Prelude

During the night of 23/24 October 1983, two C-130 Hercules aircraft of the United States Air Force (USAF) were approaching the south-west coast of the small island of Grenada in the Caribbean. Their passengers were twelve US Navy (USN) members of the Sea-Air-Land Combat Team (SEALs) and four USAF personnel. These latter four were skilled in controlling air traffic, likely to be very heavy after the forthcoming invasion. All these men were highly trained Special Forces, and they were about to make a very hazardous parachute descent in the dark, from low level, into the sea. The plan was that these men should jump from 600 feet near the USS *Clifton Sprague*, a guided missile frigate of the USN.

Then, in two 23-foot Boston Whaler boats, they would make a covert landing in Grenada, where their mission was to install guidance beacons on the partially constructed airstrip at Point Salines. The beacons were to aid an airborne assault by the United States some thirty-six hours hence.

The plan was that the Whalers would be available by the frigate and the jumpers would be guided by lights to their floating havens. The two Whalers would be returned to the frigate once the SEALs had landed.

It was a simple plan. What could possibly go wrong? The weather was an issue. The wind was gusting at 25 knots and there was a heavy swell; had this been an exercise, it would have been cancelled. The jumpers were laden with the impedimenta of modern warfare. They carried weapons, ammunition, rations, a radio and medical equipment. They did, however, wear an uninflated life jacket.

A jump into water, and especially at night, poses the question, at which time the jumper should detach his parachute. Judging height in these circumstances is difficult. Release the 'chute too early and the jumper will plunge far deeper into the water than is healthy. Too late, and he risks being enveloped in the clinging silk.

The C-130 pilots sighted the frigate, but the parachutists were given the green 'go' light too soon by an inexperienced aircrew. As a result, the jumpers fell further away from their intended target than was desirable. The sailors in the Whalers struggled to find their anticipated passengers.

Four men were never found and the force had sustained 25 per cent casualties before the operation had even begun. This was an inauspicious start to Operation

URGENT FURY, in which further misfortune, accident, operational failure and inept leadership were all to be combined.

The two airports around which much of the action took place are in the extreme south-west at Point Salines (with aircraft symbol) and at Pearls, just north of Grenville on the east coast, but not shown on this map. The major armed encounters between US and Cuban/Grenadian forces were in the very small area south of a line running east to west and south of Constantine.

Chapter 2

The Place, its People, and its Politics

To put the invasion of Grenada, and the bizarre circumstances leading up to it, into perspective it is necessary to consider the history and constitution of this island paradise, which is the southernmost of a chain of tiny islands that run for 400 miles from the east of Puerto Rico to the coast of Venezuela.[1]

The island is roughly oval; it is 21 miles (34km) long and 12 miles (19km) wide. The population in 1983 was about 90,000 strong but now, in 2024, it is 115,600. Of these, 82 per cent are of African heritage, 13 per cent of mixed ethnicity, 2 per cent East Indian, and only 0.7 per cent are Caucasian.[2]

Grenada was discovered by Christopher Columbus on 15 August 1498. He sailed past the very small island and, although he did not stop, he nevertheless named it Concepción. Quite where the name Grenada came from is unclear.

In June 1609, the first attempt at settlement by Europeans was made by an English expedition of twenty-four colonisers who arrived in the ships *Diana*, *Penelope* and *Endeavour*. Their modest settlement was attacked and destroyed by the indigenous islanders and many of the settlers were tortured and killed. The few survivors were evacuated when the ships returned on 15 December that same year.[3]

The inhabitants of Grenada in 1609 were the Carib, an aggressive tribe who, having butchered the previous indigenous Arawak, had held sway in Grenada for 150 years. On 17 March 1649, a French expedition of 203 men from Martinique, led by Jacques Dyel du Parquet, landed at a point now known as St George's. Here they built a defendable settlement that they called Fort Annunciation.[4] Du Parquet had been the governor of Martinique, and he was acting on behalf of the Compagnie des îles de l'Amérique (Company of the Islands of America).

A treaty was swiftly agreed between du Parquet and the indigenous Chief Kairouane to peacefully partition the island between the two communities.[5] Du Parquet returned to Martinique, leaving his cousin, Jean Le Comte, as Governor of Grenada.[6] Conflict broke out between the French and the indigenous islanders in November 1649 and fighting lasted for five years until 1654, when the last opposition to the French on Grenada was crushed.

Grenada remained in French hands until 1762, when it was taken by the British, without violence, during the Seven Years War. It was formally ceded to Britain in 1763 by the Treaty of Paris. In 1767, a slave uprising was firmly put down, but there was a reprise in 1775. The island was recaptured by the French, but it was restored to Britain in 1783 by the Treaty of Versailles.

Grenada was not a happy place for much of its history. In 1795, there was a further outbreak of civil unrest and violence when Julien Fédon, a mixed-race estate owner, led a rebellion against the British colonial government. He was supported by representatives of the French Revolutionary government.

Fédon and his supporters enjoyed considerable success and, at one point, had established control over of most of Grenada. During the rebellion, about 14,000 of the 28,000 slaves in Grenada at the time were allied to the revolutionary forces; some 7,000 of them were killed in action. At the time of the rebellion, Grenada still had a significant Francophone population.[7] Many French people who had seen Grenada ceded to the British in 1763 joined as well, along with some French Catholics who had been excluded from civil and political rights because of their religion and wanted to oust the British. The French had limited rights, particularly those who were considered to be mixed-race.[8]

On 8 April 1796, a brother of Fédon was killed in an encounter with British soldiers. To avenge the death of his brother, Fédon ordered the summary execution of forty-eight of the fifty-three British prisoners he was holding in the mountains, including the Lieutenant Governor, Ninian Home. This murder removed any possibility of a negotiated settlement. Fédon mounted an attack on St George's, but it failed, and that defeat triggered the eventual collapse of the rebellion on the steep hills and ridges of Mount Qua Qua, which rises to 2,346 feet (715m). Fédon was never captured, and his fate is unknown. Slavery was abolished in 1833 and the Royal Navy took the lead in the suppression of the slave trade.

From 1885, Grenada was headquarters of the British Windward Islands Government, which lasted until 1958. Grenada then joined the ill-fated West Indies Federation, which expired in 1962. It attempted, unsuccessfully, to federate with the remaining territories in the Windward Islands, as well as with Barbados and the Leeward Islands.

The capital city is St George's, which is also the main port, and is located on the south-west coast. Grenada is a constitutional monarchy, and the head of state is now King Charles III, who is represented by a governor general. There are two legislative houses.

It has been termed the 'Spice Island' as it grows and exports nutmeg, mace and cloves. It is blessed with an agreeable climate, wonderful white, sandy beaches and sufficient rain to feed the lush vegetation that cloaks the high ground. The volcanic soil is well suited to the growing of all manner of fruit and vegetables including bananas, grapefruit, limes, lemons, tangerines, pumpkins, tomatoes and cassava. Almost any plant thrives in the rich soil, and the warm sun and constant rain make Grenada a gardener's dream. It is nutmeg, however, that is at the centre of Grenada's wealth. It provides about 33 per cent of the world's nutmeg.

From 1949, and for thirty years, the dominating personality in Grenada was Eric Gairy (later Sir Eric). He turned trades union membership into a political weapon and, in 1951, early in his political career, he engineered a general strike, which paralysed the island and produced severe civil unrest. Inebriated by his oratory, encouraged by his total disrespect for the white establishment and the Governor, and delighted by his womanising cockiness, the workers of Grenada fell for the handsome, dashing Gairy.[9]

Notwithstanding Gairy's popularity, Britain used military units to restore order. Gairy was arrested but not charged. He founded the Grenada United Labour Party (GULP).[10] His political career flourished, and he was elected as a representative of Grenada's Legislative Council in 1951, 1954 and 1957. His conduct was such that he was banned from political activities and lost his seat from 1957 to 1961. He then returned to public office and served as Chief Minister and Minister of Finance from August 1961 until April 1962. It was at this point that the colonial governor dismissed him for his questionable use of state funds. Gairy was merely corrupt at this stage of his life; later he morphed into a despot.

His dismissal did not hinder his career and, although out of office, he led the opposition party from 1962 until 1967. At this point, Gairy won the 1967 general election and formed a new administration as Premier of the Associated State of Grenada. On 3 March 1967, however, Grenada became a self-governing state, in association with the United Kingdom. Grenada remained a British colony until 1974, when it was granted independence and at which time it joined the Commonwealth, the United Nations and the West Indies Associated States.

Gairy was soon to face opposition from a bright young man called Maurice Bishop, who in 1963, at age 19, was offered a place at the University of London to study law. He duly graduated and was awarded the degree of Bachelor of Law at Gray's Inn in 1966.[11]

In this formative period of his political development, Bishop was influenced by the writings of Kwame Nkrumah, Frantz Fanon, Malcolm X, Fidel Castro and Che Guevara. The Black Power revolts in the USA in the late 1960s and the Black Power uprising in Trinidad and Tobago in 1970 created a lasting impression on the young lawyer and the New Jewel Movement (NJM) that he founded in March 1973.[12]

While studying Grenadian history, Bishop focused on anti-British speeches and drew on Julien Fédon, the head of the 1795 uprising. In 1964, he participated in the UK's West Indian Standing Conference (WISC) and the Campaign Against Racial Discrimination (CARD). He travelled from the UK to socialist Czechoslovakia and the German Democratic Republic. During this period, he studied the works of Marx, Lenin, Stalin and Mao Zedong. Bishop was particularly impressed by Julius Nyerere's *Ujamaa: Essays on Socialism* (published by Oxford University Press in 1968) and the Arusha Declaration of 1967.[13]

By 1967, Bishop was a convinced Marxist and had developed a two-year plan to implement his political philosophy in Grenada. The plan called for his temporary withdrawal from participation in political activities and his work as a lawyer, in order to co-create an organisation capable of taking power on the island.[14] His personal manifesto drew on his academic thesis, 'Constitutional Development of Grenada', which he completed in 1969.

Bishop returned to Grenada in 1970 to find the island in the dirty hands of Eric Gairy, which was a positive incentive to manage change. Bishop spread himself and his political views widely. For example, in 1972, he helped organise a conference in Martinique that discussed and strategised actions for liberation movements. The philosophy of Julius Nyerere and Tanzanian socialism were guiding elements for the Movement for Assemblies of the People (MAP), which Bishop helped organise after the elections of 1972.

Bishop and co-founders Kenrick Radix and Jacqueline Creft were committed to steering MAP towards the construction of popular institutions, centred in villages, to facilitate broader participation in the country's affairs. In January 1973, MAP merged with the Joint Endeavor for Welfare, Education and Liberation (JEWEL) to form the New Jewel Movement (NJM). Bishop shared the leadership as Joint Co-ordinating Secretary with Unison Whitman.[15]

On 18 November 1973, Bishop and other leaders of the NJM were driving in two cars from St George's to Grenville, where they were to meet with businessmen of the city. Security forces, under Assistant Chief Constable Innocent Belmar, overtook Bishop's motorcade. Nine people were arrested, and were beaten by the government. In prison, the prisoners shaved their beards, revealing Bishop's broken jaw. These events became known in Grenada as 'Bloody Sunday'.[16] It was a foretaste of the violence that was to scar Grenada for the next ten years – much of it initiated by Bishop and his acolytes.

By 1973, and the run-up to independence, Gairy's hold on Grenada was total and he had become a very rich man. He no longer needed to conceal his corruption and boasted that 'he who opposes me opposes God'.[17] He consolidated his hold on public life and set about collecting honours, awards and degrees.

Gairy controlled the domestic economy of the island by placing his men in every organisation. He employed a group of thugs called the 'Mongoose Gang' who murdered and tortured at will and without any form of restraint.

Gairy was, by any yardstick, a gangster. Patronage and nepotism became rampant. Nothing of significance could be done without his knowledge or personal approval. He acquired substantial business interests and property, including the Tropical Inn, Rock Gardens and Evening Palace hotels. In 1976, his government introduced a law requiring banks in Grenada to put 5 per cent of their deposits in the treasury.[18] He had access to this money.

Sir Eric Gairy faced a determined political opponent in Maurice Bishop, whose NJM was gaining traction. Gairy, predictably, responded violently. A special commission, chaired by Sir Herbert Duffus in 1973, produced a coruscating report. Duffus confirmed what was generally acknowledged. That is to say, allegations of police brutality were well founded, and that beatings and killings were unjustified and criminal. The Mongoose Gang was described as 'an unlawfully constituted body of men paid from public funds'[19] – legal words for 'a bunch of thugs'.

Following the Duffus report, there were demands for Gairy's resignation, but he ignored them, and a nationwide strike followed. This started on 1 January 1974 and continued for months. The Governor since 1968, Dame Hilda Bynoe, DBE, a medical doctor, viewed the chaos with dismay and, on 21 January 1974, 'convinced that she could not handle the political challenges that a deeply divided society presented, she resigned'.[20] Gairy appointed Major Leo de Gale to represent Queen Elizabeth II. He served briefly as Governor and then, on independence, as Governor General.[21]

The British Government was painfully aware of the breakdown of law and order in Grenada but was anxious to relinquish its governmental role. Notwithstanding a request to delay independence until stability had been achieved, Her Majesty's Government (HMG) kept to the previously agreed timetable. This, despite the prolonged strikes that had paralysed life in Grenada. The island went to independence, on 7 February, a day marked by an electricity blackout caused by striking power workers and by hunger strikes against Gairyism.[22]

Prince Richard of Gloucester had been nominated to oversee the independence formalities and the lowering of the Union flag. However, he was deemed to be at grave risk, and he was replaced by, the presumably expendable, Peter Blacker, a parliamentary undersecretary at the Foreign and Commonwealth Office. He did the job, lowered the flag, and survived to tell the tale.

A notable absentee at the 'celebrations', if they can be so described, was Maurice Bishop, who had been incarcerated by Gairy the day before and charged with attempted assassination. It was alleged that he was holding small arms and bombs in his house. Bishop was released on bail two days later. Independence should have been a happy day, the birth of a new country, with contentment and stability at its core.

It was not like that.

The gala dinner, to mark the occasion, arranged at the Holiday Inn at Grand Anse Beach, was a debacle. The hotel management fled the scene and left behind a handful of staff, with the pastry chef in charge. Although the dinner was not of major significance, it nevertheless epitomised the shambolic nature of Grenada's independence. The UK was well out of it and, no doubt in the Foreign and Commonwealth Office, sighs of relief were breathed.

Notes

1. Adkin, Major M., *Urgent Fury: The Battle for Grenada* (London, Leo Cooper, 1989), p. 1.
2. Britannica.com.
3. Steele, B.A., *Grenada: A History of its People* (London, Macmillan, 2003), pp. 35–6.
4. Ibid., p. 39.
5. Ibid.
6. Ibid., p. 40.
7. 'Excessive Severity: Treason and the Grenadian Rebellion of 1795' (The National Archives (UK), retrieved 4 August 2023).
8. Ibid.
9. O'Shaughnessy, H., *Grenada: Revolution, Invasion and Aftermath* (London, Sphere Books, 1984), p. 35.
10. 'Eric Gairy' (Biography), Caribbean Hall of Fame (caribbean.halloffame.tripod.com).
11. Wilder, A.E., 'Maurice Robert Bishop (1944–1983), The Grenada Revolution 2019' (The Grenada Revolution Online, retrieved 6 June 2017).
12. Ambursley, F. and James, W., 'Maurice Bishop and the New Jewel Revolution in Grenada' (*New Left Review*, Nov/Dec 1983).
13. Wilder.
14. Mendoza, Jorge L., 'Granada, La Nueva Joya del Carib', *Grenada: The New Jewel of the Caribbean* (Havana, Editorial de Ciencias Sociales, 1982), pp. 72–192.
15. Ibid.
16. Wilder.
17. Obituary of Sir Eric Gairy (Hugh O'Shaughnessy, *The Independent*, 1997).
18. Adkin, p. 5.
19. *Report of the Duffus Commission of Inquiry into Breakdown of Law and Order and Policy Brutality in Grenada* (London, FCO 63/1370).
20. O'Shaughnessy, p. 53.
21. It was a curiosity of British colonies with a similar status as Grenada that the Governor was a local individual, appointed by the Prime Minister but with the Queen's agreement. The Governor's role was to represent the monarch, advise the Prime Minister, but not to exercise any authoritative function. Clearly, Gairy had rejected advice given to him by Dame Hilda.
22. O'Shaughnessy, p. 54.

Chapter 3

Independence and Revolution

In 1974, across the globe, events in Grenada were being closely observed. Other Commonwealth nations were either incredulous or appalled. The United States of America – an entirely separate foreign country, their respective capitals 2,078 miles (3,344km) apart – had no domestic or political ties with Grenada. Nevertheless, perhaps not unreasonably, the USA considered how the new regime might affect it.

Since 1823, the USA had espoused the view that European powers had no right to extend their system or direct influence into the New World. This was the so-called 'Monroe Doctrine'. At the time, it was no more than a hollow statement that could not be implemented.

Theodore Roosevelt, elected President of the United States in 1901, was an adherent to the Monroe Doctrine and in 1904 had pronounced:

> Chronic wrongdoing, or an impotence which results in a general loosening of the ties of civilized society, may in America, as elsewhere, ultimately require intervention by some civilized nation, and in the Western Hemisphere the adherence of the United States to the Monroe Doctrine may force the United States, however reluctantly, in flagrant cases of such wrongdoing or impotence, to the exercise of an international police power.[1]

He went further the next year when he issued a clarification that was markedly more specific when he averred that, when European governments began to use force to pressure Latin American countries to repay their debts:

> the United States would not just prevent but *militarily intervene* [author's emphasis] in affairs between European and Latin American governments if European pressure resulted in the Latin countries becoming chronically unstable failed states.[2]

Over the long term, the doctrine had little to do with relations between the Western Hemisphere and Europe, but it did serve as justification for US interventions in Cuba, Nicaragua, Haiti and the Dominican Republic.[3]

The United States was elastic in the implementation of its foreign policy in the Caribbean. In 1903, 'Roosevelt had prepared for his country to take strategic control of the area. He encouraged separatists in the Colombian province of

Panama to set themselves up as an independent republic – instantly recognised by the USA.'[4] The Panama Canal was completed in 1914, by which time the Americans had taken control of a strip of land on either side of the waterway. The Panama Canal Zone was, in effect, an American colony.

William Taft followed Roosevelt into the White House and, in 1912, asserted humbly:

> The day is not far distant when three Stars and Stripes at three equidistant points will mark our territory: one at the North Pole another at the Panama Canal and a third at the South Pole. The whole hemisphere will be ours in fact as, by virtue of our superiority of race, it already is ours morally.[5]

That statement was absurd when it was made, and remains so today. However, the superiority of the USA and its citizens over all lesser beings is indoctrinated in every American from birth. As children, they swear fealty to the flag every day.

Little wonder that this feeling of superiority is a factor in the dealings of the USA with the rest of the world. It lays at the heart of an unremitting 'regime change' foreign policy, which is backed up by the USA's massive, unchallenged economic and military power and its self-awarded, solitary tenancy of the moral high ground.

The USA has a lengthy history of interfering in the affairs of other sovereign states. In the early twentieth century, it occupied Honduras (1913), Haiti (1915–34), Nicaragua (1912–33), Cuba (1892–1902 and 1906–9), Dominican Republic (1916–24) and Columbia (1902). It made incursions into Panama in 1908, 1912 and 1918.[6] At Annex B (page 201) is a list of American incursions initiated by the USA since 1811. This pattern of intervention into the governance of sovereign countries continues to this day.

It is germane to reflect that the horrors inflicted on the world by Germany and Japan in the Second World War were a direct result of their shared delusion of *racial* superiority. The USA is not even remotely that extreme but, nevertheless, it does share the delusion, believing that it is *nationally* superior.

In defence of the USA, it must be appreciated that the country does not answer to any higher authority and the pursuit of its political objectives is entirely a matter for the US government of the day. It pays lip service to the UN only when it is convenient. This freedom of action is shared with every other sovereign country in the world. However, very few have the military clout to exercise that freedom.

Taft's statement reflected the expansionist ambition of the USA. In 1917, the islands of St Thomas, St John and St Croix in the Virgin Islands were purchased from Denmark. It was a start that was further embellished during the Second World War when, in exchange for fifty obsolete First World War vintage destroyers, the USA was granted a ninety-nine-year lease in seven British territories in the Caribbean. These were Jamaica, Antigua, St Lucia, Trinidad and Tobago, the Bahamas, British Guiana (now Guyana) and Newfoundland.

At the time, Great Britain was fighting for survival. Franklin Roosevelt exploited the situation ruthlessly on behalf of his country. Who can blame him? There are no 'friends' in international politics.

The USA was unquestionably the power in the Western Hemisphere, and it exercised that power in 1954 when its CIA supported a right-wing dissident who overthrew President Jacobo Árbenz of Guatemala. Five years later, Fidel Castro took control of Cuba, and he became the bogeyman who haunted US foreign policy from 1959 until his death in 2016. Castro embraced Marxism-Leninism from 1959, and his philosophy appealed to the countries of what came to be called the Third World. Inadvertently, Castro played a major role in the events that were to follow on the Spice Island of Grenada.

In 1974, although Grenada was 2,078 miles (3,344km) away and, ostensibly, absolutely nothing to do with the USA, the island was nevertheless viewed as being 'of interest'. At that time, the military power of the USA was such that it believed it had a part to play in the governance of the Western Hemisphere and beyond. This measure of self-confidence was little inhibited by the unsuccessful campaign in Vietnam.

An increasing number of Grenadians were at odds with Gairy and his machinations. It was dangerous to voice a measure of discontent but, despite that, Bishop's NJM gathered strength and began to flourish. Curiously, Gairy's ill-judged and criminal conduct was not politically counterproductive. His knighthood, granted in 1977, was almost certainly initiated by his prompting the first Governor General, Sir Leo Victor de Gale, GCMG, CBE, to nominate him. Accordingly, the *London Gazette* of 20 September 1977 proclaimed:

> The QUEEN was pleased on Tuesday, 2nd August 1977, at Buckingham Palace, to confer the Honour of Knighthood upon the undermentioned:
>
> Sir George William BARLOW.
> Sir Satcam BOOLELL, GCSK, QC.
> **The Right Honourable Sir Eric Matthew GAIRY.**
> The Honourable Sir Clifford GRANT.
> The Honourable Sir Arthur Frederick GRIFFITH.
> Sir Charles Henri Raymond HEIN, QC.
> The Honourable Sir Ross HUTCHINSON, DFC.
> Professor Sir Christopher John DEWHURST.
> Sir William Atkinson DOWNWARD.
> Sir William Allan Patrick BRANCH.

Governor General de Gale stepped down in October 1978 and was replaced by Sir Paul Scoon, who was to be an important player in the island's history. Gairy's knighthood impressed no one and did nothing to curtail his *modus operandi*.

In December of that year, the UK sent treasury officials to the island to determine the issue of immediate financial aid. Unfortunately, by now Gairy had hitched his wagon to the Chilean Pinochet regime. This was anathema to Judith Hart, the Labour government's Minister for Overseas Development. No aid was forthcoming.

Gairy's credibility dropped lower when his passion for the study of unidentified flying objects (UFOs) became public knowledge. His planned absence in March 1979, when he left Grenada to attend a debate at the United Nations to discuss UFOs, was particularly ill-judged.

Gairy's trip to the USA had a hidden agenda. It was his intention that, while away from the island, his acolytes would arrest all the principal players in the NJM and, at a stroke, cripple his vociferous opponents. However, Gairy was beaten to the punch, because twenty-four NJM members, armed with a miscellany of antiquated firearms, bombs, swords, knives and cudgels, made a pre-emptive strike on the barracks of the Defence Force. They threw some petrol bombs, caused a fire and, having achieved complete surprise, overwhelmed the sleeping men. By so doing, they almost achieved the bloodless coup hoped for by Bishop. There was just one casualty. Lieutenant Brizan, who, having been advised by telephone that the barracks was on fire, made his way to the scene by car. He came upon a group of armed men who signalled him to stop, which he did. What or why is not known, but soon after, Brizan was shot dead.

Most Grenadians welcomed the coup. They saw it as the start of a new era – one without Gairy, without corruption and without brutality. What they could not know was that they were escaping from the frying pan only to jump into the fire.[7]

The armed overthrow of an elected government in a Commonwealth country was without precedent. The eighteen English-speaking Caribbean countries greeted the news with 'shock and wariness', although conditional support was forthcoming from the Caribbean Community (CARICOM), a regional trade organisation.[8]

A witness to the rise of Bishop was the US ambassador to the Eastern Caribbean, Frank V. Ortiz, a career diplomat. Ortiz, who was based in Barbados, was instructed to visit Grenada and report on the possible or probable manner in which the new regime would conduct itself. His first of two visits was on 9–10 April 1979, for which he was well briefed by his political masters.

Ortiz revealed that the USA proposed to gift aid amounting to US$1.34 million.[9] Although he assured Bishop that America would not support any countercoup mounted by Gairy, he nevertheless warned, 'The USA would view with displeasure any tendency on the part of Grenada to develop closer ties with Cuba.'[10]

Bishop and Coard were affronted by Ortiz's blunt approach and three days later, Bishop broadcast to the island and expressed his dismay that the wealthiest country in the world would be limiting its immediate aid to a 'paltry' $5,000. He chose to contrast that with offers of aid from other left-leaning countries like Guyana and Jamaica. In this broadcast, later christened his 'backyard speech', he asserted, 'No country has the right to tell us what to do to or how to run our country, or who to be friendly with. We are not in anybody's back yard, and we are definitely not for sale.'[11]

This unnecessarily bellicose speech played well with the domestic audience, who welcomed his robust style. The fact is that no independent country ever welcomes interference in its governance, but in the real world, any aid always comes with strings attached. Bishop's speech was markedly less well received in Washington.

The next day, Grenada and Cuba established diplomatic relations. This move had been on the cards even before Bishop took ill-feigned offence at Ortiz and his offer. Indeed, the day before the speech, a Cuban ship ostensibly delivering cement also carried crates of small arms and ammunition.

Since 1962 and the Missile Crisis, Cuba had been accurately perceived in the USA as a Russian acolyte. Cuba was hostile to the USA but not aggressively so. It was patently incapable of any sort of military action against the USA. But this was all about hearts and minds, and Castro knew that no amount of military power can defeat a strongly held ideology. This was a lesson that should have been evident from Vietnam.

Bishop worked hard at fostering a relationship with Fidel Castro and Grenada became the recipient of Cuban aid in multiple forms. Castro took on the role of mentor to an acquiescent Bishop. Fifty doctors, teachers and technical specialists were sent to aid in the social, economic and political development of the island. Forty-three military advisors were also sent to shape a major expansion of the Grenadian Army. But the largest Cuban investment in Grenada in terms of both money and personnel came in the construction of a new airport.[12] Soon thereafter, and on the assurance of a constitutional form of government, the UK and Canada recognised Bishop's Marxist regime. On 22 March 1979, the USA followed suit. Bishop was now well placed, having been accepted politically by three major powers.

However, this political honeymoon was short-lived because, on 25 March, Bishop made a speech in which he promulgated ten new People's Laws. The first of these laws expunged any vestige of the Westminster style of governance he had inherited. Grenada was to be ruled by proclamation, although there was a suggestion that there would be a return to constitutional government at some unspecified time in the future.

Sir Paul Scoon had no part to play in the day-to-day governance of Grenada. He could advise, but he served at the pleasure of the Prime Minister. He tried to establish a relationship with Bishop, and they played tennis together, although the Marxist-Leninist philosophy of Bishop was anathema to Scoon. Scoon's personal distinction was useful to Bishop and the revolutionaries, who 'regarded the Governor General as a useful figurehead who would smooth international recognition for their new regime and facilitate their relations with Canada and the United Kingdom'.[13] Scoon was originally a teacher, having taken an external degree at London University. He extended his academic education with an MEd at Leeds University. He then taught at the Boys' Secondary School back home in Grenada. Moving into the administration of education, he rose to be Chief Education Officer. He changed horses and became Secretary to the Grenada Cabinet and, in effect, the head of Grenada's civil service. He was appointed to be an officer of the Most Excellent Order of the British Empire (OBE) in 1970. He was later Deputy Director of the Commonwealth Foundation, based in London. Scoon was a distinguished man with a track record of public service – a sound basis for his appointment. He was an admirable choice as governor general and a key player in the events that were to follow.

Later, in November 1979 at a public meeting, Selwyn Strachan asserted, 'Last March 13th, the people of Grenada had their fairest election ever; that is, one man, one gun! Nobody can dispute the fairness of that!' He seemed not to understand that democracy and guns are not bedfellows.

Bishop having assumed the position of prime minister, the once idealistic law student dedicated to democracy, self-determination and the rule of law was replaced by an egocentric, pathologically unbalanced tyrant. Bishop would have been advised to hold a general election to provide himself with a legally sound mandate. There is no doubt that had he done so, he would have won a massive victory at the polls for the People's Revolutionary Government (PRG). Bishop's position was inviolate and the People's Revolutionary Army (PRA) provided the necessary muscle. Meanwhile, Gairy moved to the United States, did not return to Grenada until late in 1983, and he had not been missed.

Bishop introduced a system called 'heavy manners'. Under this umbrella his subordinates inflicted the most loathsome and bestial torture on supposed opponents. 'Heavy manners' were conducted in the prison, Fort Roberts, in PRA barracks or in a police cell. Bishop appointed 23-year-old Ian St Bernard as Commissioner of Police. This young man had had no form of police training, but he was willing to use his office in unswerving support of Bishop. St Bernard insisted on being called 'comrade' and threatened those who forgot that they would 'go up the hill'. This was a euphemism for confinement and probable torture in police custody.

Bishop intended to take and hold absolute power over Grenada and its people. To this end, he 'followed Marxist-Leninist principles mirroring the Soviet system exactly, in both the PRG and the PRA'.[14] Bishop's government pursued hard-line socialist policies and, having aligned itself with Cuba and the Soviet Union, this led to concerns in Western nations, particularly the United States. Relations between Grenada and the US deteriorated, as the US worried that the island could become a communist stronghold in the Caribbean, and with Cuban support, provide Russia with a beachhead in the theatre.

Bishop shrewdly recognised that it was necessary to present an attractive front to the world and so he included in the original ruling council of the PRG several businessmen, capitalists and entrepreneurs. He was quoted as saying, 'This was done deliberately so that imperialism won't get too excited and would say "well they got some nice fellas in that thing: everything all right" and as a result they wouldn't think of sending in troops.'[15]

In practice, power in Grenada was vested in a very small group, two of whom were his close associates Bernard and Phyllis Coard. Others were General Hudson Austin, Lieutenant Colonels Joseph Ewart Layne and Liam James, Majors Chris Stroude and Leon Cornwall, Selwyn Strachan and John Ventour.[16] Membership of the PRG was closely controlled, and in May 1983, there were only eighty full members. There were many others seeking to satisfy the demanding criteria. These included ideological study, supervised political work, payment of 5 per cent of gross salary to party funds, and understanding, accepting and implementing the principles and programmes of the party. Finally, one had to accept party discipline, including in one's private life.

Under Bishop's uncompromising rule, Grenada was administered by three organisations. These were: the Central Committee, fifteen to seventeen strong; the Politburo, of seven to eight members; and the Cabinet, of about twenty, who represented the various ministries. Bishop chaired all of these, and some people, such as Hudson Austin, had membership of all three. There was not much time left for productive work after the endless committee meetings. There was, inevitably, a host of lower-level organisations and, in combination, Grenada was grotesquely overmanaged.

Bishop made a 'Line of March' speech in which he laid out his stall. He said:

> the state sector must be built to be the dominant sector … We must assume total control over all financial institutions over a period of time … We must assume total control over all foreign trade, and also some aspects of internal

> trade ... We must assume total control of all public utilities – electricity, water, transport.[17]

It is evident from this that it was the notion of 'total control' that drove Bishop, and, by inference, he would do whatever it took to achieve that aim. The tools for this control were to be the People's Revolutionary Militia (PRM). This quasi-military organisation was supplemented by the National Women's Organisation and the National Youth Organisation, and, in order to embrace the entire population, there was also a children's outfit, entitled the Young Pioneers, for those between 5 and 14.

Later, on 13 September, Bishop pronounced, in a secret session with PRG members: 'You get detained when I sign an order ... Once I sign it, like it or not, it's up the hill for them.'[18]

Two years after Grenadian independence, Bernard Coard returned home to the island and allied himself with Bishop. Coard had earlier moved to the United States to study economics and sociology at Brandeis University in Massachusetts. In 1967, he moved to England and studied political economy at Sussex University. It was during this period in the UK that Coard joined the Communist Party. He became a teacher, taught for two years, completed a doctorate and, in 1971, wrote and had published a book entitled *How the West Indian Child is Made Educationally Subnormal in the British School System*. His next move was to Trinidad, where he took a post at the University of the West Indies. Coard had a sound academic track record and was clearly the intellectual superior of most of the NJM hierarchy. On his return, he swiftly established himself as the ideological guru and he brought a deal of 'rigour to the political debate in Grenada'.[19]

Coard was a very capable, erudite individual, steeped in ideology, but he did not have the 'people skills' of Bishop, who was, without question, a charismatic personality. The contrast between these two men was marked and one Grenadian remarked, 'Maurice charmed people, Bernard convinced them.'[20]

Ere long, their differences would come to a head.

Coard set up a study group of about eighteen younger members of NJM; it was called the Organisation for Education and Liberation (OREL). They debated Leninist texts and, as a group, they developed a sense of ideological and personal commitment.

Coard had not been in Grenada during all the worst excess of Gairy and so did not share the depth of Bishop's experience. Nevertheless, as a committed Marxist-Leninist, revolution was in his blood and the unseating of Gairy in 1979 suited his book. Coard and his ideology were central to the increasingly overbearing PRG. The promotion or appointment to any senior government position was subject to rigorous political scrutiny and membership of the party was a prerequisite. In the People's Revolutionary Army, all officers were required to be from a working-class background – a doubtful criterion that probably excluded many other capable candidates.

The PRG recognised that it had to have some legalised system to back its endeavours but judged that the legal system, operated under colonial rules, albeit highly efficient, was no longer appropriate. On that basis, the well-established laws of the land were rescinded and public affairs were to be subject to proclamation.

> A series of people's laws were drawn up, all signed by Bishop. People's Law No. 2 established the PRG. People's Law No. 10 (Declaration and Effect of Laws) gave the Prime Minister his all-embracing power; and People's Law No. 46, the Terrorism (Prevention) Law, was the proclamation under which 'heavy manners' were imposed. Under this law terrorism was defined as 'the use of threat or violence for political ends', which in effect was saying that the PRG themselves were terrorists. The PRA or police could arrest a suspect without a warrant and he or she could then be detained (no bail was allowed) without trial more or less indefinitely.[21]

The indoctrination of the population was a constant aim of Bishop's government and he imported, from Cuba, experts in this dark art. They brought a degree of sophistication to the production of placards, and they fine-tuned the political slogans that were then displayed across the island on notice boards or as graffiti sprayed onto convenient walls. Grenadians were faced by the words of revolution at every turn.

The Marxist-Leninist paradise that Bishop had created worked well, initially, and Coard proved to be a capable finance minister. A senior international banker who had dealings with him at this time recalled him to be affable and approachable. Coard was, intellectually and operationally, head and shoulders above his colleagues from other islands in the Eastern Caribbean. Whereas some of the more conservative governments in the region baulked at making the economic and political sacrifices demanded by the International Monetary Fund in exchange for its aid, Coard was always willing to meet the IMF more than halfway. He also knew the way to get money quickly and efficiently out of the international lending agencies. Whilst some of the other finance ministers would rant and rave about the bureaucracy of the lending banks, Coard saved his energies to understand the system and make it work for Grenada.[22]

Initially, Coard's control of the island's finances was effective, but the economic malaise was deeply rooted, and endless political debate could not promote a healthy economy. The financial outlook in Grenada was unpromising. A surplus of US$500,000 in 1975 had turned into a deficit of US$5.3 million by 1978. Soon after Coard took economic control, he obtained financial support, to some degree, from Algeria, Syria, Iraq, Libya, Venezuela and Jamaica. However, he was burdened by his Marxist-Leninist philosophy. Having taken into public ownership many of the income-producing agencies on the island, he found that the capitalist facts of life were at odds with Marx and all his acolytes.

Notes

1. O'Shaughnessy, H., *Grenada: Revolution, Invasion and Aftermath* (London, Sphere Books, 1984), p. 57.
2. 'Our Documents – Theodore Roosevelt's Corollary to the Monroe Doctrine (1905)' (ourdocuments.gov, retrieved 9 April 2021).
3. US State Department, Office of the Historian (history.state.gov).
4. O'Shaughnessy, p. 57.
5. Ibid.
6. Paine, S.C.M., *The Wars for Asia 1911–1949* (New York, Cambridge University Press, 2012), p. 24.
7. Adkin, Major M., *Urgent Fury: The Battle for Grenada* (London, Leo Cooper, 1989), p. 7.
8. Kukielski, P., *The US Invasion of Grenada: Legacy of a Flawed Victory* (Jefferson, North Carolina, McFarland & Co., 2019), p. 162.
9. Ortiz, F.V., 'Grenada Before and After' (*Atlantic Monthly*, June 1984), p. 9.
10. Payne, A., Sutton, P.K. and Thorndike, T., *Grenada Revolution and Invasion* (New York, St Martin's Press, 1984), p. 49.
11. 'In nobody's back yard' (Bishop speaks, 13 April 1979).
12. Kukielski, p. 164.
13. Ibid., p. 163.
14. Adkin, p. 12.
15. Ibid., p. 13.
16. 'Hudson Austin, Biography' (www.thegrenadarevolutiononline.com, retrieved 9 May 2021).

    Austin was an early member of the military wing of the party and received military training in Guyana, and Trinidad and Tobago, along with eleven other Grenadians, sometimes referred to as 'the twelve apostles'. Austin was unique in this group as he also received training in the Soviet Union. Despite all this training, he hardly merited the rank of general.
17. 'Line of March' speech, 13 September 1982.
18. Ibid.
19. O'Shaughnessy, p. 71.
20. Ibid., p. 82.
21. Adkin, pp. 16–17.
22. O'Shaughnessy, pp. 86–7.

Chapter 4

The View from Washington

While the governance of Grenada moved inexorably to disintegration, the rest of the world looked on with a mixture of dismay, incredulity, concern, or a combination of all three. Nowhere was this more evident than in Washington, DC.

In the early 1980s, the USA was affected by what has been called 'the Vietnam syndrome'. This refers to a term used to describe the psychological and political impact of the Vietnam War on the people of the United States. It originated in the aftermath of the war and gained prominence during the 1970s and 1980s. It implies a sense of caution, reluctance or aversion by the American public and policymakers towards engaging in military interventions abroad and a desire to avoid any conflicts that might mirror the debacle in Southeast Asia that cost 58,220 American lives. A further estimated 70,000 veterans later committed suicide. Vietnamese losses in all three wars (1945–75) involving both North and South Vietnam, are counted in millions. The factors resulting from the Vietnam War that had combined to breed this aversion in the USA to military action were, in brief:

- it was highly unsuccessful, had been costly and had fuelled anti-war sentiment
- it had given rise to war crimes and atrocities that had shocked the American public
- there had been no clear political or military objectives
- the extensive media coverage had been graphic, which further raised anti-war sentiment
- the impact on those men who served in Vietnam, many of whom returned suffering from post-traumatic stress disorder (PTSD). They then faced a negative reception from the public – a further contribution to a broader disillusionment with the war.

However, in American political circles, attitudes over Cuba verged on paranoia, and the involvement of Cubans in the building of a new airport at Point Salines fuelled that paranoia for several years. Caribbean islands, like Grenada, are in large measure dependent, economically, upon tourism. Tourism requires tourists, tourists must travel, and air is the favoured international means of doing so. On arrival at a resort, there must be ample hotel accommodation. The airport at Point Salines was a first step in exploiting the emerging tourist market.

There was another small and inadequate airfield at Pearls, on the east coast of the island, which was British built during the Second World War. Events had overtaken Pearls, it was not well maintained and by the late 1950s, it could only service the needs of the small inter-island Leeward Islands Air Transport company. The airstrip was an uncomfortable forty-five-minute journey from the capital, St George's. Nevertheless, and despite its multiple limitations, in due course, this facility would become a major military objective.

A team of international consultants recommended the building of new facilities at Point Salines. The commercial benefits of a new airport were evident to Gairy, and later to Bishop and Coard. They all, in turn, endorsed the project and then addressed its funding.

It was only then that Cuba joined the party.

The estimated cost of the new airport was US$45 million, but on the completion of a 9,000ft long (2.743km) and 150ft wide (45.7m) runway, Grenada would be able to accept traffic from London, Washington, New York and Toronto, flying in DC-9s, and Boeing 747s and 727s. The commercial advantages of exporting Grenadian farm products via Point Salines was evident.

There was international involvement in the Point Salines project. An American company, Layne Dredging, built the runway and filled the tidal salt ponds that were an inconvenient feature of the area. METEX, a Finnish company, was contracted to install all the exterior lighting, and Plessey, a British company, was engaged to fit all the navigation and communication systems.[1]

In 1983, Representative Ron Dellums, a Democrat from California, journeyed to Grenada on a fact-finding tour, having been invited by Bishop. Later, he gave his findings to colleagues in the House:

> Based on my personal observations, discussion, and analysis of the new international airport under construction in Grenada, it is my conclusion that this project is specifically now and has always been for the purpose of economic development and is not for military use. ... It is my thought that it is absurd, patronizing, and totally unwarranted for the United States government to charge that this airport poses a military threat to the United States' national security.[2]

His view ran counter to that of President Reagan and his acolytes, and his wisdom was ignored. Meanwhile, Castro was supporting Grenada with cash and with labour. He had sent 500 labourers to work on the airport project and, like all Cubans, they had been given cursory military training, but they were not soldiers. They were not, in any way, a threat to the USA.

* * *

Washington was aware that there were hundreds of its citizens studying on the Spice Island. This was a legacy of Gairy, who, in 1976, had countenanced the establishment of a medical college that operated under the guidance of Charles R. Modica. He was an educational chancer who saw the commercial advantages in offering to baby boomers, unable to find a place at an American university, the chance to study for a medical degree. Entry levels were undemanding because this was a strictly 'for profit' arrangement. Gairy was alive to the benefits to himself, whilst committing his government to the Modica project. Modica persuaded American investors to put up $10 million and swiftly thereafter, Grenada granted Modica and his investors a 'sole and exclusive' charter to create a medical school, with access to the state hospital for teaching purposes.[3]

Gairy moved quickly to ensure the success of the medical school. Modica was granted a ten-year lease on a building and 6 acres of land at True Blue – all for $21,500 per annum. The financial machinations need not delay us here. Suffice it to say, when the first classes assembled in January 1977, there were 6 part-time professors and 152 students. The students were paying only about 30 per cent of the tuition fees charged in the USA. This was a major recruitment incentive, and by the spring of 1979, the faculty was 23 strong and the student body was around 600.

The Vice Chancellor of the medical school was Geoffrey H. Bourne, PhD, ScD, an Australian with a glittering career, who added lustre to the school. He had a personal relationship with Bishop and, after the coup that ousted Gairy, he was assured that the status of the school was secure.[4] Bishop's speech in the spring of 1982 was proof enough of that, although Bishop perceived the school perhaps to have CIA connections. The school, mindful of the rocky nature of Bishop's government, kept several options open. One of these was its campus on St Vincent. It also made approaches to other Caribbean islands, any one of which would have served as a bolthole in a crisis.

A factor in Grenadian life was the USA/Cuba/Grenada relationships. Bishop constantly berated the USA in a succession of belligerent speeches and made very public his belief that the CIA was operating in Grenada. There is no evidence that the CIA was active in Grenada – perhaps if it had been, the conduct of the later invasion, named Operation URGENT FURY, would have been less flawed.

Despite Bishop's rhetoric, the three national groups living on the island worked together amicably and effectively. The American medical students were taught by Cuban and Grenadian doctors. They played basketball against the Cuban labourers and international politics did not intrude. A measure of the harmonious domestic atmosphere was on display when, in early 1982, Bishop was invited to address the graduating class of students. Bishop avowed that, since its founding, the school had brought benefits to Grenada. He finished his speech by proclaiming: 'Long live the St George's Medical School.' Little wonder that there was a standing ovation. It was, of course, what Bishop did best.[5]

* * *

Bishop's political ambitions and his alignment with Cuba and Russia had the inevitable effect of cooling relations with the USA, which, by 1982, were best described as 'frosty', not least because formal political relations had been established with Russia in September 1979. Grenada went out on a limb in support of Russia when it opposed the UN resolution calling on a Russian withdrawal from Afghanistan on 15 January 1980. Reagan took office in February 1981; he attributed to Cuba and Grenada disproportionate attention, and he rattled his metaphorical national sabre.

Back in August 1981, the USA had conducted a vast exercise called Operation OCEAN VENTURE, the cost of which was that of a small war. All Caribbean nations were invited to participate to give the spurious impression that there was a unity of political and military purpose in the Caribbean theatre. The forces involved were 250 ships, 1,000 aircraft and 120,000 personnel, all overwhelmingly American. The exercise included the invasion of a mythical country named 'Amber and the Amberdines that bore an unmistakable similarity to Grenada and the Grenadine islands. US Marines staged an amphibious landing on the island of Vieques, off Puerto Rico; there was also a hostage rescue scenario, and an airdrop by 350 Rangers.'[6]

Predictably, the thinly veiled exercise narrative did not fool Bishop and he responded by issuing a statement describing the exercise as 'a practice run for a direct invasion of Grenada by US troops'. He was, of course, correct.

In 1982, Britain had stunned the military world when it mounted an operation to evict Argentinian invaders from the Falkland Islands. The USA had pressed Britain to negotiate some form of shared sovereignty with the invaders, but Mrs Thatcher would have none of it, and the subsequent campaign in and around the Falklands was conducted in an exemplary fashion. This was by no means a military walk in the park. Five British ships were lost, and 255 men killed, with 777 injured, but the British force achieved its aim, expelled the surviving Argentinians, and sent a strong message to potential enemies. The Argentinians lost 2 ships and 649 military personnel.

The USA provided some intelligence but played no physical part in the liberation of the Falklands. In early 1983, politically the USA needed an easy victory, somewhere, anywhere, to restore public pride in its Armed Forces. The British had demonstrated what could be achieved by resolute political direction, a sound command structure and well-trained servicemen and women.

In mid-1982, the victorious British fleet had steamed home, and Grenadian attention was on the increasingly fractious atmosphere at the head of its government. There was a faction in Bishop's party that wished to replace him. The arguments were all ideological and although Coard was the instigator, he kept a low profile and encouraged others to mount criticism of Bishop and his leadership.

* * *

Bishop entertained grandiose plans for the armed forces of Grenada (People's Revolutionary Armed Forces, PRAF). He had courted the Cubans, but his hope was that Soviet Russia would produce the hardware. Bishop anticipated the formation and equipping of 4 regular infantry battalions armed with about 60 armoured personnel carriers (APC), over 100 ZU-23 anti-aircraft guns, 50 rocket launchers, 160 military vehicles, 7 aircraft and 6 patrol vessels. He anticipated that the Russians would provide all the ancillary facilities required to service this armed force. He was sure it would be the Americans he would have to fight one day. However, his plans came to naught.

* * *

The debacle of Operation EAGLE CLAW in April 1980 (the failed attempt to free Americans held hostage in Iran) had an adverse effect on public opinion in the USA. It proved to be a factor in Carter's defeat by Reagan, who took office in 1981, and, on Reagan's election, the Cold War got very much colder.

In 1983, the possibility of a terminal conflict between East and West was exacerbated by a 'potentially lethal combination of Reaganite rhetoric and Soviet paranoia'.[7] President Reagan's assertion that he would 'leave Marxism-Leninism on the ash heap of history' lowered the temperature even more.[8] In the face of Reagan's well-publicised aggression, it was little wonder that the Russians feared a pre-emptive nuclear strike (see Chapter 22).

On 1 September 1983, a Soviet fighter plane shot down a Korean Airline's Boeing 747, killing all 269 passengers and crew. Relations between East and West plummeted to a new low. The Soviet position was that the airliner was a spy plane, an outrageous provocation and a legitimate target. Reagan was swift to condemn 'the Korean airline massacre as an act of barbarism … and inhuman brutality'. Later, a senior US public servant commented that Reagan wallowed 'in the joy of total self-righteousness'.[9] All this conjecture was despite it being clear that the incident was the unfortunate combination of the actions of two incompetent pilots. The airliner had strayed over Soviet territory and the Russian pilot had acted peremptorily.

Reagan's paranoia over Russia was matched by similar sentiments over Cuba. This Communist-led island nation was a minor player on the international stage, but loosely allied to the Russian camp. A modest Cuban presence in Grenada was accorded disproportionate importance. On his election, Reagan was determined 'to stem and ideally reverse Soviet-supported Communist expansion throughout the world – and especially in the Caribbean, which had been regarded as an American lake since the days of President Monroe. For Reagan, Cuba was a *bête noire* and Grenada was its surrogate.'[10]

* * *

During the turbulent days of September and October 1983, when self-criticism was the flavour of the month, Austin recognised that the PRAF was in bad order. He claimed that his duties overseeing the construction of the new airport at Point Salines had diverted him from his prime responsibilities.

Austin's protest was ignored, and he came under attack from officers ostensibly under his command. The most vocal were Layne, Cornwall, James and Chris de Riggs, the Minister of Health, who suggested that Austin be replaced as the commander of the PRAF. It was Lieutenant Colonel Liam James who put the ball in play, when he declared: 'We all agree that the Army is in a state of rut and demoralisation. Along with a serious ideological drift. The Army needs at this time Leninist leadership in that of Comrade Layne [Lieutenant Colonel Joseph Ewart Layne] and the political and academic work of Comrade Cornwall [Major Leon Cornwall].'[11]

To the reader with a military background this destructive criticism of the commander speaks volumes of the quality of Austin's leadership and the apparent lack of fundamental discipline. George Lewison commented later:

> James [Lieutenant Colonel Liam James] and Layne wielded the real power in the army. Austin never held that extent of power. Layne was the politburo person in the army. James was in charge of the Interior, police, and intelligence. They wanted to wield military power rather than wanting to build an army of the highest professional standards. Their militarism was a militarism bent on political power.

In the event, Austin survived and retained his position but there had to be concessions, and Layne and Cornwall's duties were adjusted so that they could focus on political issues as they affected the army.

There was no quick fix available to resolve the military deficiencies in Grenada. Morale was very low, and this was a result of a combination of deeply rooted problems. Pay was very poor; US$ 100 was the monthly pay for a private soldier – insufficient for much in the way of 'beer and skittles', and a source of much discontent. In addition, the soldiers had to cope with seriously substandard accommodation in which the plumbing, electrical and water supplies were only available intermittently. Inadequate food was available, but in insufficient quantity and of abject quality. Training was repetitive, and uninteresting. It is little wonder that recruitment could not fill the ranks as the parlous state of the army was widely understood. Soldiers were voting with their feet and did not extend their contracts. Some merely deserted.

In the militia, the situation was just as dire, perhaps worse. A mobilisation exercise in the spring of 1983 had been mounted to prepare for an anticipated American invasion. There was a marked lack of enthusiasm from the membership and that was reflected in the low turnout. The leadership of the PRM was weak and unskilled. It was evident that the PRM was not going to present any challenge to a well-trained, well-armed and very fit invading force – from anywhere.

The centralisation of militia weaponry worked against any plans for rapid deployment, exacerbated by a dearth of troop-carrying vehicles. The Cuban instructors had a difficult job on their hands. An example was when a ZU-23 AA gun was used to practise on a target some 200 yards (183m) away. This was close-range shooting but, having fired twenty-five rounds, the target was unscathed. This performance was symptomatic of a wider malaise and did not bode well for the future.

Volunteer soldiers need particularly capable officers. Regardless of nationality, volunteers have to be encouraged, cajoled and stimulated. An order to a volunteer is best delivered with a smile and sometimes an explanation. The weaknesses in both regular and militia units were of long standing and, as far back as April 1982, a meeting had been held in Havana to consider the issue. General Arnaldo Ochoa, a minister of the Revolutionary Armed Forces, met with a group of Grenadians. The party included Austin, James, Layne, Einstein Louison, Coard and Strachan.

It was agreed that Cuban construction workers would be armed, more Cuban officers were to be sent to train militia units, and state-of-the-art radio links between Grenada and Cuba were to be established. Mark Adkin, who was a professional soldier and involved in Grenadian affairs, judged that:

> The conference concluded with General Ochoa's highlighting what he felt were the Grenadian military weaknesses. In his view, the Americans would

> eventually invade; therefore, some financial cutbacks in other areas might be necessary to boost defence. He did not consider, rightly, the unwieldly BTR-60 APC suitable for the island's terrain. The PRA was unstable, lacked training and was not ready for combat. Command lacked continuity, with personnel being shifted too often. The PRA's structure and composition were wrong and Grenadian defence plans did not reflect a proper combat organisation or take account of the difficult, mountainous terrain. Ochoa ended with a recommendation that had the support of everyone: more political indoctrination for the soldiers.[12]

Clearly, the PRAF only presented a threat to the people it served. It was not a viable adversary to any external force – least of all the massively powerful United States. Eighteen months after General Ochoa's coruscating review, the PRAF had made little or no significant improvements.

The strength of Grenadian armed forces in 1983 was 1,300 troops of varying quality and commitment, 8 APCs, 2 armoured cars and 12 AA guns, no aircraft and no navy.[13] However, the Pentagon planners estimated that the 'island might be defended by a force close to 4,500 composed of 1,500 regular Grenadian soldiers, 2,000 Grenadian reservists, and 1,000 Cuban advisors and construction workers'.[14]

Bolger comments that the PRA also had 'seven 130mm towed artillery pieces'.[15] This mélange did not constitute a threat to world peace. In addition, and employed in Grenada, working on the airport, there were 636 Cuban labourers. These men all had had cursory military training, and they were equipped with small arms – one wonders why. There were 148 other Cubans in Grenada filling diplomatic, advisory or commercial appointments.

In October 1983, the United States would confront the Grenadian/Cuban forces, listed above, with 7,300 troops, 4 tanks, a helicopter carrier (USS *Guam*), an amphibious assault ship (USS *Saipan*), an aircraft carrier (USS *Independence*), 3 destroyers, 2 frigates, 1 ammunition ship and 27 Tomcat F-14A fighter aircraft. Also present in a non-combatant role would be 353 individuals from the Caribbean Peacekeeping Force (CPKF).[16]

This might perhaps be described as 'overkill'?

However, as Napoleon said, 'Nothing succeeds in war except in consequence of a well-prepared plan' – and the planning of URGENT FURY was not well prepared.

Notes

1. Schoenhals, K.P. and Melanson, R.A., *Revolution, and Intervention in Grenada: The New Jewel Movement, the United States and the Caribbean* (New York, Routledge, 1986), p. 56.
2. Collier, P. and Horowitz, D., 'Another "Low Dishonest Decade" on the Left' (*Commentary*, January 1987).
3. Leventhal, M.A., 'Entrepreneurship and Nation Building: Proprietary Medical Schools and Development in the Caribbean 1976–1990' (doctoral dissertation, University of Chicago, 1995), pp. 74–6.
4. Bourne, G.H., 'Revolution, Intervention & Nutrition: What happened in Grenada' (*Nutrition Today*, Jan–Feb 1985), p. 18.
5. Leventhal, p. 119.
6. 'Atlantic Exercise involves 214 Countries' (*All Hands*, March 1982), p. 172. This quote is from Kukielski, p. 167. The alleged participation of 214 countries in 1981 is challenged. In 2023, there are only 195 in the whole world. Nevertheless, the exercise did take place and similar exercises were conducted in 1982 and 1983.
7. Macintyre, B., *The Spy and the Traitor* (London, Penguin Books, 2018), p. 179.
8. Reagan, President R.W., speech to the House of Commons, 8 June 1983.
9. Catto, H.E., US Assistant Secretary of Defense (*Los Angeles Times*, 11 November 1990).
10. Kukielski, P., *The US Invasion of Grenada: Legacy of a Flawed Victory* (Jefferson, North Carolina, McFarland & Co., 2019), p. 167.
11. Adkin, Major M., *Urgent Fury: The Battle for Grenada* (London, Leo Cooper, 1989), p. 153.
12. Ibid., p. 157.
13. Cole, R.H., *Operation Urgent Fury: The Planning and Execution of Joint Operations in Grenada 1983* (Joint History Office, Office of the Chairman of the Joint Chiefs of Staff, 1997).
14. Ibid.
15. Bolger, D.P., 'Operation Urgent Fury and its Critics' (*Military Review*, July 1986).
16. Ibid.

Chapter 5

The Violent Coup

The relationship between Bishop and Coard had been based upon their shared Marxist-Leninist ideology. However, Coard was dissatisfied with the manner that the NJM, under Bishop, conducted its affairs. He was unhappy to be the focus of all intellectual and theoretical problems faced by the party, although, in large measure, this was a product of his intellectual grip on political ideology. He was overworked and was conscious that other 'members of the Central Committee shirked their responsibilities'.[1] Nevertheless, Coard was only too aware of the key role he played in Grenadian affairs.

Coard recognised that an opportunity existed for him to supplant Bishop if he moved covertly. Meanwhile, Bishop, unaware of Coard's ambitions, was intent on cultivating international relations, and, to some extent, he had been successful. Bishop was sufficiently pragmatic that he spread his brand of bonhomie widely. He had participated in the aims of the London-based Socialist International. (SI). In July 1981, he organised and hosted a meeting of the committee of the SI in St George's. The SI promoted democratic socialism; not that Bishop would have recognised democracy if he saw it. Nevertheless, membership gave access to a wider world. This is evidenced by the European Economic Community (EEC) giving Grenada aid to the tune of EC$ 8.2 million in the period 1979–82. Ties with both the SI and EEC, although directed by Bishop, were co-ordinated by Unison Whiteman, the Minister for External Relations, and a member of the Central Committee of the NJM.

On 27 July 1982, the NJM and the Communist Party of the Soviet Union signed a formal agreement between themselves. That same month, Coard commenced his campaign by resigning his membership of the Political Bureau, the Central Committee, and the Organising Committee. He retained his role as deputy premier and his responsibility for planning and finance. Coard was betting that his resignations would leave a void that was difficult to fill, and that ere long, his comrades would clamour for his return.

On 12 October 1982, about ten weeks after Coard's carefully staged resignation, the Central Committee of the NJM met to debate the issue and to review the state of the party and the performance of its higher organs. The delay was perhaps because the NJM had continued to function, after a fashion, despite Coard's absence from some of its activities.

Coard did not attend but he sent Selwyn Strachan to represent him at the four-day meeting of the seventeen most senior party members. Strachan explained that Coard had resigned for a combination of reasons. He listed overwork, the reduction of his (Coard's) authority as chairman of the Organising Committee, and his concern about the slackness of the Central Committee, which he judged to be inefficient. Finally, he expressed Coard's view that what was needed was 'the introduction of Leninist measures, including a change in the chairmanship of the central Committee, chopping of dead wood, putting all members to actually do some work on outside committees and the expansion of the Politburo'.[2]

During this interminable talking shop, the focus switched from Coard to Bishop and his closest supporters. In characteristic Marxist style, the meeting degenerated into 'an orgy of self-criticism'. The multiple failings of Grenadian governance were attributed to Bishop. General Austin declared that more 'heavy manners' were required. That is to say, more non-judicial killings and torture. This was some way from the Westminster style of government bequeathed to Grenada on independence. The remark by Austin was indicative of his intellectual gifts.

Bishop was on the back foot; he accepted the criticism and made excuses. His supporters were taken to task, and in an apparently arbitrary manner, four were demoted, not least Unison Whiteman. The soul-searching reached the point when all those present were required to grade their own performance on a 1–5 scale. The criteria for this self-evaluation were to be based on 'discipline, ideological level, work performance, relations with the masses, character, analysing ability, dues, and functioning ability'.[3]

This bizarre exercise concluded when Coard agreed to hold an eight-week crash course in Marxism-Leninism for those whose grasp of hard-left philosophy was lacking. During this period, Bishop seemed to be blithely unaware of his vulnerability. Coard had skilfully directed attention to strictly political aims and had concealed his personal ambition – in which he was strongly supported by his wife. The process by which Coard sought to take control of Grenada was convoluted and lengthy, and it had an impact beyond the shores of the island – not least in the USA.

The thoughts and words of all US presidents are enshrined after they leave office. President Reagan, by his own well-documented account, accorded Grenada disproportionate attention and he clearly had wildly misinterpreted the need for the new airport at Point Salines. In the spring of 1983, the Cold War was at its most frigid and Reagan exacerbated international tension when, on 8 March, he declared the Soviet Union to be an 'evil empire', one that is godless and indifferent to morality that springs from religion.[4] He viewed Grenada as being part of a Soviet plan, with Cuban help, to establish a military base from which the USA could be threatened. Later that week, on 10 March, while speaking to a group of manufactures, he rejected criticism of his posture on Grenada, saying:

> People who make these arguments haven't taken a good look at a map lately or followed the extraordinary build-up of Soviet and Cuban military power in the region or read the Soviet's discussion about why the region is important to them and how they intend to use it. … It isn't nutmeg that is at stake in the Caribbean and Central America. It is the United States' national security.[5]

From these remarks, it is evident that Reagan would favour any chance to effect change in the governance of the Spice Island if it presented itself. On 23 March 1983, Reagan returned to the topic of the Soviet threat and made his 'Star Wars' speech, during which he made further reference to the military potential of the Point Salines Airport.

The President's view of this construction was coloured by the advice he was given by his advisors. They insisted that the new airport would enable MiG-23s to operate from Grenada and would extend the operating range of these Cuban fighter-bombers right across the Caribbean. The new facility would be almost 1,600 miles closer than Havana to Angola. The runway at Point Salines could facilitate both eastbound flights supporting the nearly 50,000 Cubans in Africa, and flights from Libya and the Soviet bloc to Central America.[6]

Bishop responded by broadcasting to his people and he asserted, without evidence, that there was a CIA plot to invade Grenada. Bishop was nevertheless correct to forecast an American invasion. Reagan continued to gnaw on the Grenadian bone and, on 27 April, 'appealed to federal lawmakers to support his foreign aid programs that would hold the line against externally supported aggression in the Caribbean basin'.[7]

Reagan's constant and ill-found remarks on the Point Salines project were so egregious that participants rebutted his criticism, albeit in the case of Plessey, the electrical contractor, not until after the invasion. However, then Plessey pointed out that the new airport lacked eleven of the critical characteristics of a military installation. It made mention, among others, of radar, hardened aircraft shelters, underground fuel, weapons and ammunition storage – all 'must haves' in a military air base.

The fact was that, in the spring and summer of 1983, American cruise ships docked in St George's and excursions from the ships visited the airport site – there was little else of interest on the island. Students from the medical school were observed using the uncompleted runway as a racetrack.

Vice President Bush, speaking at a conference on the Caribbean in Miami on 5 December 1982, had pronounced that Grenada was a dependency of Cuba and the Soviet Union. Bishop immediately refuted the assertion and took a positive approach to the matter. He approached the USA with a proposal that he send a 'high-level emissary' to debate the issue directly with the Vice President. In the event, that emissary would be Bishop himself.

The negotiations eventually led to an eleven-day visit, which would culminate, on 7 June 1983, with a meeting at the State Department in Washington with William Clark, at that time National Security Advisor, and Kenneth Dam, Assistant Secretary of State.

Clark and Dam made it clear to Bishop that, much as they were prepared to talk, they required a change in Grenadian conduct – especially in respect of its relations with Cuba and the Soviet Union. A moderation in the language used by Bishop in his observations on the USA was a 'must have'. The Americans conceded that there was room for the normalisation of relations.

Dam later reported to Reagan that Bishop had given assurances that Grenada 'would not be a security threat to the US or any other government in the hemisphere'. He concluded that the meeting had achieved its aim and that in future, Bishop's sincerity would be judged by the actions he took.[8]

The meeting had several consequences. Predictably, the Soviet Union was discommoded not to have been part of the loop; the Grenadian ambassador in Moscow was the recipient of their ire. The modest diplomatic success of the trip to Washington had reflected well on Bishop domestically, and that, in turn, placed pressure on Coard.

> The discord in the Central Committee was unabated and it festered. The parlous state of the country fed discontent. Public services functioned intermittently, roads went unrepaired, the part trained, amateur militia was not fit for purpose, national morale, generally, was low, and the few productive individuals were exhausted. The Revolution was on the verge of collapse.[9]

On 14 September, the Central Committee met for three days, during which Bishop found himself, once again, under sustained attack. The main antagonists were Lieutenant Colonels Liam James and Joseph Ewart Layne. Phyllis Coard, who was head of the National Women's Organisation and sat in the Central Committee, was a significant player and enthusiastically threw fuel on the flames.

At some stage in the proceedings, it was suggested that the party and government should be headed by a shared leadership of Bishop and Coard. A vote was taken, and the suggestion approved by a vote of 9:1. Bishop and two others abstained. However, Coard was not present and ostensibly, he would have to be consulted. Bishop asked for time to consider the proposal, having no doubt as to the probable result.

A full party meeting was convened on 25 September but only 50 of a total membership of 300 attended. Bishop could see that he had few options, and so he seized the chance to endorse 'shared leadership'. It all became very fraternal, the attendees sang 'The Internationale'. Bishop and Coard embraced, and bogus sweetness and light prevailed – for the moment. However, it was clear that Coard was the victor.

By dint of his chairmanship of the Politburo, Coard had control over party and government. Bishop retained his title of prime minister but, in effect, he was little more than a figurehead. He was painfully aware that he had been sidelined. Soon after the meeting, Bishop and two of his supporters, Whiteman and Louison, left on a trip to Eastern Europe. They paid an unscheduled, thirty-six-hour visit to Cuba on the way home. Bishop took this as the chance to build on his relationship with Castro – his political mentor.

It had been a mistake to leave the scene; it gave Coard the opportunity to consolidate his grip on power. That was amply demonstrated when Bishop's party returned to Pearls Airport. They were met only by Strachan, who had dressed down for their arrival.

This was a studied insult.

Bishop resolved to reopen the shared leadership issue at the first opportunity. That arose four days later when there was a meeting in Fort Rupert. The eight attendees included Bishop and Coard. This group was the executive of the NJM. However, during Bishop's absence, Coard had altered the structure of the committee by adding to it the fifteen-strong Central Committee.[10] By doing this, Coard had further reduced Bishop's grip on the levers of power.

Notes

1. O'Shaughnessy, H., *Grenada: Revolution, Invasion and Aftermath* (London, Sphere Books, 1984), p. 109.
2. Adkin, Major M., *Urgent Fury: The Battle for Grenada* (London, Leo Cooper, 1989), p. 29.
3. Ibid., p. 30.
4. Reagan, R.W., *The Public Papers of President Ronald W. Reagan* (Reagan Presidential Library), quoted by Kukielski, pp. 168–9.
5. Reagan, R.W., remarks on Central America and El Salvador at the Annual Meeting of the National Association of Manufacturers, 23 March 1983.
6. Cole, R.H., *Operation Urgent Fury: The Planning and Execution of Joint Operations in Grenada 1983* (Joint History Office, Office of the Chairman of the Joint Chiefs of Staff, 1997), p. 9.
7. Reagan, R.W., address to a Joint Session of the Congress on Central America.
8. Confidential memorandum from Dam to Reagan. 'Meeting with Prime Minister Maurice Bishop of Grenada', 7 June 1983 (Department of State, declassified and accessed by Kukielski, 16 July 2018).
9. Seabury, P. and McDougall, W.A., 'Extraordinary General Meeting, 25 September 1983' (San Francisco, Institute for Contemporary Studies. The Grenada Papers), pp. 300–15.
10. Louison, G., *George Louison and Kenrick Radix discuss: Internal events Leading to the U.S. Invasion of Grenada* (New York, Grenada Foundation, 1984), p. 28.

Chapter 6

Confrontation and Killing

The tension between Bishop and Coard was acute. Bishop recognised that violence was a possibility and he started to fear for his life. He told his two bodyguards that he thought that Coard and his wife were planning his death.[1]

Bishop confided in Vincent Noel that he had heard talk of an 'Afghanistan solution' where the moderate prime minister had been assassinated in a coup. Further to that, Noel later said that he had heard 'Chalky' Ventour remark that 'there would be a solution like Afghanistan if the Chief fucked around on the question of joint leadership'.[2] On the evidence, it is clear that for some, violence was perceived as being a viable solution to resolve political issues.

In the early hours of 12 October, Major Keith Roberts, the head of the security service, met with Bishop's bodyguards and told them that Bishop was exhibiting dictatorial traits and that their first loyalty was to the Central Committee.[3]

Several hours before the meeting was planned to start, party members assembled and agreed that they were united behind Coard. They prepared a written statement confirming their solidarity and concluded by averring that 'the People's Revolutionary Armed Forces Branch of the NJM awaits the decision and orders of the Central Committee'.

At this meeting, to be chaired by Coard, it was Bishop's intention to raise the shared leadership issue, and the way it could be efficiently employed.[4] However, Coard and his supporters considered shared leadership to be 'a done deal' and were not prepared to debate the matter. The meeting did not go well for Bishop as his opponents, well briefed and of like mind, provided implacable opposition. One of Bishop's principal supporters drew fire and, after a vote, George Louison was summarily dismissed from both the Central Committee and the Politburo.[5]

It was circulated that Bishop had started a rumour that the Coards were planning to murder him. The rumour had some traction and there was unrest at St Paul's by members of the militia. This minor show of support for Bishop was rapidly suppressed and the Army Command disarmed the St Paul's and the St David's militia.

Bishop denied emphatically that he had started the rumour, but he was not believed, and the meeting collapsed into sufficient chaos that the Chairman (now John Ventour) drew a gun to enforce a degree of discipline.[6] Bishop was obliged to broadcast a rebuttal of the rumour and, despite the reality, advised listeners that the party was united. After a long and stressing day, he was badly shaken, and only returned to his home at midnight.

The next morning, the Central Committee met yet again, this time at Coard's house. Bishop was not present when his former colleagues decided that he should be arrested and confined to his home. A Lieutenant Callistus Bernard, who was serving on the island of Carriacou, was ordered to return to Grenada, where he was to be responsible for the incarceration of Bishop. He relished the job and made it clear to his men that Bishop was to have no visitors except with his, Bernard's, express permission.

On the afternoon of 13 October, Bishop, closely guarded, was taken to Butler House to attend yet another party meeting. Bishop looked 'exhausted and ill'.[7] Vincent Noel tried to get Bishop some medical attention but was put under house arrest for his trouble. Noel thought that Bishop was possibly suicidal.

The party meeting was a huge event and about 250 had come together to witness the fall of Bishop. Noel observed that it was a 'horrendous display of militarism, hatred and emotional vilification'. Ventour chaired the meeting, at which, thirty-one people spoke. Coard said nothing and left others to speak for him. Bishop arrived at the meeting and was greeted with an ovation. He defended himself, speaking for forty-five minutes. He agreed that he had rejected the joint leadership directive but emphatically denied spreading rumours about the intentions of the Coards. At that point he was totally undone when one of his security guards contradicted him and, moreover, said he had been a participant in spreading the rumour.

The mood of the meeting underwent a radical change. Some of Bishop's supporters wept, but others were hostile and sought his immediate expulsion from the party he had formed. He was formally expelled the next day and, in protest, Kenrick Radix, the Justice Minister, resigned and started to campaign for Bishop's release from arrest. The Cuban ambassador heard the news and asked to be briefed on the situation. The people of Grenada were shocked by the turn of events but were unaware of the detail and responded by mounting relatively small, pro-Bishop demonstrations of several hundred supporters.

Coad realised that his average citizens would not appreciate the governmental chaos. He acknowledged the unpalatable fact that, as yet, he did not have a majority support among Grenadians. The public's response to Strachan, when he opted to visit the offices of the *Free West Indian* newspaper, illustrated that lack of support. Strachan was made most unwelcome and obliged to flee the building. Coard moved quickly to counter the demonstrations and announced that he had resigned as Deputy Prime Minister. In these circumstances there was a political gap and Hudson Austin abandoned his hitherto support for Bishop, and, on Thursday, 13 October, realigned himself with the majority of the Central Committee. Austin had a positive and well-established reputation as the builder of the PRA and as a key player in the overthrow of Gairy.

Three days later, on Sunday, 16 October, Austin broadcasted to the nation. In his speech, he made it clear that Bishop was the cause of the current political instability. He lambasted Bishop but did not get round to admitting that the (still) Prime Minister was under house arrest. The consensus was that Coard had written the speech, which ended with an appeal 'to maintain unity in order to ensure that imperialism does not take advantage of this moment of difficulty'.[8]

The imprisonment of Bishop was not a secret, and it was fuelling his support. Notwithstanding, the majority of the Central Committee had made it clear that, if need be, it would use force to impose its will.

* * *

In Washington, as early as 14 October, the Joint Chiefs of Staff (JCS) had been working with Admiral Wesley L. McDonald, the Commander-in-Chief of Atlantic Command (CINCLANT) on plans to invade Grenada. All that was needed was a presidential order, but President Reagan needed a *casus belli* before he issued that order. A *casus belli* is defined as 'an act or situation that justifies or allegedly justifies a reason for going to war'.[9] Libraries around the world are replete with philosophical texts on the topic of *casus belli* and the 'just war' they provoke. Reagan realised that any action he took would draw detailed post-operation analysis. He promulgated his view that the protection of American medical students, resident in Grenada, was to be his *casus belli*.

The reality was that the students were not at risk, and it might be argued that Reagan was motivated to remove a Marxist-Leninist regime and to eradicate Cuban influence in Grenada. Although this was highly desirable from Reagan's point of view, nevertheless, it would not be a plausible *casus belli*.

While Grenada wallowed in chaos, on 17 October, 1,700 men of the 22nd Marine Amphibious Unit (MAU) moved from Camp Lejeune in North Carolina and boarded five ships of the United States Navy (USN). The reinforced battalion was supported by a squadron of helicopters, a platoon of tanks and a battery of artillery. This balanced force was well equipped to meet any eventuality it was likely to encounter. Soon after, it headed east towards the Mediterranean and Lebanon, where it would replace the 24th MAU, currently undertaking 'peacekeeping duties' centred on Beirut. (President Reagan had previously deployed Marines to Lebanon in August 1982 in an attempt to counter the blood being spilt in a civil war that had escalated and drawn in Israel and Syria.)

The flagship of this force was the USS *Guam*. She was, in effect, an aircraft carrier for helicopters, of which she bore twenty-two transport and attack aircraft.

The Marines and their equipment were accommodated on four transport ships, namely, USS *Barnstable County*, *Fort Snelling*, *Manitowoc* and *Trenton*.

* * *

The idea of a rescue mission to release Bishop was first mooted on 15 October in the US Embassy in Bridgetown, Barbados. The proposal was picked up by the Chief of Staff of the Barbados Defence Force and, on 16 October, he sent for Major Mark Adkin, a British contract officer, employed as a staff officer responsible for 'operations and training'. Adkin was tasked to construct an outline plan to rescue Bishop from house arrest. His brief was to determine the size of force required and how it would be transported. He was not to consider the provision of that transport, but both officers realised that any airlift would be furnished by the USA.

Adkin obtained one of the scarce maps of Grenada and promptly consulted two officers with detailed knowledge of the island. One of these was Lieutenant Commander Peter Tomlin, who knew Bishop well and had been the captain of a Barbados Coast Guard vessel that had carried a CIA operator and a Canadian representative into St George's following Bishop's coup in 1979. Tomlin's information was supplemented by that of Major Mike Hartland, a former British regular officer now serving in the Barbados Defence Force. Hartland had lived and worked in Grenada in the period 1968–79, when he was the manager of Point Salines estate.[10]

The draft plan was based on a surprise *coup de main* operation and presumed a hostile scenario. In outline, the initial helicopter-borne assault would take place under the cover of darkness. The key targets were the houses of Bishop and the Governor General, the two airfields at Pearl and Point Salines, and the radio station. First estimates were that two battalions would be sufficient, with a third deployed once beachheads were secured. It is noteworthy that it was not intended to attack any PRA installations, but rather the PRA was to be confined by the establishment of strategic blocking positions. This would put the initiative for aggressive action firmly in the court of the PRA and possibly the Cubans.

Adkin submitted his plan to Colonel Rudyard Lewis, the Chief of Staff. He endorsed the plan and took it to the Prime Minister, Tom Adams. Subsequently, the plan was debated with Adams's cabinet. However, and although Adkin's plan went no further, the Barbados Government took particular interest in events in Grenada.

* * *

On Sunday, 16 October, Fitzroy Bain, President of the Agricultural Workers' Union, applied himself to organising a demonstration against the incarceration of Bishop. Bain was successful, and the demonstrations were duly staged but with little practical effect. The Cuban Ambassador, one Torres Rizo, offered to mediate in the matter, but Coard rejected the offer, very well aware of Bishop's relationship with Castro and all things Cuban.

By Tuesday, 18 October, it was clear to the Central Committee that it had failed to win Grenadian hearts and minds. Moreover, the tide of public opinion was running against it. There was yet another lengthy meeting attended by Coard and his closest supporters. Austin, Layne, Cornwall, McBarnette, James Strachan, St Bernard, Ventour, and later, Buxo, were all present and, in a feverish atmosphere, a six-point proposal was drafted that sought a compromise of sorts with Bishop. While this proposal was being drafted, Whiteman was whipping up the crowds to endorse Bishop and enjoyed considerable success with his efforts.

On Wednesday, 19 October, Bishop, heartened by the manifestation of public backing and indeed affection, roundly rejected the humiliating proposals. Later that same day, a crowd estimated at between 2,000 and 3,000 gathered in Grenville and displayed its advocacy for Bishop. Placards were in evidence, proclaiming 'We want democracy' and 'C for Coard. C for Communism'. Many shouts of 'We want Maurice' were heard. The demonstration was peaceful and relatively good-humoured. Whiteman built on that when he broadcast on Radio Antilles, located on Montserrat. His broadcast struck a very responsive chord with many young people, who abandoned school, turned out in force and began to drift from Market Square to Mount Royal, the residence of the Prime Minister and Governor General Sir Paul Scoon. For Coard, the situation was desperate; he feared for his future at the hands of the masses, who clearly detested him but held Bishop in affection.

The crowd presumed that the PRA would not fire on schoolchildren, and it did not. Instead, Major Leon Cornwall, past member of OREL and now ambassador in Havana, confronted the crowd and sought to defuse the rising tension. He misread the situation and struck a wrong note when he shouted, 'Maurice Bishop has betrayed the masses.'[11] He drew a hostile response, and in the face of catcalls, he retreated.

The crowd drew closer to Bishop's house and shots were fired over their heads, which caused panic in some and greater resolution in others. A young man called Thompson Cadore, who had been a leader of the crowd, now pushed forward and with others made his way to Bishop's house, where he found the Prime Minister tied to a bed. Jacqueline Creft, Bishop's long-term mistress and mother of his son, was tied to another bed.

Bishop showed signs of acute mental stress and had lost his usual commanding presence. 'Fear of being poisoned had prevented him from eating; incessant smoking, lack of sleep and the endless mental turmoil had sapped him physically.'[12] Creft was exhausted but in better condition. The pair were ushered, part carried, through the mass of cheering humanity to vehicles that would bear them to the centre of St George's. Bishop vacillated over which vehicle to take. He was curiously indecisive and eventually selected one of the cars. On their brief journey, Creft's mother, Lynne, ran to the roadside to greet her passing daughter. They exchanged a few words before Creft and Bishop were moved on.

Lynne would never see her daughter again.

Bishop's priority was to find a place that offered physical security and the thick walls of Fort Rupert fitted the bill. This was named in honour of his father, who had been killed while opposing Gairy, some nine years previously. When Bishop and Creft arrived at the fort, the small PRA garrison was at a loss, not knowing where their duty lay. However, the size of the crowd, its fervour, and the fact that some were armed, were, in combination, sufficient motivation for the soldiers to stand aside and allow Bishop and his party entry.

Fort Rupert was the headquarters of the PRA. It was about 350ft (106m) above sea level and had commanding views. About sixty soldiers were employed in the fort, largely on administrative duties. The Chief of Staff, Major Einstein Louison, had his office there, as did Major Christopher Stroude, who was, in effect, the political commissar of the PRA. He was the senior officer in Fort Rupert, and he could see that there was no point in opening fire on the masses demonstrating outside. He ordered his soldiers to hand in their weapons and change out of uniform.

Bishop and his closest aides had to establish some priorities. They determined that the PRA garrison should be disarmed and that weapons should be redistributed to Bishop's supporters. A second priority was the need to communicate with the Grenadian people and the wider world – not least the Cubans. Finally, Coard and his henchmen must surrender and accept the judicial process that would follow.

Stroude was told to hand over his revolver and explain the situation to all the other officers. One of these was Captain Redhead, who had previously been detailed to collect tear gas from Grand Anse police station, about 2 miles (3km) away, but having dashed there, he found no tear gas. He then did stock up with tear gas at the police headquarters on Melville Street. On his return, he found Bishop already in place.

The operations room of the PRA was on the first floor, and it was here that the Central Committee had met to debate Bishop's fate. Now the room was full of excited and jubilant supporters. The anticipation was that Bishop would address the crowd, but he did not. He instructed Peter Thomas, an immigration official, to take a party and collect the weapons held in the immigration department. Quite why an immigration department needed firearms has never been explained. Thomas did as he was bidden and within fifteen minutes, he returned with automatic rifles and light machine guns.

Coard and the Central Committee's manoeuvring had not worked, and they concluded that the only remaining option was violence. In the meantime, they moved to Fort Frederick, located on a ridge about 1½ miles (2km) from Coard's residence. Fort Frederick was the base of 'a motorised company and with two of its three platoons mounted in six Soviet, BTR-60 Armoured Personnel Carriers'.[13]

The soldiers were called on parade and Lieutenant Colonel Joseph Ewart Layne addressed them. He said that there was considerable civil unrest and that a mob was seeking to turn back the revolution. Officer Cadet Myers warned

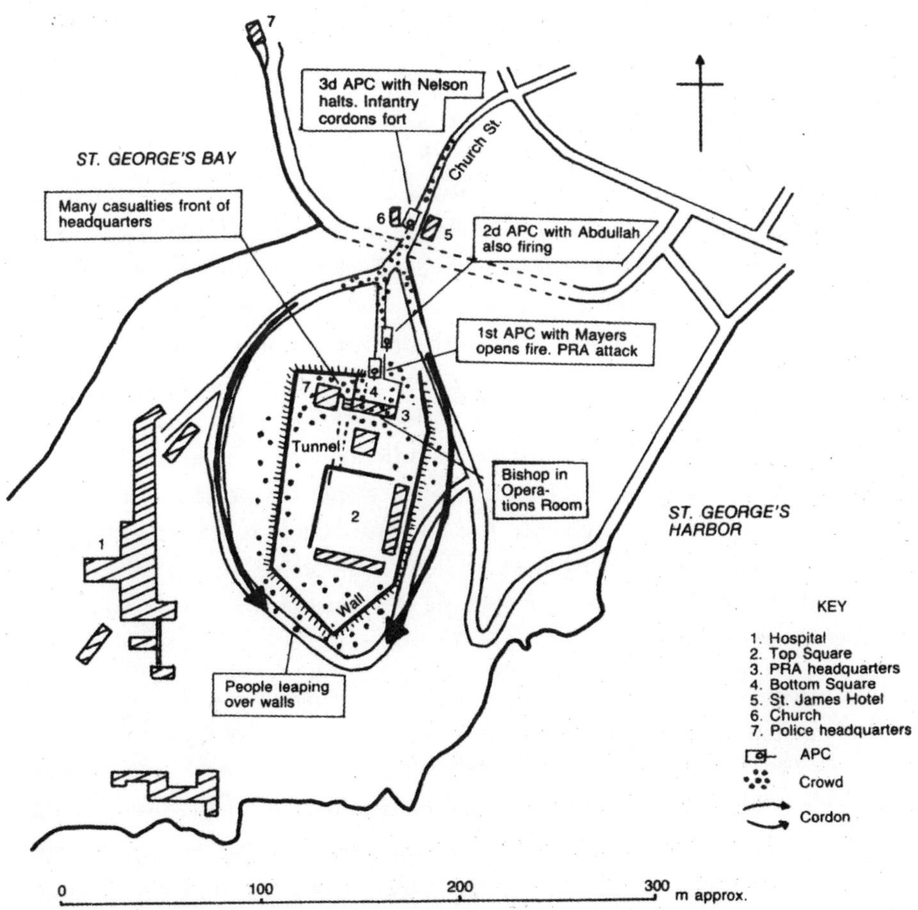

The PRA attack on Fort Rupert and the indiscriminate killing of civilian demonstrators. (*Adkin*)

that the operation they were about to launch could cost them their lives – in the event, it was to cost Meyers his. The soldiers, fired by the rhetoric, changed into combat gear and drew weapons and ammunition. A platoon of twenty-five boarded a truck and left Fort Frederick as Coard and his wife arrived.

There was a telephone link to Fort Rupert, but Coard was told that Bishop was in control of the operations room. It was at this stage that the decision was taken to kill Bishop and his acolytes. Coard realised that Bishop's popularity could not be lightly overturned and, as a consequence, his life was at risk if Bishop was reinstated. Hitherto, Coard and others had been fighting for the revolution; now, much more pragmatically, they were going to have to fight for their lives.

Major Einstein Louison had broken out of house arrest and when he reported to Bishop, he was told to open the Fort's armoury and distribute the weapons to the cheering mob outside so that they could defend themselves if that became necessary. The Cuban Ambassador Rizo was approached at some stage during 19 October and was asked for assistance. Rizo recognised the delicacy of the situation and radioed Havana for guidance. Within the hour, Castro replied, telling Rizo that 'under no circumstances were Cuban personnel, civil or military, to become involved in the internal turmoil of Grenada'.[14]

The situation changed when three PRA armoured cars and a large East German truck were seen speeding towards Fort Rupert from Fort Frederick. Initially, this convoy was presumed to be reinforcements for Bishop, but the converse was the case. This small force was commanded by Officer Cadet Conrad Myers. His assumption of command was based on his three years' service in the US Army, which included time in the Berlin garrison. He had under his command Lieutenant Callistus Bernard and Lieutenant Raeburn Nelson and ten PRA soldiers.[15]

The convoy halted and Myers gave his orders – it was 1.03pm. The soldiers dismounted, fanned out and advanced up the slope. The armoured cars revved their engines and accelerated into the courtyard of Fort Rupert unopposed. The operations room was just ahead. Then, without any form of warning, the armoured cars opened fire with automatic weapons on the crowd and Vincent Noel was one of the first to fall.

> The effect of this volume of fire at such close range was devastating. The heavy bullets literally chopped people to pieces. There was indescribable panic as people sought to escape. The APCs blocked the only exit, so demented fugitives, some grievously injured, sought to throw themselves over the walls or scramble up the steps leading to the top square. Even there, many were compelled to leap 20ft [6m] or more onto rocks, breaking bones in the process. Women and children were cut down with the men. In the first few

> moments, pandemonium reigned. Within two minutes, the bottom square and headquarters balcony were deserted except for the dead and crippled. The firing became more intermittent, though still heavy. Some soldiers had run up the stairs behind the headquarters and were shooting into the rear of the building.[16]

The thin internal walls of the building were shredded by the fire and killed and wounded the occupants. At this point, Myers was shot in the groin with a burst of four rounds from an AK47.[17] Hugh O'Shaughnessy speculated that he was possibly shot by one of his own men in the third armoured car who was disgusted by the orders he had been given. Meyers died in hospital. By any yardstick, he had committed a monstrous war crime and so there was an element of rough justice in his demise.

As the automatic fire penetrated the building, Bishop was bereft and he was heard to say, 'Oh God, Oh God, they have turned their guns on the masses.' He ordered his defenders to cease their fire and instructed those able to walk to give themselves up. The wounded dragged themselves into the open, where there was a total dearth of compassion. The majority made their way down the hill and back to town, leaving behind the dead, wounded and the broken bodies below the walls of the fort.

However, not all were given that opportunity and some were detained. These were:

Maurice Bishop	Prime Minister
Jacqueline Creft	Minister of Education and Minister of Women's Affairs
Keith Hailing	Marketing and Import Board
Evelyn Bullen	a business supporter of Bishop
Evelyn Maitland	the proprietor of Maitland's garage
Unison Whiteman	supporter of Bishop and Foreign Minister
Norris Bain	Minister of Housing
Fitzroy Bain	President of the Agricultural and General Workers' Union.

The eight realised that their lives hung by a thread and were able to note that Lester Redhead was an enthusiastic and vociferous advocate for their early execution. He was the officer directly responsible for the security of army headquarters but was outranked by Stroude. The plan that Meyers had been given was that Bishop and his group should be killed in the assault. Only Vincent Noel had succumbed to the fusillade and taking these eight prisoners was an unwanted complication.

Stroude consulted Bernard (now Abdullah) and Cecil Prime. They agreed that the Central Committee had to make any decision on execution. They left

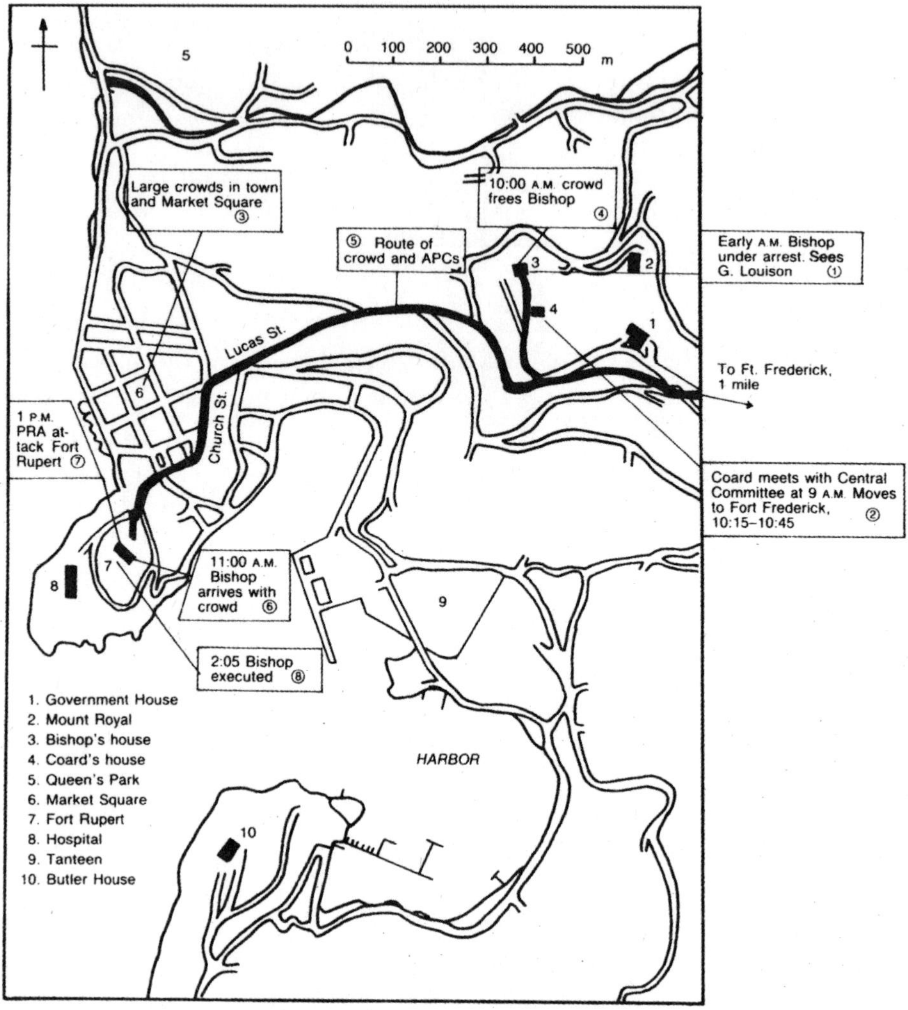

The events of 19 October 1983. (*Adkin*)

the prisoners standing by the wall in the top square under an armed guard. Stroude, Abdullah, Prime and Redhead hastened to Fort Frederick only a few hundred yards away and there they were able to shift responsibility to the Central Committee. Coard and his associates were not best pleased with Abdullah's report because now that Bishop lived, his demise would be difficult to conceal.

Coard, Layne, Austin, James Strachan, Ventour, McBarnette, Bartholomew, Ian St Bernard and Phyllis Coard knew that any decision they made had to be unanimous.

It was – at 2pm on 19 October.

Swiftly, they all agreed that Bishop and the other seven were to be shot, at once. Redhead was to make the arrangements and Abdullah was to command the firing party.

Events moved quickly thereafter. Abdullah was the centre of three firers; Andy Mitchell and Cosmos Richardson were the other two. Abdullah ordered the eight to turn around and then he produced what purported to be a death warrant. He said, 'This is an order from the Central Committee that you shall be executed by fire. It is not my order; it is the Central Committee's.' At this point, Jackie Creft half turned and said, 'Wait, wait, hold on. I'm pregnant.'

Her plea fell on deaf ears and Mitchell grunted, 'No fucking comrade at this time.' Abdullah commanded, 'Prepare to fire.' Weapons were cocked, aimed and when Abdullah ordered 'Fire', three automatic weapons sprayed the group.

The firing went on long after all eight were prone. The bodies were cut to bits. Bishop's back, stomach and neck had all been hit. Creft had one hand shot away as well as other multiple wounds. Fitzroy Bain's body was split and his intestines had spilled out. Flesh and blood were stuck to the wall. It was a scene of total carnage as puddles of blood formed. Abdullah ordered 'Cease fire' and he went forward to view his handiwork. Incredibly, despite his ghastly wounds, Bain was still alive. Abdullah ordered Fabien Gabriel to finish him off and Gabriel fired one round into Bain's head.

The whole dreadful business was complete. But it was to be the trigger for Operation URGENT FURY – the invasion of Grenada by the USA, predicted by Maurice Bishop some years before.

Later, Major Christopher Stroude, the Political Chief of the PRA, pronounced: 'It was a unanimous decision that all had to die.'[18]

* * *

Before the murders, two young Barbadians arrived at Pearls Airport and were closely questioned by immigration officials as to the nature of their business. The young man claimed to have been a regular visitor to Grenada. The cover story that they were holidaymakers was convincing and Second Lieutenant Alvin Quintyne and Lance Corporal Marita Browne of the Barbados Defence Force were free to move about Grenada and report on the situation to Colonel Lewis.

They found that local people were loath to engage in conversation with strangers, and they observed a measure of military activity but were unable to get to the new airport at Point Salines. Quintyne surmised that their cover was broken and decided to cut the mission short. The immigration official commented on the brevity of their holiday, but they were permitted to leave.[19] The two Barbadians were fortunate because the next day, Bishop and his associates were murdered, and Grenada plunged into a domestic abyss.

Notes

1. Handwritten statement by W. Errol George, 12 October 1983. Archived in the Grenada Documents Collection, Georgetown University. Booth family Centre for Washington Special Collections. Quoted by Kukielski, p. 173 and endorsed by Adkin, p. 41.
2. Adkin, Major M., *Urgent Fury: The Battle for Grenada* (London, Leo Cooper, 1989), p. 41.
3. Radix, K., *George Louison and Kenrick Radix discuss …*
4. Davidson, J.S., *Grenada: A Study in Politics and the Limits of International Law (*Aldershot, Gower Publishing, 1987), p. 68.
5. Adkin, p. 42.
6. Ibid.
7. Ibid.
8. O'Shaughnessy, H., *Grenada: Revolution, Invasion and Aftermath* (London, Sphere Books, 1984), p. 128.
9. https://languages.oup.com/google-dictionary-en.
10. Adkin, pp. 92–3.
11. O'Shaughnessy, p. 133.
12. Adkin, p. 48.
13. Ibid., p. 59.
14. Ibid., p. 53.
15. Ibid., p. 66.
16. Ibid., p. 69.
17. O'Shaughnessy, p. 137.
18. Stroude, in a statement to the police, November 1983. Quoted by Adkin, p. 63.
19. Adkin, p. 94.

Chapter 7

After the Killing

At Fort Frederick, there was an atmosphere of exultation after the killing of the eight people. However, there were practical difficulties to be faced. The hospital was overwhelmed with injured people. In response, there was an immediate appeal for all retired nurses and Salvation Army personnel to give assistance.

A Revolutionary Military Council (RMC) was formed. It was composed of sixteen of the most politically active members of the PRA. Coard did not want to be identified as being in control and what was needed was a front man. Who better than General Hudson Austin? The RMC members were:

General Hudson Austin
Lieutenant Colonel Liam James
Lieutenant Colonel Joseph Ewart Layne
Major Leon Cornwall
Major Tan Bartholomew
Major Keith Roberts
Major Christopher Stroude
Major Basil Gahagan
Captain Lester Redhead
Captain Huey Romain
Captain Cecil Prime
Lieutenant Ashley Foulkes
Lieutenant Rudolph Ogilvey
Lieutenant Iman Abdullah
2/Lieutenant Kenrick Fraser
2/Lieutenant Raeburn Nelson.

However, it was Coard who, with his wife Phyllis, directed matters. The military regime assumed control of the island and Austin addressed the nation late that evening. He said that the RMC 'would govern the country until normalcy is restored'.[1] He then gave a completely sanitised, unbalanced version of the events at Fort Rupert.

Austin was 45 years old and had played a key role in Bishop's overthrow of Gairy, but 'was unprepared by intellect, education or temperament to be the effective leader of a nation'.[2] His uniformed service was limited to that of a prison guard as a young man, when he met Bishop. In his youth, he had aspirations in construction engineering and embarked on a testing correspondence course with the Jamaica Institute of Science and Technology, but this led nowhere. It was reported that 'you only have to talk to Austin to know that he was barely more than literate'.[3]

Austin sported the badges of rank of a general and revelled in his appointment as head of the army and the security services. Notwithstanding his elevated position, the British High Commission in Barbados judged him to be 'a man of erratic judgment, fickle loyalties and no particular intellect'.[4]

This was the man who, nominally, was now the head of the Grenadian Government. However, British observers were well aware of whose hands were on the levers of power. Clearly, Bernard Coard, Liam James, Joseph Layne and Leon Cornwall were the decision makers and Austin was no more than a front man.

In Barbados, American Ambassador Milan Bish sent a priority telegram, which was labelled CRITIC (critical intelligence), to the State Department. The telegram said:

> there appears to be imminent danger to US citizens resident on Grenada due to the current deteriorating situation which includes reports of rioting, personnel casualties … Embassy Bridgetown recommends that the United States should now be prepared to conduct an emergency evacuation of US citizens residing in Grenada.[5]

This was grist to President Reagan's mill and he got important political support from Prime Minister Eugenia Charles of Dominica. She was a formidable and capable person and was invited to meet Reagan at the White House on 25 October. She travelled with Ambassador Francis McNeil, Reagan's emissary to the Organisation of Eastern Caribbean States (OECS), who was returning from consultations with likely allies in an invasion.

Charles proved to be an excellent advocate for military intervention, impressed Reagan, and shared a press conference with him. The press conference was symptomatic of Operation URGENT FURY. Reagan initially referred to the 'five member nations of the OECS' and, thereafter, promptly made mention of six. This he then clarified, as Jamaica and Barbados were not members of OECS. This clarification reduced to four the number of OECS members participating. Reagan added to the confusion by pronouncing that 'all of them had joined unanimously'. This was emphatically not the case: Montserrat and St Kitts and Nevis did not sign up and, of course, nor did Grenada.

The press conference served to muddy the waters further when President Reagan asserted, 'Early this morning, forces from six Caribbean democracies and the United States began landings on the island of Grenada in the Eastern Caribbean.'[6] In fact, the first Caribbean representative did not come ashore until 1100 hrs – and none was exposed to any armed action. Their presence was purely symbolic.

At this conference, President Reagan justified the invasion on three grounds. These were: a) to protect innocent lives, particularly American, b) to forestall further chaos, and c) to restore law and order and democratic government.[7] He made no mention of opposing Cuban/Russian ambitions and nor did he draw attention to the alleged verbal request from Sir Paul Scone for assistance.

In 1997, the historian Ronald Cole was charged by the Joint Chiefs of Staff to write the definitive history of the invasion of Grenada. He observed:

> Memories of the Iranian hostage crisis and the aborted rescue attempt at Desert One were fresh. Anxious to avoid a similar experience, policymakers mounted URGENT FURY in haste [and] in response to a threat to American medical students on Grenada.
>
> The operation succeeded, but flaws in its execution revealed weaknesses in joint operations. Together with the bombing of the Marine Corps barracks in Beirut that same month, the experience of Operation URGENT FURY added impetus to efforts to reform the joint system which were already under way.[8]

It was on 19 October that Lieutenant Cecil Prime, flushed with the apparent success of overthrowing and murdering about fifty people, pronounced, 'Long live martial law!'[9] The manifestation of this brand of governance was the decision of the Revolutionary Military Council (RMC) to impose an all-embracing curfew across the island, with a shoot-on-sight provision for those breaking the restrictions.

The RMC was faced with several pressing issues, the first of which was internal security. The overwhelming majority of Grenadians held Coard and his henchmen in very low regard, and there existed the possibility that supporters of Bishop might yet make an armed response to his murder.

The curfew was a draconian measure applied without any appreciation of the consequences. The RMC did not have the trained manpower nor the transport to conduct police patrols during an island-wide twenty-four-hour curfew. The closure of all business activity was patently absurd, and hundreds made nocturnal and dangerous forays to obtain food.

Some Grenadians, anticipating arrest and confinement, abandoned their homes and decamped to the forest or to an address of no interest to the police. The country ground to a halt. The RMC eventually recognised that public services had to function. Hospitals as well as electrical, water and telephone systems were critical and those employed in these areas had to be provided with a pass.

The original four-day curfew was relaxed on the second day to allow people to shop between 10am and 2pm. But this window was too short, and chaos was the inevitable result. Banks were overrun and shops ran out of stock. By Monday, 24 October, the curfew was completely degraded, and it was abandoned.

Dr Geoffrey Bourne, Vice Chancellor of St George's University School of Medicine, was one of many caught up in the curfew. He was conscious of the importance of the school to the Grenadian economy and that was emphasised when, on 20 October, two armed members of the security service called at his house. His apprehension was allayed when they explained that they were checking to ensure that he, his students and faculty had sufficient food and water at True Blue and Grand Anse, his two campuses.

Notwithstanding the hard-line Leninist-Marxist philosophy of the RMC, the economic importance of Bourne and his school was an unhappy capitalist necessity. The school was a valuable source of foreign exchange and:

> Direct annual payments included a general fee of US$ 75k, plus rent for the 'True Blue' facility, US$ 100k for upgrading work at the hospital, US$ 300k in wages for local employees ... Bourne quoted 'colossal gas, electricity, telephone, and water bills' ... He estimated indirect payments of EC$ 60k for postage and EC$ 100k for air travel. Students spent US$ 2.5 million.[10]

Little wonder then, that the wellbeing of Bourne and his school was a priority for the RMC and neither Bourne nor his students were ever at risk. This being the case, Reagan's *casus belli* was seriously damaged.

* * *

At Fort Rupert, the aftermath was dreadful. 'There were bodies, bits of bodies and blood everywhere.'[11] The fire brigade was summoned to quell the fires still burning in some vehicles but also to wash away the puddles of blood.

Roberts was posturing amid the carnage and fired his Kalashnikov to dissuade spectators. Horribly wounded Vincent Noel was carried down from the balcony, where he had been shot in the opening moments of the attack. Abdullah, noting that Noel was not dead, pointed his pistol at the dying man's head but was restrained by Raeburn Nelson. Noel died soon after.

In late afternoon, Gabriel, who had been given the grisly and stomach-turning job of disposing of the bodies, completed his task. The cadavers and unidentified body parts were stacked in a truck and covered with a blanket. Austin, who assumed command of the situation, told Redhead that under cover of darkness and the anonymity derived from the curfew, the bodies were to be burnt in a pit behind the latrines at Camp Calivigny.

Later, Austin came to check on progress and view the bodies. He remarked to Gabriel, 'These fucking troublemakers were supposed to be dead long.' He added, 'Maurice, bring that about for himself because he was not true.'[12] At 1.30 the next morning, the truck carrying the bodies bogged down and the corpses had to be transferred to a smaller vehicle. It was a revolting job, but eventually the dead were all dumped in the pit, and Abdullah took on the task of burning them. The fire consumed the bodies, but it took until noon on 20 October. Meanwhile, the PRA issued a communique that was blatantly dishonest. It said:

> Today our People's Revolutionary Army has gained victory over the right opportunists and reactionary forces which attacked the Headquarters of our Ministry of Defence. These anti-worker elements using the working people as a shield entered Fort Rupert. Our patriotic men, loving the masses and, rather than killing them since we understood that they were being used, we held our fire …

The author of this nonsense warmed to his work and the communique continued, saying:

> Comrades, these men who preached for us that they had the interests of the Grenadian people at heart did not have one member of the working class controlling their criminal operations. These elements, although they used the working class and working people to gain their objective, did not have any confidence in them and therefore had only businessmen, nuns, nurses and lumpen elements in the operations theatre …

There was more in a similar tone, all bristling with self-justification and Marxist -Leninist rhetoric. The following day there was more of the same and the PRA Political Department justified its position by pronouncing, 'Maurice Bishop and his other petty bourgeois and upper bourgeois friends had deserted the working class and working people of Grenada.'[13]

The overthrow of Bishop alarmed the Castro government in Havana on three counts. First, Bishop was a valued friend of Cuba. He had just visited when he was accorded considerable public respect. He was presented to the Cuban people as a popular Marxist-Leninist hero. Only three months earlier, he had attended the opening of a new textile mill, at which time he presented Castro with a rifle used in his overthrow of Gairy. All very symbolic. The second reason was that President Castro and Bishop had a strong personal relationship. The third, and perhaps the most important, was that 'the Cubans suspected that Bishop's overthrow was the work of the Reagan government executing another regime change. If the worse came to the worse it could be the signal for US landings in Nicaragua, El Salvador and perhaps in Cuba itself.'[14]

If Coard, Austin and the others of that group hoped for Cuban support, they were to be sadly disappointed because Castro released an unequivocal statement condemning the coup and its violent outcome. The statement read:

> Bishop was one of the political leaders best liked and most respected because of his talent, modesty, sincerity, revolutionary honesty and proven friendship with our country. He also enjoyed great international prestige. The news of his death deeply moved the Party leadership, and we pay the most heartfelt tribute to his memory.
>
> Unfortunately, the division among Grenadian revolutionists led to this bloody drama.
>
> No doctrine, no principle or proclaimed revolutionary position and no internal division can justify atrocious acts such as the physical elimination of Bishop and the prominent group of honest and worthy leaders who died yesterday.
>
> The deaths of Bishop and his comrades must be cleared up. If they were executed in cold blood, the guilty should receive exemplary punishment.[15]

The strength of that statement was such that the new regime had clearly lost the support of its only effective international ally. To his credit, Fidel Castro then made every effort to prevent a shooting war, and on 22 October, he contacted the USA by way of the Swiss Embassy in Havana.

The Cuban position was that it recognised the concern felt in the USA for American citizens but explained that there was also concern for Cubans working in Grenada. The message urged the USA to stay in contact, saying, 'It is convenient to keep in touch on this matter, so as to solve favourably any difficulty that may arise or action that may be taken relating to the security of these individuals, without violence or intervention in the country.'[16] By the time this message was received, planning was complete and the USA was set on war. There was no reply to the Cuban message for three days.

About three hours after US troops had landed, Havana was advised that the USA was acceding to a request from OECS for assistance. The reply went on to agree with the need to stay in contact and to ensure that every consideration would be given to the safety of Cuban personnel. These were weasel words because by now, the battle for Point Salines Airport was under way and some Cubans were already dead.

It might well be argued that, with a more determined negotiating effort, a shooting war could have been avoided, and lives and treasure saved. However, Reagan and the hawks around him saw the crushing of the insignificant regime in Grenada as a crusade, a means of enhancing the reputation and standing of the USA. The advertised *casus belli* was the bogus rescue of the medical students, who were never at any physical risk.

Castro was a shrewd politician and a few days later, on 24 October, he sent Colonel Pedro Comas, a seasoned regular officer, and Carlos Andres Larrañaga, a diplomat, to the island. They were to implement Castro's direction to Cubans in Grenada, which was:

> If the USA intervenes, we must vigorously defend ourselves as if we were in Cuba, in our camp sites, in our workplace close by, but only if we are directly attacked. I repeat, ***only if we are directly attacked*** [author's emphasis]. We would thus be defending ourselves, not the government nor its deeds. If the Yankees land on the [Point Salines] runway section near the University or its surroundings to evacuate their citizens, fully refrain from interfering.[17]

These are not the sentiments to be expected from a dedicated and aggressive enemy.

* * *

During the brief period 19–25 October, there was a great deal of activity in several different locations involving different groups of people. At this point, it is necessary to backtrack to 20 October.

It took until noon of that day for the bodies of the murdered eight at Camp Calivigny to be crudely cremated. At that time, the Lebanon-bound ships of the US Navy, led by USS *Guam*, were passing tranquil, prosperous Bermuda. Unexpectedly, the Pentagon issued orders for the Commodore to alter course and take up station east of Puerto Rico, in the Atlantic. In addition, an American, six-strong carrier battlegroup, led by the carrier USS *Independence*, 'was directed to take a holding position around Dominica'.[18] The USN was in the process of assembling a thirteen-strong task force in the Caribbean for an as yet undefined mission.

The situation in Grenada worsened and as it did so, the implementation of a plan came closer and the arrangements more specific. On 20 October, the Chairman of the Joint Chiefs, General John W. Vessey, contacted Major General Richard A. Scholtes, the commander of Joint Special Operations Command (JSOC). He asked Scholtes for his views on how an invasion of Grenada might be conducted.[19] The official history observed:

> After Grenada moved into the orbit of the Soviet Union and Cuba in 1979, US agencies had few opportunities to collect intelligence. Admiral McDonald's staff had inadequate tactical intelligence concerning Grenada. Aerial photography

indicated numerous sites for landing zones and parachute drops. An old intelligence estimate calculated Grenadian forces at about twelve hundred regulars with more than twice that number of militia and four torpedo boats. Since the precise deployment of Grenadian forces was unknown, picking the sites to land troops would be a risky business.[20]

On 21 October, CBS Evening News led with a report of USN activity in the Caribbean. It speculated that, ere long, the fleet would evacuate the estimated 600 US citizens at the Medical College in Grenada. The report alerted the media around the world, and at a stroke, any strategic surprise was lost.

At sea, communications between ships of the *Guam* group were being conducted using lights and the Morse code – a technology invented in 1830 by the American Samuel Morse. The need for Morse code reflected the 'communications limitations that would plague the impending operation for days to come'.[21]

This was not the only deficiency that would inhibit operations. Colonel Faulkner, commanding 22 MAU, presumed that his force would be the instrument to rescue the medical students. The only available map was a tourist brochure of Grenada, and the *Guam*'s navigating officer was working with a chart of Grenadian waters dated 1936. However, all was not lost because there were three officers who had some knowledge of Grenada. One was a yachtsman who had sailed in Grenadian waters. A second officer had spent his honeymoon on the island. Between them, they were able to provide a small measure of intelligence on the island's only operational airport at Pearls. A third officer, Lieutenant Colonel Ray L. Smith, now commanding one of the Marine battalions, when a student at the Armed Forces Staff College had written a study on a hypothetical landing on the island, initiated by the paranoiac Reagan government's view of Grenada.

By 22 October, the Pentagon had created two draft invasion plans and was considering its command-and-control options. Whatever military plan finally evolved, it would have to have the unqualified support of George Shultz, the Secretary of State, and Caspar Weinberger, the Secretary of Defense.

The two plans were: a) a marine assault by 22 Mau with air support from USS *Independence* or b) a cross-beach or airborne assault by Army Rangers supported by USN SEALS and Delta Force commandoes.[22]

The two civilian politicians were not prepared to endorse either plan, which committed about 1,800 troops. It was tacitly agreed that the parachute soldiers of 82nd Airborne Division would supplement the invaders as 'mop-up' troops. The politicians wanted the force to be enlarged. However, this aspiration flew in the face of the aims of the Chairman of the Joint Chiefs, who wanted to limit the number of senior officers on the battlefield. To this end, General John Vessey ruled that the involvement of 82nd Airborne Division should be limited to two battalions. This would, at a stroke, separate those battalions from the normal command chain of XVIII Airborne Corps.

This decision had far-reaching consequences, not least of which, it would remove those two battalions from their logistic support; but no compensating addition had been made. In a post-operation assessment, Jonathan House commented:

> In retrospect General Vessey's decision to exclude the XVIII Airborne Corps from the chain of command was the single most important cause of problems in URGENT FURY. The arbitrary elimination of the Corps level of command and staff from URGENT FURY made the accomplishment of the mission more difficult.[23]

General Vessey made two further far-reaching decisions. To ensure maximum operational security, he imposed special category (SPECAT) restrictions on all planning message traffic; this limited planning information to selected members of the Intelligence (J2) and Operations (J3) Directorates.

Vessey then approved the course of action, which specified a *coup de main* in which Rangers or Marines and airborne troops would conduct multiple simultaneous rescue and combat operations.[24] After the diversion of US warships to Grenada became news on 21 October, US intelligence agencies reported that the Grenadians and Cubans were organising to resist. The President then approved the Chairman's recommendation that the US ground forces include both Rangers and Marines.[25]

That same day, 22 October, Admiral McDonald was assembling his team that would exercise command over the invasion force. The commander of Joint Force 120 was to be Vice Admiral Joseph R. Metcalf III and, as such, he would have overall responsibility for every aspect of the operation. He was vastly experienced, very assertive and widely admired for his sense of urgency. However, he had no expertise in land operations, and, on that basis, McDonald appointed Major General H. Norman Schwarzkopf to be Metcalf's ground operations advisor, with a brief to ensure that the navy used the soldiers correctly. Schwarzkopf was doubtful and commented, 'It doesn't sound as if I'm exactly going to be welcome.' In reply, the operations chief at Fort McPherson said, 'As a matter of fact, you're not. The navy doesn't like the fact that you are being sent.'[26]

It was not a happy marriage, and with 20/20 hindsight, one wonders why the operation was navy led from the beginning. Metcalf had under his command a mixed bag from all four services – the Coast Guard was employed later. The representatives had not worked together before, did not know each other and, in some cases, where they did there was a degree of animosity. All intended to push the interests of their service or unit. No decision had been taken on which plan was to be selected and so every formation had to be represented. The glaring omission was that of Lieutenant General Jack Mackmull, the commander of XVIII Airborne Corps.

> Although perhaps not apparent to the subordinate commanders at the time, on Saturday, 22 October, URGENT FURY had the makings of a fiasco. The 82nd Airborne, the rangers under JSOC and the Marines at sea were all simultaneously planning to take the same objectives.[27]

All those present were aware of the deleterious effect that the media had had in Vietnam (1956–73) and which contributed hugely to the loss of public support for the war. With this in mind, McDonald had ruled that the most stringent secrecy rules were to be applied. Discussion was limited to face-to-face meetings or on secure telephone lines. The media was to be totally excluded.

It was against this backdrop of mistrust that, at 5am on the morning of Saturday, 22 October, President Reagan met with Secretary of State George Schultz and National Security Advisor Robert McFarlane – with a photographer present. The object of the exercise was to discuss a request from the Organisation of Eastern Caribbean States for the USA to intervene in Grenada to restore order and democracy.

Schultz was firmly in favour of a military response and, later, in his memoirs, he commented, 'The entire Grenada operation was driven by the State Department,' i.e., Schultz.[28]

At 1645 hrs, the JCS issued an 'execute' order to CINCLANT to 'launch a multi-national, multi-service operation on Grenada to restore order, neutralize Grenadian and Cuban forces and protect American citizens no later than dawn on Tuesday October 25'.[29]

The reference to 'multi-national' needs to be clarified. It is the usual practice for the United States, when it engages in military operations, to form a coalition of other interested parties. This perfectly reasonable but entirely political arrangement seeks to emphasise the international composition of the armed force and to refute any suggestion that the USA is pursuing its own agenda.

In practice, the other 'interested parties' are not part of any strategic planning and their function is to cast a veil of respectability and shared responsibility over the operation. This was the case in October 1983, when the coalition consisted of a very small token representation from the OECS. That body was composed of Antigua and Barbuda, Dominica, Grenada, Montserrat, St Kitts and Nevis, St Lucia, and St Vincent and the Grenadines. The military capacity of OECS was minimal and, in the event, its involvement in URGENT FURY was no more that symbolic. It contributed less than 5 per cent of the manpower, and none of the major weapons of war. It would not engage in combat and was actually no more than a cynical PR exercise.

Reagan's position was publicly unequivocal. There were American citizens in Grenada and their safety was paramount. With a shared interest, Ken Kurze and Linda Flohr, from the US Embassy in Barbados, with David Montgomery, the Deputy British High Commissioner in Barbados, flew to Pearls to discuss the evacuation of their citizens. Montgomery had the additional task of visiting Sir Paul Scones – the only viable political/diplomatic person with a capacity to represent the people of Grenada and provide leadership, albeit with difficulty.

Adams would later allege that Scones asked Montgomery for military assistance from the UK. However, a verbal request would not suffice, and it was necessary for Sir Paul to put such a request in writing. That would be sufficient to legitimise any foreign incursion. However, *he did not put his request in writing* (author's emphasis) and one wonders, why not? It would only take a moment to do with Montgomery standing beside him. This simple failure to act would later prove to be of enormous significance. The US State Department helpfully drafted the sort of request they would like to receive, and they sent the draft to Barbados unsigned and undated.

The position of Sir Paul Scones was tenuous. He had to live alongside murderous thugs like Austin and, although his life had not been threatened, it was quite reasonable for him to be apprehensive. He was bereft of ideas as to how he could usefully contribute to the situation.

Negotiations for the evacuation of foreign nationals were held but were fruitless and the US and British emissaries returned from Grenada empty-handed.

Later, on Saturday, 22 October, the *Guam* Amphibious Group received signals from its base in Norfolk, Virginia. One directed the group to turn towards Grenada, another advised the Commodore that the US Army intended to invade Grenada with airborne troops.[30] There was no mention of Marine participation, to the consternation of Colonel Faulkner, the commander of 22 MAU.

* * *

The President of the USA, Ronald Reagan, was beset with a range of issues in October 1983, all of which required urgent attention. The situation in Grenada was 'work in progress' and on Sunday, 23 October, events on the other side of the world forced themselves to the forefront.

At Beirut Airport, the US had established a barracks for its troops who were part of a United Nations peacekeeping force. That day, a truck bearing about 9,500lb of TNT, or its equivalent, crashed a path through the security barriers and breached the walls of a barrack building. The truck exploded with devastating effect. The death toll was enormous: 241 Americans died on the spot, and a further 13 died later of wounds.

Moments later, a second truck bomb was exploded at the French base, killing fifty-eight soldiers. In both attacks, a total of six civilians were killed. US losses were on a par with the losses of day one of the Tet Offensive in 1968. Reagan and his close advisors, faced with this major act of war, took no military action in response.

The strain Reagan was under was evident when he flew back to Washington from a golfing weekend that had been held to allay public suspicion that 'something was up'. He was reported as saying, 'If this [Grenada] was right yesterday, it's right today and we shouldn't let the act of a couple of terrorists dissuade us from going ahead.'[31] The two situations, of course, were not remotely linked.

* * *

Reagan's claim that he authorised the invasion of Grenada to ensure the safety of US citizens was treated with a degree of scepticism at the time. Later, Lawrence Eagleburger, the Under Secretary of State for Foreign Affairs, commented that on 20 October in a Crisis Pre-planning Group meeting, a rescue plan for the students was discussed, but so too was the overthrow of the hostile Grenadian regime. He said, 'The prime motivation was to "get rid" of that son of a bitch [General Austin] before the Cubans got any further embedded. ... The students were the pretext ... but we would not have done it simply because of the students.'[32]

On Sunday, 23 October, small contingents of OECS troops and police started to arrive in Barbados, and in Grenada, the militia and PRA were being mobilised. The RMC telexed the UK asking that it intervene to prevent an invasion by the USA. That communication was either not received or it was ignored. The former colonial power appeared to take the view that it was not appropriate for any foreign intervention in a domestic situation best left to the Grenadians.[33]

Reagan called a top-secret meeting at about 8pm on Monday, 24 October. Present were the top five congressional leaders from both sides of the House. These luminaries were delivered to the White House by covert means so that they could be briefed on Reagan's intentions but without attracting public or media attention. The President delivered a summary of Grenadian events, albeit from his perspective. He told the meeting that Grenada's Caribbean neighbours had pleaded for the USA to intervene. He opined, 'We have absolutely no alternative but to comply with this request. I think the risks of not moving are far greater than the risks of taking the action we have planned.'[34]

Under the terms of the 1973 War Powers Resolution, the President of the United States is obliged to consult with Congress before committing American armed forces to any form of violent activity. One of the attendees was Thomas 'Tip' O'Neill, the Speaker of the House of Congress, a powerful political figure and a committed supporter of President Reagan. At one point, O'Neill remarked, 'It's your show, Mr President.' Edwin Meese III took this to mean that Reagan would bear, personally, the political and diplomatic responsibility for any military action that was taken. As the meeting broke up, O'Neill commented, 'Well, Mr President, this isn't consultation, this is notification. Good luck.'[35]

The meeting closed at about 10am and Reagan was left alone with Admiral Vessey. Reagan asked the Chairman of the Joint Chiefs to review the envisaged timeline. Vessey advised, 'Now is the time you have to say go ahead now or we can't make it until tomorrow morning.' In addition, he added that the operation could be cancelled up to a few hours before the planned landings.

The planners of the operation were beset with doubts. The official history commented:

> Landings by Rangers or Marines might prompt the Grenadians or Cubans to kill the students or hold them hostage. The Cuban construction workers might reinforce Grenadian troops and inflict significant casualties upon US forces; the Soviet Union might exert pressure on US forces or those of US allies in Europe or the Middle East. If any of those events occurred, the Reagan administration could expect criticism from Congress, the media, and foreign governments. Some critics would focus on the casualties or hostages; others might accuse the President of disregard for international law.
>
> The Joint Staff concluded that the rewards of a successful operation offset the risks. A swift, precise strike probably would rescue most of the students and avert a hostage situation. Removal of the pro-Cuban junta would eliminate a threat to US strategic interests in the Caribbean. A well-executed display of US military prowess would convey US determination to protect its vital interests. In Western Europe where US willingness to fight for European soil was questioned, such action might inspire confidence in the United States.[36]

The Joint Chiefs were concerned that any expeditionary force sent into Grenada should have sound legal footing and it emphasised that the President should consult Congress in advance of the operation – this was a pre-requisite of Section 3 of the War Powers Resolution. The Chiefs' concern is to their credit, but Reagan was fully aware of his constitutional responsibilities – he just chose to ignore them.

The US Constitution was quite specific and if, for some reason, it was not possible to consult Congress within forty-eight hours of the invasion the President should explain the necessity and the legal basis for his decision.

In order to comply with Article 51 of the UN Charter and Article 5 of the Rio Treaty, the State Department should inform the Security Council and the signatories of the Rio Treaty of the proposed action and the reasons for it.

It was recognised that Grenada was a Commonwealth country and that it was desirable to seek assistance, or at the least the approval, of the United Kingdom.

President Reagan grasped the nettle said 'Go', and by so doing brought down a storm of international criticism. Nowhere was the anger more in evidence than in the British House of Commons. *Hansard* recorded that anger.

Notes

1. Adkin, Major M., *Urgent Fury: The Battle for Grenada* (London, Leo Cooper, 1989), p. 78.
2. Kukielski, P., *The US Invasion of Grenada: Legacy of a Flawed Victory* (Jefferson, North Carolina, McFarland & Co., 2019), p. 185.
3. Montalbano, W.D., 'Coup Began as a Debate among Leftists' (*Los Angeles Times*, 21 October 1983).
4. Telegram, 'Grenada Revolutionary Council' (British High Commission to HMG Foreign and Commonwealth Office, London, 24 October 1983).
5. Kukielski, p. 186, quotes Motley, L.A., *Lessons Learned*, p. 11. Adkin, p. 98, also applies.
6. President Reagan, press conference, Washington, 25 October 1983.
7. Cole, R.H., *Operation Urgent Fury: The Planning and Execution of Joint Operations in Grenada 1983* (Joint History Office, Office of the Chairman of the Joint Chiefs of Staff, 1997).
8. Ibid.
9. Adkin, p. 83.
10. Ibid., p. 87.
11. Ibid., p. 79.
12. Ibid., p. 80.
13. O'Shaughnessy, H., *Grenada: Revolution, Invasion and Aftermath* (London, Sphere Books, 1984), p. 139.
14. Ibid. p. 149.
15. Ibid, pp. 149–50.
16. Adkin, p. 160.
17. 'Documents on the invasion of Grenada' (*Caribbean Monthly Bulletin*, October 1983). Supplement No. 1. Quoted by Kukielski, p. 43.
18. Cole, p. 18.
19. Carney, J.T. and Schemmer, B.F., *No Room for Error: The Covert Operations of America's Special Tactics Units from Iran to Afghanistan* (New York, Ballantine Books, 2002), p. 117.
20. Cole, p. 14.
21. Kukielski, p. 12.
22. Cole, p. 23.

23. House, J.M., *The United States Army in Joint Operations 1950–1983* (Washington, DC, US Army Center of Military History, 1992), p. 174.
24. Department of State and Department of Defense Preliminary Report, 16 December 1983.
25. Cole. This is, in effect, the official history of the operation.
26. Kukielski, p. 25.
27. Adkin, p. 137.
28. Schultz, G.P., *Turmoil and Triumph: My Years as Secretary of State* (New York, Charles Scribner's Sons, 1993), p. 343.
29. Kallander, D.C. and Matthews, J.K., *Urgent Fury: The United States Air Force and the Grenada Operation* (Military Airlift Command, Office of History, Scott AFB, 1988), p. 22.
30. Spector, R.H., *Marines in Grenada, 1983* (Washington, DC, History and Museums Division, HQ USMC, 1987), p. 3.
31. Adkin, p. 121.
32. Moore, C., *Margaret Thatcher: The Authorised Biography* (London, Alan Lane, Vol. 2, Chapter 5, 'Reagan Plays her False', 2015), pp. 118–19.
33. Sir Geoffrey Howe, speaking in the House of Commons, 24 October 1983.
34. Weinberger, C., *Fighting for Peace: Seven Critical Years in the Pentagon* (New York, Warner Books, 1990), p. 118.
35. Baker, J.A., Chief of Staff to President Reagan, in an interview by Chidester, J., Knott, S.F. and Young, J.S., 15–16 June 2004 (Transcript, University of Virginia).
36. Cole, p. 24.

Chapter 8

Communications

During the evening of Sunday, 23 October, President Reagan signed the National Security Decision Directive (NSDD) and by so doing authorised the invasion of Grenada. Soon after, the sixteen-strong SEAL team who were to initiate URGENT FURY took off.

In Washington, British Ambassador Sir Oliver Wright was told by Lawrence Eagleburger, Under Secretary of State for Political Affairs, that 'all was calm'.[1] Taking that statement at face value, HMG was hoodwinked – a matter made all the more bitter by the action of the US Government in taking into its confidence the governments of small, independent Commonwealth Caribbean countries and the administration of the British Crown colony of Montserrat.

At this point, communications faltered. Reagan did not inform Adams and waited for twenty-four hours until he did so. At 1pm on Monday, 24 October, he sent a cable to UK Prime Minister Margaret Thatcher to advise her of the OECS request for assistance signed by seven Commonwealth countries – Jamaica, Barbados, Antigua, Dominica, St Lucia, St Kitts and Nevis, and St Vincent. This request was opposed by Guyana, Trinidad and Tobago, the Bahamas, Belize and, of course, Grenada.

Immediately, Montserrat, still a Crown colony and a member of OECS, was expressly forbidden to participate in any future invasion of Grenada. Were it to do so it would implicate HMG in the operation, and that was totally unacceptable.

The constitution of OECS as determined by the 1981 Treaty of Basseterre was quite categorical and Article 3.1 (b) stated that the second major purpose of the organisation is simply 'to promote unity and solidarity among the member states and to *defend their sovereignty, integrity and independence*' (author's emphasis). 'OECS was conceived as primarily an instrument for foreign policy co-ordination and harmonisation, in particular joint overseas representation among its Member States. It rationalised the institutional structure of integration among Eastern Caribbean States, by creating one organisation for functional and political cooperation and economic integration in the sub region.'[2]

At 4pm on 24 October, Sir Geoffrey Howe, Secretary of State for Foreign and Commonwealth Affairs, addressed the House of Commons. He was clearly on the back foot, and he ran very close to misleading the House – a most egregious offence. Slightly edited here, in the interests of brevity, *Hansard* recorded the exchanges, as below. Sir Geoffrey Howe rose to address the House of Commons, which then subjected him to a stern examination.

Sir Geoffrey Howe: With permission, Mr. Speaker, I will make a statement on the situation in Grenada. The House will be aware of the violent events of last week on the independent Commonwealth island of Grenada. Her Majesty's Government join with those in the Caribbean region and elsewhere who have deplored the killings, and we view with grave concern the existing state of unconstitutional government and insecurity on the island.

We are particularly conscious that there are some 200 British citizens on Grenada, including a number of British tourists. The resident representative of the British High Commission has been active in maintaining contact with this community and reports that no British citizens appear to be in immediate danger. The Deputy High Commissioner also visited Grenada from Barbados yesterday to make contact with the new authorities and to speak with the Governor-General. He found the island calm but tense and confirmed that neither the Governor-General nor members of the British community appeared to be in any imminent danger. None the less, the position remains extremely volatile.

It is for this reason that Her Majesty's Government *have instructed HMS* Antrim *to be prepared to evacuate our community should the situation worsen and make this necessary* [author's emphasis]. Meanwhile, we remain in close touch with the Governments of the other Commonwealth Caribbean countries, whose leaders have been meeting in Trinidad. We shall be discussing with them, and with other interested states, the best prospects of helping to achieve a restoration of constitutional government, peace and security in Grenada. I shall keep the House informed of developments.

Mr. Denis Healey (Leeds, East), the opposition 'shadow' to Howe, observed: Military dictatorships are all too common in that part of the world. I think that I am correct in saying that this is the first time that anything like one has been established in a Commonwealth country in the Caribbean. I welcome the steps that the Government have taken to ensure the evacuation of any British citizens who wish to leave the island and his intention to concert policy with other Commonwealth members in the Caribbean. *Can the Foreign Secretary assure us that there is no question of American military intervention on the island? It could only make the position worse* [author's emphasis].

Sir Geoffrey Howe: *I know of no such intention* [author's emphasis]. [This poses the question, what did Thatcher tell her right-hand man?]

Mr. Peter Tapsell (East Lindsey): Has my right hon. and learned Friend any information about the alleged Cuban presence on Grenada and the role that it has played or is playing? Is he aware of the widespread belief in the Caribbean during the past two or three years that Grenada should be regarded as part of a Soviet game-plan, and the new airports as a jumping-off ground aimed primarily at Trinidad and Venezuela? Should we not, therefore, see the incident as a serious development in the global struggle for power and not just as an isolated seizure of power by a group of the military?

Sir Geoffrey Howe: One must take account of all those factors in considering such a matter. It must be remembered that Prime Minister Bishop, who lost his life in the recent *coup d'état*, was a close friend and associate of Dr. Castro, that there are several hundred Cuban advisers on the island already, and that the Cuban Government have lamented the death of Prime Minister Bishop and deplored the recent events. It is difficult to conclude—although my hon. Friend is correct to remind us of the facts—that in that respect the matter has changed significantly.

Mr. Russell Johnston (Inverness, Nairn and Lochaber): Does the Secretary of State think that, where a group has seized power in a Commonwealth country with a small population, the British Government have any responsibility to do anything?

Sir Geoffrey Howe: The British Government obviously are concerned with such an event in any independent country, particularly one that has only recently secured that independence and freedom as a result of decisions of the House, but Grenada is an independent country. Our concern and what we are prepared to do about it must be determined by recognition of that fact.

Mr. Eldon Griffiths (Bury St. Edmunds): In view of the desirability of avoiding any American intervention to safeguard American citizens, can the Foreign Secretary say whether HMS *Antrim* would have the appropriate authority to assist also in the removal of any Americans who might be at risk?

Sir Geoffrey Howe: The United States Government have explained that their own naval forces in the area are in that position *solely because of the requirement that may arise to rescue their own very sizeable community in Grenada* [author's emphasis]. There is no reason to doubt that their forces would be sufficient to achieve that purpose, but I take account of the point raised by my hon. Friend.

Mr. John Fraser (Norwood): As I represent tens of thousands of West Indians, may I tell the Foreign Secretary of their openly expressed sense of outrage and grief at what has happened in Grenada? Will it be the aim of the Foreign

Secretary's policy, in conjunction with his Commonwealth colleagues, to seek not only the restoration of constitutional government but democracy in Grenada, without undue veto or pressure from the United States, Cuba or any other country?

Sir Geoffrey Howe: I confirm what the hon. Gentleman said about the sense of outrage felt by members of the Caribbean population in Britain, as in the Caribbean itself, at what has taken place. It must be remembered that the Government who have been ousted came to power, in 1979, as a result of a military coup. I am sure that it would be right for us to take counsel with the Caribbean Commonwealth Governments to see whether there are any steps which can be taken to help promote the prospects of the return of democratic government in the island of Grenada.

Mr. Nigel Spearing (Newham, South): Has the Foreign Secretary been told that last year members of the Select Committee on Foreign Affairs visited Havana and Grenada and produced a report with recommendations?

Is he aware that among those recommendations in respect of Grenada was a recommendation that Her Majesty's Government should strengthen diplomatic presence there, and that they should initiate talks with a view to starting a bilateral aid programme? Has he been told that those recommendations were turned down? Does he agree that the Select Committee might have been right?

Sir Geoffrey Howe: I am, of course, aware of the recommendations of that Select Committee. The decisions taken in respect of them have been explained in the White Paper to which the hon. Gentleman referred. However, I do not believe that an event of this kind would have been significantly influenced by acting on those recommendations.

Mr. George Foulkes: Is the Foreign Secretary aware that his reply to my right hon. Friend the Member for Leeds, East (Mr. Healey) about possible American intervention was not at all reassuring? *Will he and the British Government advise the American Government than any intervention by the United States would be unhelpful?* [Author's emphasis.] Is he aware that progress towards democracy, such as my right hon. and hon. Friends have spoken of, will not be achieved by any form of external military intervention?

Sir Geoffrey Howe: I assure the hon. Gentleman that we are keeping in the closest possible touch with the United States Government and the Caribbean Governments to which I have referred. *I have no reason to think that American military intervention is likely. The United States Government have explained that the movement and presence of their naval vessels in the area is prompted solely by*

> *the same reasoning which led us to consider the positioning of HMS* Antrim—*to rescue a sizeable American community in Grenada if circumstances deteriorate and evacuation is necessary* [author's emphasis].
>
> **Mr. Jeremy Corby** (Islington, North): Is the Foreign Secretary making representations to the United States Government to withdraw their fleet, which is anchored off Grenada? Its presence can only exacerbate the situation and be a prelude to a possible landing on Grenada by American forces?
>
> **Sir Geoffrey Howe**: I have already explained twice that *the presence of the United States naval vessels is not prompted by the consideration that the hon. Gentleman has in mind. The vessels are there for the reason that the United States Government and we have given. There are more than 1,000 United States citizens and several hundred British citizens on Grenada. It is only prudent that when Governments of democratic countries are faced with such circumstances, they take steps to provide for the rescue of their citizens if necessary. That is the reason for the presence of the naval vessels* [author's emphasis].

In its usual civilised manner, the House had warned Howe, and the Thatcher government, that any American invasion would be the source of extreme anger. Howe left the House only to learn, at about 6pm, that a second telegram told the UK Government that the USA with Jamaica and Barbados were going to intervene in Grenada.

Predictably, Thatcher's response was forceful and thoroughly disapproving. At 2am on 25 October, President Reagan sent another telegram thanking Thatcher for her response but confirming that the invasion would proceed. Thatcher promptly telephoned Reagan and expressed her anger and distress that an ally should invade a Commonwealth country. Senator Howard Baker was in an adjoining room when Reagan took the call. He recalled, 'He said, "Margaret", long pause. "But Margaret", and he went through that about three times and came back sort of sheepish and said, "Mrs Thatcher has some reservations about this."'[3]

Bernard Ingham, Press Secretary to Margaret Thatcher, later put this exchange into a wider context, and with the benefit of hindsight, he said:

> Margaret Thatcher had the great ability to tell people off in the bluntest possible way without giving terminal offence. It would have been difficult to give terminal offence to President Reagan who was the sunniest man alive at the time. She did not mince words with her colleagues, but in a curious way they tolerated that because they reckoned that she was pretty straight with it, apart from Mr Gorbachev who just liked arguing.[4] Let's not kid ourselves that the tremendous ructions over Grenada caused any damage to her relations

> with President Reagan as such. It was something that she recognised that relationships had to go through, but they survived. They probably survived all the more because she was so frank about matters.[5]

In the UK, there was widespread anger and disbelief that the USA would invade a Commonwealth country of which Queen Elizabeth II was the head of state. There is no record of HM's opinion but, curiously, she cancelled her normal weekly meeting with her prime minister. This was interpreted by some as a measure of her displeasure. The Commonwealth was one of her abiding priorities but, as ever the exemplary constitutional monarch, she never expressed a view. It is reasonable to suppose that the Queen was not a little discommoded.

George Schultz, US Secretary of State, somewhat patronisingly and apparently inaccurately, opined the following day, 'We are, of course, always impressed with the views of the British Government and Mrs Thatcher, but that doesn't mean that we always have to agree with them and, of course, we also have to make decisions in the light of the security situation of our citizens as we see it.'

The invasion had made Thatcher and her government look not only incompetent, but also very foolish. It was nothing less than a national humiliation inflicted by an alleged ally with whom the UK had a 'special relationship'. The situation was exacerbated by the previous denials by Sir Geoffrey Howe of any likely US invasion.

The charge of incompetence is valid. In Bridgetown, Barbados, the High Commissioner, Giles Bullard (later Sir Giles Bullard, KCVO, CMG), was aware of the strong feelings about the regime in Grenada in other Caribbean countries. He had advised London to act with the Americans, or at least doing nothing to hamper them. The fact that his advice was ignored was something that irked him, although he never referred to it later in his life.

Bullard and his staff sent thirty telegrams to London between 19 and 24 October and made it clear that some Caribbean leaders were pressing for a military solution to the Grenada issue. On 22 October, Bullard advised the Foreign and Commonwealth Office that, following a meeting of the OECS, the UK was invited to join the coalition and a formal request would follow – it never did.

During 22–23 October, the Foreign and Commonwealth Office in London was working at a pace commensurate with the weekend! Everything was conducted at a slower pace and cables from around the world were dealt with by the duty officer, a third-ranking official called Richard Luce. He had to determine the criticality of a plethora of incoming cables and redirect them appropriately. He was able to confirm to Barbados that the West Indian guardship, HMS *Antrim*, was to sail to Grenadian waters. That was scant comfort in the circumstances.

On Monday, 24 October, Thatcher chaired a Cabinet meeting that was to discuss current events. The consensus was that HMG was opposed to taking any military action considering the legal, constitutional and practical difficulties that were entailed. It also opposed military intervention by any other power.

* * *

The position of the UK was crystal clear to the US Government, but preparations for war were very advanced although the fine detail remained unclear. To clarify the situation, and at about the same time that the first SEAL mission had failed, Admiral McDonald called a meeting of all the senior commanders, many of whom were meeting for the first time.

The first encounter between Admiral Metcalf and Major General Schwarzkopf did not go well, as Metcalf emphasised his seniority and treated the general with scant courtesy.[6] He treated Major General Richard Scholtes of Joint Special Operations Command in much the same manner.

McDonald's meeting was filled with general officers, among whom was Major General Edward Trobaugh, the commander of 82nd Airborne Division. Curiously and inexplicably absent were any representatives of the navy or marine forces currently at sea. Metcalf was unconcerned and explained later that he 'knew how they operated'.[7] Deputy Assistant Secretary of State L. Craig Johnstone was present. He was the political appointee, ranked as a general officer, and played a full part in the discussions.

The meeting did not address any number of fundamental issues. There was, incredibly, a total dearth of intelligence. How the Cubans and Russians might react if, where and when was not considered. A complex operation such as that now envisaged required detailed and meticulous planning, a flexible and reliable communication system, a professionally adept and decisive command system and, in this case, a high level of interservice cooperation. It was Admiral McDonald's role to ensure that these elements were all in place. However, they were not before his meeting, and they were still absent when the meeting broke up.

Logistic support was not mentioned. There were no maps of the island. The attackers did not know the strength, deployment, morale or likely response of either the PRA or the Cubans. There was no information as to the location of PRA headquarters, its communication network or its supply system. There was no information available on anti-aircraft defences. The location of the alleged 'at risk' American citizens and the presence or not of armed guards with these citizens was yet another unknown. 'From the military point of view, the lack of accurate intelligence was to be the most serious failure of the operation.

Intelligence shortcomings were directly or indirectly responsible for URGENT FURY'S delayed H-Hour, loss of surprise, slow development, tactical failure, and unnecessary casualties.'[8]

The USA had in place all the elements it required to take and hold the miniscule Spice Island. There was a contingency plan in place, numbered 2360. This plan made provision for an intervention in Grenada. The plan specified the structure for such an operation and command was to be invested in the Commander US Forces Caribbean at Key West in Florida. This worthy, in 1983, was Lieutenant General Jack Mackmull, commanding XVIII Airborne Corps. In the event, he was completely excluded from Operation URGENT FURY.

Plan 2,360 was not implemented; it continued to gather dust in the Pentagon and an *ad hoc* command organisation was created instead. This decision was a serious and fundamental error of judgement. The Pentagon developed a vast military sledgehammer to crack a very, very small Grenadian nut. The force had thirteen ships, thousands of soldiers and Marines, all backed by vast airpower. The opposition was tiny, poorly untrained, ill-equipped and badly led. The smart money was on an American victory.

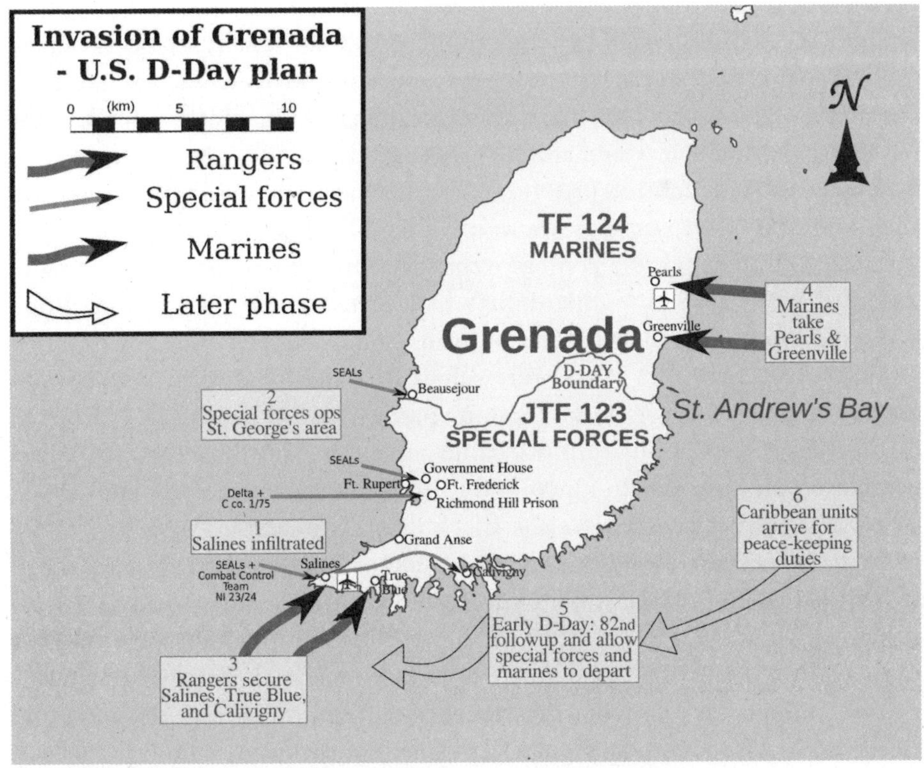

The plan, revealed by McDonald, and which Metcalf had to implement, predictably and correctly intended to overwhelm any opposition by sheer weight of numbers, firepower and technology. The USN was to ring-fence the island, and Marines from USS *Guam* would be delivered by helicopters to the north-eastern coast to seize and hold the airstrip at Pearls and the nearby town of Grenville.

Concurrently with the marine attack, Army Rangers, flying from bases in the south-east of the USA, would take Point Salines and its incomplete airstrip. Their further mission was to contact the medical students at True Blue campus, adjacent to the airstrip. The existence of a second campus at Grand Anse was unknown. True Blue accommodated only about a third of the student population. The other two-thirds lived about a mile and a half away (2.5km) over the hill to the north-west or lived in houses or apartments in the Lance aux Epines peninsula and elsewhere. The existence of two campuses was not a secret, and hundreds of parents were aware of the location of their offspring. On the face of it, this mission was straightforward and achievable. However, possible enemy response and countermeasures were not factored into the JSOC plan.

The Pentagon and Metcalf were in blissful ignorance.

Another facet of the operational plan was entrusted to Special Forces, SEALs, Delta Force and Rangers. They were to move, at 0400 hrs, in nine helicopters, reassembled in Barbados. Two of the UH-60A Blackhawks, each with eleven passengers, would head for the Beausejour transmitting station, north of St George's; another pair would aim for Government House. The remaining five would first, release political prisoners being held at Richmond Hill Prison, and then find, and take to safety, Governor General Sir Paul Scones.

These Black Hawk helicopters were state-of-the-art aircraft. Originally designed for service in Vietnam, they had been further developed and one of their features was their protection from small arms fire. The cockpit area was armoured, the fuel tanks were self-sealing, and the rotor blades were constructed around a hollow titanium spar. This gave the Black Hawk the capacity to survive a hit from projectiles of up to 23mm calibre. The main gearbox would continue to function for thirty minutes after the loss of all oil. The sophisticated design gave the Black Hawk a low noise signature, a low radar cross section, low engine exhaust signature and an infrared suppressor. It had dual flight controls, twin engines and triple electrical and hydraulic systems.[9] All in all, this was an incredible war machine and probably the best of its type in the world.

Two of the Special Forces targets were of doubtful value. The seizure of the radio station and the freeing of political prisoners in Richmond Hill Prison would not contribute to the success of the operation. The radio station was installed by

Russian technicians and, even if taken by the US, Radio Free Grenada would continue to broadcast from studios behind Gran Anse Beach. It was another intelligence gap that the invaders were unaware of this second studio. As it happened, the PRA continued to broadcast until almost noon on 25 October.

The political prisoners were accorded a much higher priority than perhaps they merited. The US deployed its most highly trained servicemen to the release of Grenadian citizens when its stated aim was to secure the safety of the medical students. The selection of these two objectives 'must remain one of the most extraordinary decisions of URGENT FURY'.[10]

The plan discomforted several of the participants at the meeting. There was an air of complacency and an attitude that the operation 'would be a piece of cake'.[11] Scholtes asked for time for his SEALs to make a further attempt to reach and reconnoitre Point Salines. This was agreed and the timing for the invasion was put back to 0500 hrs, which meant that Rangers, Marines and JSOC forces would assault simultaneously. The decision to delay H-hour until 0500 hrs destroyed any possibility of the JSOC activities achieving surprise. They would strive to take advantage of darkness but there was no room for error.

The object of inserting SEALs at Point Salines was to install navigational aids for the incoming aircraft bearing the airborne element of the invasion and to report on the status of the airstrip. The MC-130 crews were perfectly competent to find Point Salines without the aid of ground radio beacons. However, they did need to know if the runway was clear for them to land and offload the soldiers. If it was not, then they would execute a parachute insertion.

It was necessary to construct a timetable and co-ordination plan to get the right men, in the right aircraft, over the correct target. It was like a three-dimensional jigsaw puzzle. The UH-60 Black Hawk and the two MH-6 Little Birds had a limited range and so they had to be transported as near to the action as possible. Barbados was selected as the staging post and the Black Hawks were packed into C-5A Galaxies. Barbados was about forty-five minutes' flying time from Grenada.

The manpower and their equipment came together from several different military installations in the USA. The C-5As were based in Dover AFB in Delaware, nine Black Hawks with their crews and ground staff were from Fort Campbell, Kentucky, and JSOC troops journeyed from Fort Bragg, in North Carolina.

The Black Hawks were disassembled for the move to Barbados on Monday night and, at 4am on 25 October, they would launch their assaults. Simultaneously, two Ranger battalions would land or parachute onto Point Salines and the Marines would storm ashore at Pearls.

It was a complex operation with lots of moving parts, and the great unknown was the quality and number of the enemy. It is enemy activity that is the ruination of any plan.

* * *

It is germane to explain that it is normal practice for military operations to share the same time frame. On this basis, military plans usually employ ZULU time, which is Greenwich Mean Time (GMT). This avoids any confusion that 'local time' might cause.

Grenada is one time zone ahead of the Eastern United States. The rotation of the planet causes the sun to rise and set in Grenada about an hour before it does in the Eastern USA. During the US period of Daylight Saving Time, the USA advances its clocks by an hour. The effect of this is that, from spring to autumn, the clocks in Grenada and the Eastern USA *show* the same time. However, changing clocks does not negate the arrival of dawn and dusk in Grenada an hour in advance of their appearance in Washington, notwithstanding what the clocks might say. This fact was not factored into the insertion of those sixteen men into Grenada.

* * *

The revised start time negotiated by Scholtes was arguably the 'start of a slippery slope'.[12] The operation was to be subject to constant amendment, and secrecy served to slow the passage of information. 'The fighting units were deployed widely and their movement and the transit distances too long for everything to come off precisely on time.'[13]

The USAF planners, who had dropped the first SEALs at 1800 hrs local time, cast them into a moonless and very dark Eastern Caribbean night instead of the anticipated thirty minutes before dusk (see page XXX). Captain Robert Gormly, the leader of SEAL team Six, observed later, 'In all my years with the SEALs, URGENT FURY was the only occasion on which the standard military procedure of using ZULU time was violated. Doing that had caused us to jump in the dark instead of day light as we had planned.'[14]

Darkness was an issue but in the SEAL mission there were other factors. They included heavy seas, and unseaworthy, open boats. None of the USAF or USN personnel were trained in their role. Failure did not stop there.

In accordance with Scholtes's instructions, the surviving SEALs were to make a second attempt at reaching Point Salines. They were despatched from USS *Sprague* in the frigate's open Boston Whaler, towing a 15ft rigid, inflatable Zodiac.

When the party was still about 30 miles (48km) short of the Grenadian shore, it encountered a ship scanning the sea with a searchlight. The reasonable assumption was that this was a Grenadian patrol vessel. At this point, one of the Whaler's engines failed and the boat, not fully under control, started to take on water. The mission was aborted and the party returned to *Sprague*.

A third attempt, this time with two Whalers, was made to land and survey the airstrip at Point Salines, and that too failed. Engine malfunction, loss of radio communication and hazardous sea conditions combined to cause the abandonment of the landing.

The insertion of six SEALs from SEAL Team 4 during the night of 24/25 October to reconnoitre the beach at the eastern end of Pearls Airport was marginally more successful. The party left the USS *Fort Snelling* in two 36ft fibreglass Sea Fox boats, and each towed a much smaller Zodiac. The passage was more than 20 miles in a rough sea. As they closed on the beach, they spotted a vessel that they assumed to be a Grenadian patrol craft, which they evaded.[15] The party reached Grenada at about midnight.

The commander, Lieutenant Michael Walsh, sent two of his swimmers to the proposed landing beach while the other four examined the beach, from the sea, in the small Zodiac. The two swimmers reached the beach undetected but on leaving the sea, came upon soldiers digging what were presumed to be defensive trenches. The two men were not seen and fortuitously, a burst of tropical rain sent the Grenadian soldiers off to find cover.

At 4am on 25 October, the SEAL team sent the message 'Walking track shoes'. This meant that tracked amphibious vehicles would find landing conditions difficult and hazardous. It was impossible for landing craft. On the basis of this advice the amphibious follow-up to the heliborne assault was abandoned.

A radio message summoned the remainder of the team and all of Team 4 occupied the trenches to wait for dawn and the marine invasion. For JSOC, the Pearl expedition helped to offset the debacle at Point Salines. This had been the first combat mission for the SEALs since their formation in October 1980 and it had not been a crashing success.

* * *

The strength of US Special Forces shrank swiftly during the ten years following the withdrawal from Vietnam in 1973 but, by 1983, it was about 13,000 strong, with a budget of $1 billion plus. This apparent return to a position of operational importance was unfortunately accompanied by allegations of criminal malpractice and financial fraud on a heroic scale, both of which were being investigated. The only post-Vietnam operation in which Special Forces had been employed was the disastrous Operation EAGLE CLAW in the Iranian desert in early 1980.

The command structure to wield the military sledgehammer mentioned earlier was complex, top heavy and highly inefficient. The command arrangements over key units deployed on Operation URGENT FURY were described by Kukielski as being 'fluid and fuzzy'. It was military nonsense when 'Rangers units were chopped back and forth on short notice under different operational commanders before and during the fighting'. Kukielski commented further that 'Intelligence was short on "D" day, two different generals believed that they were the principal forward Air Force airlift commanders for the operation. No one was ever sure how the Caribbean Peacekeeping Forces figured in the formal chain of command.'

Vice Admiral Joseph Metcalf III, USN, the designated commander of the forces committed to the invasion of Grenada, titled Task Force 120 (TF120), had not been included in the planning process. He was described by one of his peers as 'a rock-hard, salt-stained dyed in the wool, surface warrior'.[16] He was a capable officer but the victim of inept planning.

The staff officers required to manage TF120 numbered eighty-eight, and, in combination, these men would have all the specific skills to make most effective use of the force at their commander's disposal. Unfortunately, there was insufficient time to muster a team of this size. Even if it had been possible, they would not fit into the scant available space on USS *Guam*, where Metcalf would fly his flag. He selected just seventeen – the most he could squeeze into one USN helicopter.

Metcalf realised that the forthcoming operation would be subject to the closest scrutiny in Washington, and he selected one senior officer, Captain Robert R. Reading, USN, to act as his representative with higher commands. Reading's job was to produce copious situation reports (SITREPS). Metcalf commented that Reading was 'the officer in charge of keeping them off my back'.[17] Reading and his three subordinates who were to carry out this function left only thirteen staff officers to co-ordinate the myriad logistic, communication, fire control and wounded evacuation tasks.

Later, Lieutenant General Richard L. Prillaman, the Pentagon Director of Operations, commented that Metcalf 'had no air component or any adviser on air operations. He had essentially an administrative staff capable of moving boats around but not capable of running a tactical operation.'

Notes

1. O'Shaughnessy, H., *Grenada: Revolution, Invasion and Aftermath* (London, Sphere Books, 1984), p. 171.
2. Treaty of Basseterre, 1981. The OECS had no authority to suggest or cause the invasion of a member state.
3. Kukielski, P., *The US Invasion of Grenada: Legacy of a Flawed Victory* (Jefferson, North Carolina, McFarland & Co., 2019), p. 36.
4. Mikhail Gorbachev, Soviet and Russian leader, 1985–91.
5. Caribbean Witness Seminar, 29 May 2009.
6. Raines, E.F., *Rucksack War: US Army Operational Logistics in Grenada 1983* (Washington, DC., Center of Military History, 2010, pp. 138–9).
7. Metcalf, Admiral J., 'Decision Making and the Grenada Rescue' (Marshfield Mass, Pitman Publishing, *Ambiguity and Command: Organizational Perspectives on Military Decision Making*, ed., Marsh, J.G.), p. 284.
8. Adkin, Major M., *Urgent Fury: The Battle for Grenada* (London, Leo Cooper, 1989), p. 128.
9. Ibid., p. 178.
10. Adkin, p. 175.
11. Metcalf, p. 284.
12. Kukielski, p. 33.
13. Ibid.
14. Gormly, R.A., *Combat Swimmer: Memoirs of a Navy SEAL* (New York, Penguin Books, 1998), p. 185.
15. Walker, G., *At the Hurricane's Eye: US Special Forces from Vietnam to Desert Storm* (New York, Ivy Books, 1994), pp. 124–6.
16. Schudel, M., 'Joseph Metcalf: Led Invasion of Grenada' (*Washington Post*, 11 March 2007).
17. Kukielski, p. 27.

Chapter 9

Invasion – Pearls and Grenville

22 Marine Amphibious Unit (22 MAU), commanded by Colonel James Faulkner, was designated to take Pearls Airport and, to the south, the nearby town of Grenville. The MAU was 2,000 men strong, well equipped, well trained, but unaware of the physical conditions facing it. The commander had not the least idea of the size of the opposition nor where it was likely to be located. This was an intelligence-free zone and, consequently and arguably, a demonstration of how not to mount an invasion. The plan was to land a heliborne company at Pearls and Grenville simultaneously. The third company was to make a Beach landing.

The cutting edge of the Pearls/Granville operation was Lieutenant Colonel Ray Smith's 2nd/8th Battle Landing Team (BLT). Essentially an infantry battalion, it was supplemented with other specialist units to meet the current need. Smith had three rifle companies, titled E, F and G. Each rifle company was composed of three platoons, each of thirty-six men. Smith had in addition the usual headquarters and a supply company to meet his logistic needs.

For this operation, attached to Smith were H Battery 3rd/10th Artillery, with its eight 155mm towed howitzers – formidable weapons with a range of 22,000 metres. Armoured support was available in the shape of five M-60 tanks from 2nd Tank Battalion and fourteen amphibious assault vehicles – LVTP-7s – from 2nd Assault Amphibious Battalion. To complete the party, 2nd/8th had a reconnaissance platoon and engineer platoons.

By any yardstick, Smith had his own small army, which would be taken to war by the helicopters of 261 Medium Helicopter Squadron (HMM261), commanded by Lieutenant Colonel Granville Amos. The helicopter lift was provided by twelve CH-46E Sea Knights, each able to carry twenty-five fully equipped infantrymen. It could lift two companies at a time. Amos also had at his disposal four CH-53D Sea Stallions, which could carry heavy resupply loads or howitzers underslung. More firepower was provided by four AH-1 Cobra gunships.

The first of the invading Marines lifted off the deck of *Guam* at 0315 hrs on 25 October. It was a moonless night and although the pilots were equipped with night vision glasses, incredibly not all the pilots were qualified to use them.[1] It was almost 0500 hrs before all twenty-one helicopters were fuelled, loaded and on their way to war – about 10 miles (16 km) away. By now, the recent abandonment of a beach landing was causing Smith and Amos to rejig their plans.

The selected landing zone (LZ), about 500 yards (half a km) south of the airport, proved unsuitable. Dawn was breaking and the pilots could see that there were trees in the designated area. The SEALs, inserted to recce the beach, had not provided a warning, probably because it was just not part of their mission, and the LZ had been selected from recce photographs. However, the trees were not a crisis and the LZ was moved without incident, although it was 0520 hrs before the first marine boots hit Grenadian soil – twenty minutes behind schedule.

Dawn had broken when the following wave of aircraft arrived and two 12.7mm anti-aircraft guns engaged them. The guns were quickly silenced by a Marine AH-1T Sea Cobra gunship. This brief exchange of fire unsettled the Marine pilots and their passengers. The exchange of gunfire injected a sense of urgency into pilots and Marines.

What was needed was more haste and less speed because, in the unloading of aircraft, there were several avoidable accidents. Two jeeps with tube-launched, optically tracked, wire-guided (TOW) anti-tank weapons mounted were being offloaded from a Sea Stallion. They were inextricably jammed into each other and in the attempts to separate them, one Marine broke a leg; another broke an arm and one of the jeeps made an involuntary exit from the aircraft and was wrecked.

The assault on Pearls Airport was a major military non-event. A platoon advancing from the LZ was fired upon. It was ineffective fire and caused no injuries. The return fire was equally ineffective, but it did cause a party of Grenadians to run towards the western end of the runway.

The airport had a 5,151ft (1,570m) runway and was described as being 'a squalid leftover from colonial days which for all the world looked like a Victorian railway station transported to the tropics'. It was inadequate in every way: it lacked landing lights and electronic navigational aids.[2] This was a prize hardly worth taking.

At the airport, the Marines found a Russian-built AN-26, which had flown in the day before, bringing two senior Cuban officials. One of these was Colonel Pedro Comas, a professional soldier who had led the Cuban military mission in Grenada up until April 1983. His task was to enforce Castro's edict and prevent Cubans getting involved in a shooting war. The other passenger was Carlos Andres Larrañaga, a Cuban diplomat who was Castro's Caribbean section chief. It was highly unlikely that Coard and Austin *et al.* would take his advice – even if he could find them. The two Cubans were missing but the twelve-man crew of the aircraft were taken into custody. These men were not engaged in any military activity; they were civilian non-combatants, the USA was not at war with their country and their arrest is difficult to justify.

Colonel Smith was now with his Echo Company and directing American affairs. He ordered a platoon to take hill 275, from which, earlier, two 12.7mm guns had been discharged. As the Marines toiled up the hill, the PRA made their escape down the reverse slope. The PRA was, ostensibly, 906 strong, but only about half of them, 463, had responded to the call to arms. These men were trained and equipped by Cubans, but you can't teach courage, and the men on hill 275 were found wanting when put to the test.

While Echo Company enjoyed its success, Fox Company had made its heliborne arrival at Grenville, but not until 6.30am. Again, the selected LZ was unsuitable, and Colonel Amos selected an alternative. This was a playing field ringed by a high wall. The wall would provide cover and protection for any defenders who would be well placed to wreak serious damage to Marines as they exited their aircraft. Amos weighed up the factors, not least the negligible opposition so far. He overflew the town, saw people waving in a decidedly non-aggressive manner and opted to make use of the playing field.

The Marines were welcomed by the people of Grenville, who viewed them as liberators. The citizens were only too anxious to identify members of the militia and the location of their arms caches; they loaned their private vehicles to carry captured weapons.[3]

Pearls and Grenville had been secured at the cost of two broken limbs and one jeep. It had all been so very easy after days of anxious and stressful planning. The US forces of URGENT FURY had chalked up their first victory.

Notes

1. Spector, R.H., *Marines in Grenada 1983* (Washington, DC, History and Museums Division, HQ, US Marine Corps, 1987).
2. Payne, A., Sutton, P.K. and Thorndike, T., *Grenada: Revolution and Invasion* (New York, St Martin's Press, 1984), pp. 31–2.
3. Adkin, Major M., *Urgent Fury: The Battle for Grenada* (London, Leo Cooper, 1989), p. 241.

Chapter 10

Invasion – Point Salines and Camp Calivigny

On Saturday, 22 October, Lieutenant Colonel Ralph Hagler, commanding 2nd/75th Ranger Battalion, a veteran of the Vietnam War, was briefed by Major General Scholtes of JSOC. He was told that his battalion was to take and hold Pearls Airport and link up with the Marines of 22 MAU. H-hour was to be at 0200 hrs on 25 October.

Lieutenant Colonel Wesley Taylor, commanding 1st/75th Battalion, was tasked by Scholtes to land or parachute onto Point Salines Airport and was then to find and protect the medical students at True Blue campus.

These two officers had just over two days to ready their men and make appropriate plans. There was no intelligence, and no maps other than an out-of-date British tourist map. They were given black-and-white photocopies to work with.

It came as an unwelcome shock to both officers when they were told that they were to employ only half of their normal strength. It was explained that the USAF did not have sufficient personnel trained in the use of the MC-130 and C-130 troop-carrying aircraft. Taylor was also told that his C Company would be detached to support a 'special operation'.

US Rangers are well-trained and skilful light infantry. They are all qualified airborne soldiers and able to execute HALO insertions as and when required.[1] Rangers are intended to be used in quick, in-and-out type operations. They are lightly armed and as such, have to be supported. They are not intended to engage a major and determined enemy.

2nd/75th flew to Hunter Army airfield near Fort Stewart, Georgia, the home of the 1st Battalion, and arrived at 1400 hrs on 23 October. Taylor, despite the loss of Charlie Company, could still muster 300 men from his Alpha and Bravo companies. All up, with his headquarters and tactical element, Taylor had a fighting strength of 350.

Hagler, of 2nd Battalion, had far fewer; he was only able to take a few of his most capable soldiers from his Alpha, Bravo and Charlie companies. His fighting strength, including two tactical headquarters, was about 150. On the afternoon of 23 October, Hagler had completed his plan to take Pearls when he was told that his mission had completely changed. He was now to follow

Taylor into Point Salines and was then to attack Camp Calivigny, allegedly the well-protected, main PRA installation.

This new plan was not without its difficulties. Hagler's men, probably having jumped in darkness onto Point Salines and engaged the enemy on and around the landing zone, was then to march the 7½ miles (12km) across country, without maps, to engage an enemy whose strength, deployment and weaponry were all unknown. The assault on Camp Calivigny was to go in at dawn. This plan had all the makings of a disaster – and it got worse.

On Monday, 24 October, the two commanding officers had to rejig their plans again. H-hour had been put back from 0200 hrs to 0400 hrs and then finally to 0500 hrs. The new timing was to accommodate two further attempts by the SEALs to reconnoitre the Point Salines airstrip.

This was a curious decision as the Ranger pathfinder group was also tasked to reconnoitre Point Salines, albeit about three hours later. It might be concluded that the delay of the entire operation was inspired either by a 'belt-and-braces' attitude or by the need to justify the role of Special Forces in the future, and that of the SEALs in particular. Come what may, 0500 hrs was a bare fifteen minutes before dawn. An assault planned for execution in darkness was likely to be implemented in daylight, which was entirely to the advantage of any defenders. There was now no possibility of surprise.

On the evening of 24 October, as both Ranger battalions prepared themselves for departure in two hours' time, they were abruptly told to board their aircraft and depart at once. It transpired that the Rangers' flight schedule was at odds with that of the USAF 1st Special Operations Wing. Suddenly, the well-ordered calm was altered by the urgency of this latest order. The first of the Rangers' aircraft was airborne by 2130 hrs – about twenty-five minutes later than the USAF schedule had demanded. This significant change of plan was to be the first of many.

Once again, the absence of intelligence was a burden to the Rangers, as it was to be for the Marines at Pearls. It now seemed likely that a decision would have to be made mid-flight. That was indeed the case, and soon after Taylor and his battalion started their seven-and-a-half-hour journey to Grenada, he was told that the third and final SEAL mission had failed. Then the latest photographs of Point Salines were analysed, and they revealed that the runways were obstructed by three construction vehicles parked in the centre of the runway and several more blocking it at the west.[2] In addition to the vehicles, there was an assortment of 'smaller items which were later found to include 55-gallon barrels filled with coral, spikes and concertina wire'.[3]

Five C-130s and two MC-130Es were allocated to lift 1st/75th. The MC-130Es were fundamentally the same as the C-130s, except that they were fitted with more sophisticated navigational equipment. Five more C-130s were earmarked to transport 2nd/75th. To provide protection, four AS-130 Spectre gunships were included in the fleet. These were state-of-the-art and very powerful aircraft. Heavily armed, with multiple weapon systems, they would suppress enemy activity around the LZ. Grenada was not in any way equipped to resist an invasion. It had no viable anti-aircraft capability and no air force. The Spectres were the icing on this US military cake.

This latest situation report meant that both the Ranger battalions would have to jump onto their objective. Taylor decided that given the timescale, his men would jump from 500 feet (152m). They would be in the air for only between fifteen and twelve seconds; in the event of a parachute failure there would not be time to deploy any reserve 'chute. 'This was now a very hazardous operation. In peacetime exercise conditions, the minimum jump height was 1,200 feet (366m) with a wind speed of 13 knots. In Grenada on the morning of 25 October, the wind was a steady 20 knots, gusting to 25.'[4]

The soldiers on the MC-130s were cramped and uncomfortable. Airsickness affected some and the smell of vomit and sweat was stomach-turning. To add to the misery, they now had to struggle into their parachutes.

Sometime around 0300 hrs, Major Michael Couvillon was piloting an AC-30 Spectre gunship 9,000 feet above Grenada. His passengers were the pathfinder group whose task was to lead the seizure of Point Salines airstrip. Their function was to free-fall onto Point Salines at 0330 hrs, about ninety minutes ahead of Alpha Company of 1st/75th. They would report on the situation on the ground to the soon-to-arrive airborne troops. If possible, they would install navigation aids such as marker lights for the guidance of the incoming air traffic, and advise on enemy movement and locations. They were to make a covert reconnaissance of the True Blue campus.

Alpha Company of 1st/75th, led by Captain John Abizaid, was embarked in two MC-130E aircraft and their first function was to clear the runways of any obstructions. They had been allocated only thirty minutes for this unmeasured task. Enemy interference could well negate the plan. Behind Alpha Company, the remainder of 1st/75th were aboard the five MC-130s. Taylor was accompanied in the third of the MC-130s by Major General William Mall, the senior MAC representative on the operation. His presence would have inhibited the much more junior Taylor.

Taylor's task was to take control of the airstrip east of Hardy Bay and then move swiftly to secure the US citizens at True Blue. 1st/75th had been expecting to disembark their aircraft as and when they landed, but that had all changed.

At 0330 hrs, Couvillon's pathfinder passengers made their exit from his aircraft, and two men were killed when their parachutes malfunctioned. The invasion force had now lost six dead before the operation had really started. The surviving pathfinders confirmed the bad news that the airstrip was cluttered with obstacles.

It was blindingly obvious to Austin and his Cuban advisors that Point Salines was a high priority US target. Accordingly, they anticipated a cross-beach landing at the western (sea) end of the runway. On that basis they had fortified the south of the east–west runway. Their scarce, obsolete anti-aircraft guns were located on the low hills to the north of the runway.

The runway clearance team in the two leading MC-130Es were approaching from the west but, when around 20 miles short of the LZ, the leading aircraft started to experience a failure in its, previously mentioned, sophisticated navigational system. The pilot was unable to establish the critical airdrop calculations. The LZ had water on both sides and a miscalculation could well put the Rangers at extreme risk. The issue was such that the pilot said he could not guarantee to find the drop zone (DZ) in the dark. To compound the problem the weather took a turn for the worse and heavy rain reduced visibility even further.[5]

It was at 0454 hrs that Captain Abizaid saw the jumpmaster indicate 'no jump'. This called for a rapid change of plan and the USAF colonel who had command of the air component ordered the third MC-130 (Taylor's) to take the lead. General Scholtes authorised a thirty-minute delay to H-hour, putting it back to 0530 hrs and in broad daylight. The master plan was in shreds. The official history observed:

> Problems beset the operation from the start. The loss of the inertial navigation system in the lead C-130 aircraft meant that the flow of C-130s had to be adjusted in the air and delayed the parachute assault by the Rangers at Point Salines.
>
> Delay of the airdrop until daylight put it thirty-six minutes behind the Marine assault at Pearls and cost the Rangers and other Joint Special Operations Command [JSOC] forces tactical surprise. Adjusting the airflow changed the order of the C-130 airdrop, which mixed the Ranger units on the landing zone. The delay of the airdrop and confusion resulting from the unplanned sequence of the airdrop was a major operational slip-up.[6]

Taylor, who was geared to jump, had nevertheless been hoping to land on a cleared runway. He now found that he was leading the charge and would be first on the ground. At 0400 hrs, he had made the decision that his battalion would jump into action and the only exception would be those men crewing jeeps. Taylor passed his order for it to be sent by the onboard radio. He was given a thumbs-up sign by the radio operator, from which, not unreasonably, he deduced that his order had been communicated. However, the fifth, sixth and seventh aircraft did not understand the message and did not send an affirmative response. From this time, confusion took centre stage.

On the fifth aircraft, anticipating an order to jump, Nix, the company commander, already had his men rigged to do so. Inexplicably, the jumpmaster announced that the aeroplane would land and that the troops should de-rig. This was a highly unpopular situation. The men were tired, cramped, and some were airsick. All the parachute equipment was pushed to the front of the aircraft. This irritating and laborious exercise had just been completed when the jumpmaster added to the corporate unhappiness by shouting, 'Only thirty minutes of fuel left. Rangers are fighting. Jump in twenty minutes.'[7] The Rangers were not best pleased, and some probably offered an opinion on the matter.

On the fifth aircraft, chaos came to join confusion at the party. Preparing for an operational parachute landing is usually a precise, meticulous exercise. Now the men who had just de-rigged had to prepare, again, to jump. The floor space was crammed with unwanted kit as the Rangers struggled into the basic parachuting kit, which included a reserve 'chute worn on the chest. There was an overwhelming sense of urgency. There was insufficient space for movement and the normal safety checks by the jumpmaster could not be carried out, so the Rangers relied on a comrade to check them out.

The situation in the air above Grenada had reached the level of farce. Taylor was unaware that, in the first four of his troop-carrying aircraft, his Rangers were prepared to jump but, in the last three, the presumption was still that they would land. When this latter group got the 'jump' warning order, they experienced the same stressing confusion as their comrades flying ahead of them.

General Scholtes was not having a good day. His SEALs had failed three times to infiltrate Point Salines and two of his pathfinders had died in a fourth attempt. He ordered the two leading aircraft, carrying Alpha Company, to abort their approach and go into a holding pattern. For Lieutenant Colonel Taylor commanding 1st/75th, this was the final straw and he responded angrily to the combination of being told to leave two hours before schedule, the conflicting orders to jump or land and now finding his plane load was to jump into Point Salines – ahead of the Alpha Company, the designated clearance party.

Taylor had to make some swift changes. The third aircraft would lead the eight, at one-minute intervals, to the DZ – it was at this very late stage that Taylor learned that aircraft numbers six, seven and eight had all re-rigged and anticipated a landing. To give time for the men to don their parachutes, the three aircraft were told to hold off.

Taylor's C-130 made its final approach at about 150 knots and at the stipulated 500 feet. It was 0531 hrs and the sky was getting brighter every moment, but there was that hazardous and brisk 20-knot wind that added to the mix. A searchlight swept across the sky and locked onto the cockpit. The co-pilot, Captain P.R. Helm, remarked to the pilot, Lieutenant Colonel J.L. Hobson, 'Jim I don't think this is going to be a big surprise.'[8]

The Rangers all carried very heavy backpacks and Lieutenant R.T. Thomas of 2nd/75th said:

> Most people jumped with excessive loads ... I jumped with an M-60 machine gun and my .45. I also had about 1,000 rounds of 7.62mm ammunition and some frags. It was probably the heaviest rucksack I'd ever carried. A guy in front of me thought he had a hernia. He didn't think he'd be able to get out. They would just have climbed over him.[9]

The Rangers did not really jump; rather, they stumbled out of the two doors and by this method, four men would be in the air every second. Both battalions were equipped with the T-10 parachute, not the more usual MC1-1B. The difference was that the T-10 was the less steerable of the two. The thinking behind this decision was that there was less likelihood to be any mid-air entanglements using the more stable T-10. Hagler's 2nd Battalion wore their reserve 'chutes but, happily, none needed to use them.

Taylor's aircraft drew ineffective fire from a 12.7mm four-barrelled heavy AA machine gun sited on the ridge north of the terminal building. Hobson held his nerve and decanted Taylor and his forty-two comrades over Point Salines. They had boots on the ground at 0534 hrs.

URGENT FURY was to involve 20,000 American servicemen. A fundamental military precept is the need to concentrate force. Taylor and his small group emphatically did not fill that requirement. The Rangers were very exposed, and they were very fortunate that the enemy was not entrenched in strength on the low hills about 220 yards (183m) to the north of the runway. Only the AA weapons were in that situation. Had the insertion been opposed by the PRA, the probability is that all forty-three Rangers, and first to arrive, would have been eliminated. As it was, the only opposition were Cubans and they had strict orders not to in initiate any fighting.

The pilots of the two following aircraft were sufficiently discommoded by the AA fire that they opted out and pulled away. Seconds later, Taylor and his men were all alone on the runway, which was obstructed by the miscellany of detritus mentioned on page 78. It was a long, lonely twenty minutes before Taylor saw his Alpha Company approaching and providing a target for AA and small arms fire. This fire was ineffective, and a part of Alpha Company joined the CO on the ground. At about 0630 hrs, the battalion was complete.

It is remarkable that, given the lack of the normal pre-jump precautions, of the total of 497 Rangers, only one was injured, and he had a broken leg. Many others had minor contusions, but the lack of injuries is testament to the training and resolve of this Ranger force. It is also remarkable that, despite identifying the airports as likely invasion points, Austin had not deployed more of his scant resources to defend them. Had he done so, Pearls and Point Salines would have seen considerable bloodshed.

On the ground, the two Ranger battalions were inextricably mixed. The plan had called for the 1st Battalion to secure the eastern half of the airport, from the lagoon to the area of the True Blue campus, and the 2nd Battalion the western end of the runway, to the beach and the sea beyond. However, the immediate priority for both was to clear the runway of obstacles. The bulldozer that was needed on the ground was in an aircraft that had aborted the drop. To his credit, a young soldier, William Richardson from 82nd Airborne Division, with a comrade, took possession of Cuban heavy plant and moved it off the runway. An asphalt roller was pressed into service and used to flatten the steel rods that had been driven into the runway.[10] A Cuban bulldozer pushed the obstacles off the runway.

Captain Abizaid, commanding Alpha Company, determined that he had to clear the enemy from the low hills to the north towards the village of Calliste and that there was a need to send a platoon along the beach to the True Blue Campus. The approach towards the hill drew fire, and a Ranger, Mark Yamane, was hit and killed – the only Ranger to die in Grenada.

It was 0725 hrs when the Point Salines airstrip was pronounced secure.[11] From 0737 hrs, fixed-wing aircraft started to land and at the front of the queue were four C-130s carrying Alpha Squadron of Delta Force and Charlie Company of 1st/75th, which had been detached from its battalion at the operation planning stage (see p. 77). Cargo in these aircraft were eight OH-6 light helicopters, their rotors neatly folded. These helicopters could be used in the gunship role or that of troop carriers. Initially, two equipped as gunships set off to attack Fort Rupert (also known as Fort George). This was perceived to be the location of the main Grenadian headquarters and, as such, a significant target.

The OH-6s found that Fort Rupert had some modest AA defence and the AA fire sufficiently disagreeable that they returned to Point Salines within ten minutes. Accordingly, the assault on Fort Rupert was postponed.[12] This was another example of the intelligence gap because Coard and his acolytes had moved their military headquarters from Fort Rupert to Fort Frederick after the bloodletting of 19 October.

Major General Scholtes, the JSOC commander, arrived, set up his headquarters and reviewed the situation. He was decisive, and straight away cancelled the 2nd/75th attack on Camp Calivigny and the SEAL mission to take the diesel-powered electricity plant.

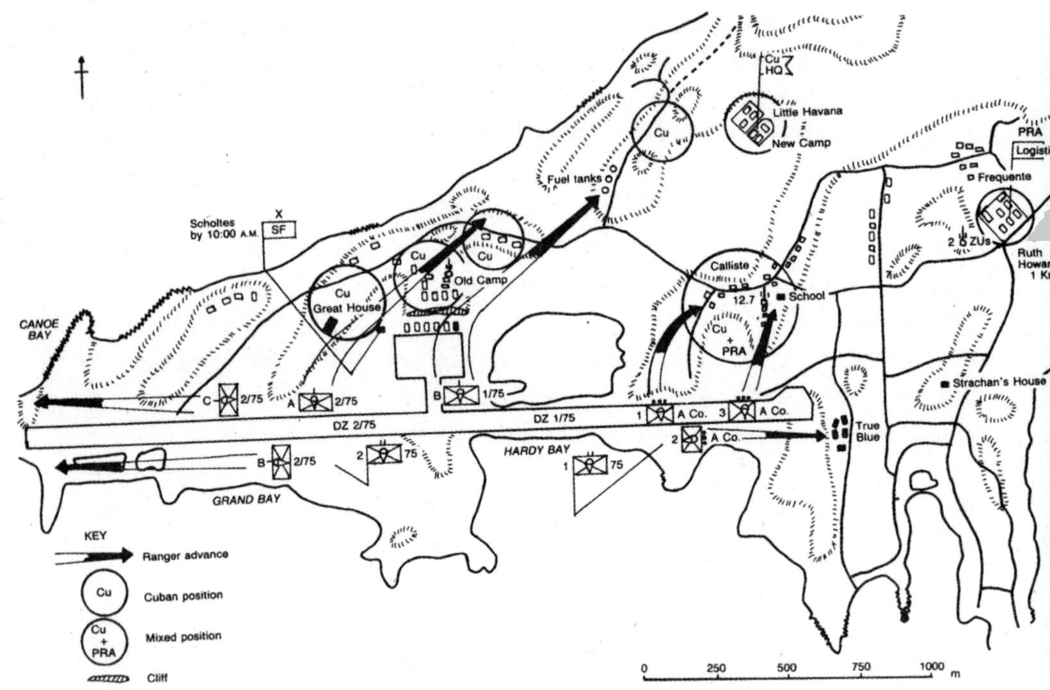

The map shows the juxtaposition of True Blue (middle right), the fuel tanks (top middle) and, at 1000 hrs on 25 October, the advance north by US forces. (*Adkin*)

Notes

1. HALO – high altitude, low opening.
2. Kallander, D.C. and Matthews, J.K., *Urgent Fury: The United States Air Force and the Grenada Operation* (Military Airlift Command Office of History, 1988), p. 40.
3. Couvillon, M.J., *Grenada Grinder: The Complete Story of AC-130H Spectre Gunships in Operation Urgent Fury* (Marietta, Georgia, Deeds Publishing, 2011), p. 65.
4. Lieutenant Colonel R. Hagler, interviewed by Major C.R. Bishop, 30 October 1983 (transcript archived at US Army Center of Military History).
5. Ibid., p. 204.
6. Cole, R.H., *Operation Urgent Fury: The Planning and Execution of Joint Operations in Grenada 1983* (US Joint Chiefs of Staff, Washington, DC, Joint History Office, 1997), p. 3.
7. Adkin, Major M., *Urgent Fury: The Battle for Grenada* (London, Leo Cooper, 1989), p. 203.
8. Hobson, J.L., 'Operation Urgent Fury' (*Air Commando Journal*, spring 2012), p. 29.
9. Adkin, p. 208.
10. Russell, L. and Mendez, M.A., *Grenada 1983* (London, Osprey, 1985), p. 17.
11. Pirnie, B.R., *Operation Urgent Fury: The United States in Joint Operations* (Washington, DC, US Army Center of Military History, 1986), p. 216.
12. Haney, E.L., *Inside Delta Force: The Story of America's Elite Counterforce Unit* (New York, Dell Publishing, 2003), p. 380.

Chapter 11

Reaction

News of the invasion spread across the globe and reaction was mixed, depending upon political persuasion. However, the international consensus was that President Reagan had overstepped the mark. At the United Nations, there was a majority who considered President Reagan's act to be counter to the ethics of the organisation. A resolution was framed that read: 'This resolution, deeply deplores the armed intervention in Grenada, which constitutes a flagrant violation of international law and of the independence, sovereignty and territorial integrity of Grenada.'[1]

The vote was later carried by a majority of 108 to 9. The US Government defended its invasion of Grenada as an action to protect American citizens living on the island, including medical students, and had been carried out at the request of the Governor General.[2] This was patently not the case, and the unvarnished truth is that it was a lie – and widely perceived to be so.

The Deputy Secretary of State, Kenneth Dam, averred that the invasion was necessary to 'resolve' what Article 28 of the Organisation of American States (OAS) refers to as a 'a situation that might endanger peace'. Dam went further and claimed that both the OAS and the UN Charter 'recognise the competence of regional security bodies in ensuring regional peace and stability'.[3]

One of the features of Operation URGENT FURY was the facile attempt at secrecy and thus the total exclusion of the media from Grenada. Hugh O'Shaughnessy, a journalist, was present in Grenadian waters throughout the 'war', but he was prevented from landing. Later he concluded that, the invasion, 'by acting illegally and by doing a job that would sooner or later be done by the Grenadian people themselves Ronald Reagan was weakening respect for international law'.[4]

One of the unexpected consequences of the invasion by the United States was that it embarrassed and humiliated the UK, its principal ally. HMG wriggled under acute public scrutiny. On 25 October, a visibly uncomfortable Sir Geoffrey Howe had to face the House of Commons – not least, his formidable shadow opposition, the vastly experienced Denis Healey, the member for Leeds East. *Hansard* recorded his opening remarks. He said:

The Foreign Secretary has made a serious and disturbing statement which contrasts oddly with the statement that he made to the House only 24 hours ago. Yesterday, he rightly told us: 'Grenada is an independent country. Our concern and what we are prepared to do about it must be determined by that fact'. [*Official Report*, 24 October 1983; Vol. 33, c. 28.]

The military regime in Grenada is repulsive to all hon. Members, and has seized power in a bloody coup, but, as I reminded the House yesterday, there are many other such Governments who seized power by similar methods, especially in that part of the world.

President Reagan made it clear this morning that he was invited on Sunday by a number of Caribbean Commonwealth countries to join them in invading the island, and in his statement, which was reported in the BBC news at one o'clock, he placed little importance on the risk to American citizens on the island. He described the purpose of the invasion as threefold. First, it was to protect innocent lives—I wonder how many lives have already been lost, and how many of those lives were those of British citizens. The second purpose was to forestall further chaos, and the third to restore law and order.

None of those objectives justifies the invasion of an independent state, particularly when, as the Foreign Secretary told us yesterday, the lives of foreign citizens on Grenada were not in imminent danger. The noble Baroness Young told the other place [the House of Lords] yesterday that the Grenada Government were putting no difficulties in the way of those who wished to leave the island. I must ask the Foreign Secretary some questions about what has happened.

What steps is HMS *Antrim* taking now to protect British citizens, as the latest news report suggests that fighting is continuing? *Secondly, what has been the role of the Governor-General, representing Her Majesty the Queen, in this affair? It is a serious matter, I hope that the House will agree, when a Commonwealth country subject to the Queen is invaded by a foreign state, and the British Government are informed of the intention to invade at the very moment when the invasion is taking place, and their protestations are brushed aside* [author's emphasis].

The Foreign Secretary has some questions to answer about what he told us yesterday. It appears that a number of Commonwealth Governments invited President Reagan to intervene as long ago as Sunday, although many Commonwealth Caribbean Governments did not, including Trinidad, the Bahamas and Belize, all of which refused to participate in the conspiracy. Were the Commonwealth Governments who took part in the invasion and invited the United States troops to intervene the Governments with which the Foreign Secretary told us yesterday he was closely in touch? The decision was apparently taken in Trinidad by the Commonwealth Governments concerned as long ago as Saturday. Were Her Majesty's Government informed of what was going on? The Grenada Government knew yesterday because they reported the happenings in the Trinidad discussions, in detail on radio, and their report was published in this morning's *Daily Telegraph*. Did those Governments invite Her Majesty's Government to join in the invasion and, if so, what reply did Her Majesty's Government give?

Yesterday, the Foreign Secretary told us that there was no reason to think that American military intervention was likely, and that he knew of no American intention to invade. That is an extraordinary statement by a representative of a Government who pride themselves on being America's most loyal ally. Were Her Majesty's Government informed in advance that this request had been made by the United States Government? Was a similar request made of Her Majesty's Government? If so, when, and what response was given?

It is clear from what the Foreign Secretary has told us that Her Majesty's Government have, on this occasion, been deceived by their American allies and by some of their Commonwealth partners. *Many of us will think twice about the credence to give joint decision on other matters. I hope that the Secretary of State for Defence will think carefully about the line that he has been taking on other matters in the light of what has happened on an island where British forces were known to be offshore* [author's emphasis.].

This refers to the proposal to site American missiles in the UK. The condition was that HMG would have the right to veto their use. Reagan's actions and his duplicity over Grenada went towards negating any assurances on the issue of missile use. Healey ended his speech by saying, 'The American decision has already split the Commonwealth states in the Caribbean. It represents an unpardonable humiliation of an ally. I must ask the Foreign Secretary, indeed the Prime Minister, to protest directly in the clearest possible terms.'

Notwithstanding the relatively temperate tenor of Healey's remarks, he had hit most of the available targets. The debate that followed was lengthy and not entirely one-sided. For example, Mr Peter Tapsell (East Lindsey), expressing a minority view, observed:

Does my right hon. and learned Friend accept that, for the reasons that I briefly summarised in my question to him yesterday, American intervention was inevitable and desirable? Does he agree that those countries in the Caribbean most completely wedded to democracy will be strong supporters of the action that has been taken?

Is it not time that those who are for ever blathering on about the dangers posed by Soviet imperialism should, for once, support the United States in defending our freedom?

The Times, on the other hand, had no doubt as to the rectitude or otherwise of Reagan's invasion, and in its edition of 25 October, 'The Thunderer' pronounced, 'There is no getting around the fact that the United States and its Caribbean allies have committed aggression against Grenada. They are in breach of international law and the Charter of the United Nations.'

Howe and Thatcher struggled not to criticise the USA, presumably to defend the 'special relationship'. That was, then, and still is today, entirely mythical. The reality is that there are no friends in international relations There are allies, but any relationship between them is invariably dependent upon treaty obligations and a shared enemy. Back in 1848, Lord Palmerston had judged, 'We have no eternal allies, and we have no perpetual enemies. Our interests are eternal and perpetual, and these interests it is our duty to follow.'[5]

Henry Kissinger expressed a similar sentiment when he said accurately, 'America has no permanent friends or enemies – only interests.'[6]

On that entirely reasonable basis, all countries are at liberty to behave as they think fit. During the eighteenth and nineteenth centuries, Great Britain was powerful enough to do just that. However, in order to ride roughshod over the sovereignty of other nations the prerequisite is vast military power and a willingness to use force for political ends. In the twentieth and now twenty-first centuries, it is the United States with that power. Waiting in the wings to succeed the USA are India and China.

Notes

1. United Nations General Assembly Resolution 38/7, 2 November 1983.
2. Murphy, P., *Monarchy and the End of Empire* (Oxford, Oxford University Press, 2013), p. 169.
3. Smith, H., 'US Defending Grenada Action before OAS' (*New York Times*, 15 November 1983).
4. O'Shaughnessy, H., *Grenada: Revolution, Invasion and Aftermath* (London, Sphere Books, 1984), p. 4.
5. Lord Palmerston (British Prime Minister 1855–8 and 1859–65), speaking in the House of Commons, 1 March 1848, when he was Foreign Secretary.
6. Henry Kissinger (1923–2023), US Secretary of State 1973–7, quoted in his book *The White House Years* (London, Simon & Schuster, 2011).

Chapter 12

25 October 1983
Special Forces Assault on Beausejour Radio Station and Richmond Hill Prison

The medical students, resident at the True Blue campus, had been woken by the sound of aircraft and a little after 0730 hrs, American voices were heard shouting to the students asking them to identify themselves. They were told to lie on the floor, an instruction quickly obeyed.

There was an exchange of gunfire between the advancing Rangers and a small detachment of PRA soldiers manning the main gate to the campus. Neither side delivered effective fire but, in the process, windows were broken and bullets pierced the building. The PRA broke off the engagement and, within fifteen minutes, the campus was in American hands. There had been no casualties on either side and there was general rejoicing as the Rangers greeted their fellow compatriots.

It came as an unwelcome surprise to the Rangers when they found that they had only 'liberated' less than half of the student body. The Grand Anse campus had never featured in the URGENT FURY planning, but it was now a priority.

Down on the airstrip, Bravo Company had been ordered to take the control tower and then to move on north-west into the hills beyond. Adkins speaks of 'heavy fire' from the Cubans as the company advanced.[1] Like so many of the engagements during this war, the fire of both sides was ill-directed, and the Cubans withdrew, leaving one dead. Twenty-two surrendered. Bravo Company moved on and by 0955 hrs it had gained about 650 yards (600m) and reached the high ground on which were the fuel storage tanks. Alpha Company held the Calliste high ground.

* * *

Operation Urgent Fury was shrouded in secrecy, the media were totally excluded, and the most closely guarded secret was to be the role of US elite Special Forces. When these Delta Force and SEAL teams arrived above the Spice Island, American boots were already on the ground at the two airstrips.

The slippage of H-hour to 0530 hrs had robbed the Special Forces of their two principal attributes – stealth and surprise. They were absent from the initial planning for the invasion of Grenada and it was not until 20 October that Major General Scholtes was invited to join the party. And it was not until Sunday, 23 October that it was 'firmly decided in Washington that regime change was the ultimate gaol of the intervention, not merely rescuing American citizens'.[2]

The Special Forces were to leave the suppression of the PRA and any belligerent Cubans to the Rangers and Marines. Their role was to resolve three sensitive, political situations. A new and, inevitably, secret army aviation unit, the 160th Special Operations Aviation Regiment (SOAR), was to deliver the soldiers of JSOC to their targets. This regiment had risen from the debacle of Operation EAGLE CLAW and its sole function was to provide the commando type soldiers of JSOC with the means to get to any target, anywhere, with stealth and efficiency. Its aircraft, the UH-60A Black Hawk, was a derivative of the Vietnam workhorse, the UH-1 Huey. It was intended to be resistant to small arms fire and able to lift a fully equipped eleven-man squad.

In Barbados, the nine Black Hawks of 160th SOAR (A) were offloaded from the Galaxies that had brought them to this staging area. They had to be reassembled, the crews briefed, and the weapons loaded. The planners had allowed an hour for this reassembling process, which was hopelessly optimistic. The ammunition for the M-60 machine guns had been placed on the Galaxies as cargo but it was discovered that it was unbelted, and this glitch had to be fixed. It all took time, and H-hour came and went. 160th had provided thirty-six pilots for the nine Black Hawks: eighteen sat in the pilot or co-pilot seats, nine were employed as navigators, and the other nine acted as door gunners.[3]

The Delta Force Rangers in SEAL team 6 were embarked on the two aircraft heading for the radio station and Government House. Two other Black Hawks were to take on Richmond Hill Prison. There was no intelligence on either objective and any available maps were of no practical use. The pilot of one of the Black Hawks, Captain Keith Lucas, was told that all he had to do was to decant his passengers on a field near to the prison. There was an air of complacency, and the presumption was that 'the operation would be a walkover'.

The prime minister of Barbados, Tom Adams, a leading light in the Caribbean support of invasion, visited the Black Hawks at 0530 hrs and was able to see them off on their missions, 156 miles (251km) away.

Any of the pilots tuning in his radio would be discomforted to pick up Radio Free Grenada, which was telling the world that the invasion had started and that American troops were taking possession of the airstrips at Point Salines and Pearls. The guns on Captain Keith Lucas's aircraft were tested and one of the M-60s jammed. It was after 0600 hrs and by the time the weapon was cleared, after just over an hour's flying time, the prison lay ahead.

* * *

The last helicopter turned away when it crossed the coastline and made for its objective, the radio station at Beausejour, about 5 miles (8km) north of St George's, the capital of Grenada. Lieutenant Donald Erskine, a seasoned Vietnam veteran, was leading this small team. He considered that 'so far his mission had violated just about everything he had been taught about planning and rehearsing a surprise assault'.[4] He described the intelligence as 'comically inadequate', as it comprised a photograph of the objective and a tourist map. Erskine's team included three men who had been part of the failed insertion at Point Salines, but he did not know them.

Erskine was tired, having had little sleep in the previous forty-eight hours, and frustrated by the constant revisions to his mission. Originally, he was to have participated in the taking of Point Salines and the 'rescue' of the medical students. But with the change of emphasis from rescue to regime change, his team were redirected to Beausejour. As Erskine and his men approached their objective, a rubber bladder of fuel stored inside the aircraft sprang a leak. Aviation fuel was washing around the feet of the SEAL team; a spark would have cremated them all, and the crew of the Black Hawk.

There was no spark.

The pilot found the radio station in a field at Beausejour Farm. As he positioned his aircraft to land about 50 yards (45m) from the building, it became a target for small arms fire. The onboard gunners responded and doused the target in effective machine-gun fire. The Grenadian opposition fled, mounted a truck and disappeared.

Erskine's orders were to defend the facility until he was relieved by CIA operatives, who would arrive from St George's with Sir Paul Scoon. The Governor General would then broadcast to the nation, appeal for calm and tell Grenadian belligerents to lay down their arms.

That was the plan.

It had several components, and for it to work, these components all had to be achieved sequentially. The freeing of Sir Paul Scoon and his broadcast to the nation was simple in concept but more difficult in practice. In fact, and although Erskine did not know, the plan had already gone seriously pear-shaped.

Erskine had been furnished with the usual encrypted radio that SEALs used on operations, together with the critical frequencies and codes required to communicate with his chain of command. He did not know that all of these had been changed overnight – but no one thought to tell him. Erskine could hear radio traffic but could not transmit. This was just one of many communication failures during Operation URGENT FURY. However, this one was life-threatening because Erskine and his small team were alone, in enemy territory, unsupported, and without communications. Erskine had no way of knowing that the rescue of Sir Paul Scoon had gone badly wrong and that the Governor General would not be arriving to make a broadcast. Bereft of any information, his team were out on a limb.

There was no Plan 'B'.

A station wagon carrying a family of civilians, including three children and a dog, was stopped and the family taken into custody to prevent them spreading the news of the SEAL presence. Later that morning, at approximately 0900 hrs, a party of about fifteen Grenadian militia, riding in a Soviet-built truck and a civilian vehicle, approached the radio station. Erskine halted the convoy, and meticulously conforming to his 'rules of engagement', identified himself. He called on the militia to surrender their weapons. This was followed by a brief, acrimonious debate. At this point, one, very foolish, Grenadian ducked behind a convenient tractor and opened fire. He was at very short range, but nevertheless, his opening round missed. The response was instantaneous, brief and ruthless: 'it lasted only fifteen seconds but left the [Grenadian] soldiers dead or wounded. The truck was a smoking wreck and, as it burnt, sending a tell-tale plume of smoke into the air.'[5]

The ten wounded were treated by the SEALs with medical training and the five dead were separated from the living. The radio station was transformed into a casualty ward, its floor slippery with blood. The family, previously arrested, were witness to the awful scene and exposed to the shrieks from the wounded men.

Erskine realised that the presence of his team at Beausejour was no longer a secret, and on that basis, he released the family, who took to the coast road that bypassed the radio station. This road was much travelled and, as the family fled, a truck with a mounted searchlight was stopped and the three occupants, thought to be Cuban, were added to the ranks of the captured.

By this time, it was clear to Erskine that the master plan had failed miserably and that his SEAL team was committed to a defence of a radio station that had no strategic value. They were lightly armed, with only short-range, automatic weapons and pistols. They had no anti-tank or mortars and their only protection from sight and fire were the thin walls of the radio station. They were very vulnerable.

The PRA, alerted to the situation at Beausejour, selected Lieutenant Cecil Prime to retake the radio station. This officer was a professional soldier and a member of the ruling junta. He already had blood on his hands as he was a participant in the murder of Bishop and his seven associates.

Prime put together a composite force for the task. It was composed of a platoon of soldiers, an armoured personnel carrier (APC), an 82mm mortar team, a jeep, a van and a minibus. It was sometime just after 0900 hrs, when Prime's convoy made its way along the coast road to the crest of the Happy Hill ridgeline, about 550 yards (500m) from the radio station that lay to the north-east, on the flat ground on the left of the road. Prime sited his mortar on the ridge, close to a local school. He ordered part of his force to advance up the road, less fifteen of his men who were to stay in their vehicles and dismount before the river bridge, and then deploy left of the road. The eight-wheeled BTR-60 APC, with Prime in command, would cross the bridge and move forward from the south-east until it could engage the target building with its heavy machine gun.

The dismounted troops approached the SEAL position from the south-west as part of a simple pincer movement. The APC halted, and the radio station came under its sustained fire from the powerful machine gun. This fire was directed by Prime, and it was devastating: machine-gun rounds penetrated the wall of the building.

Erskine was now in a situation that JSOC troops would always seek to avoid. He could not match either the firepower or the strength of his now very aggressive enemy. He determined that the station should be abandoned and the SEALs would regroup around the transmitter. Under constant fire, the SEALs, one at a time, ducked out of the radio station and set off across the meadow. They adopted the 'fire and movement' tactic in which some moved while the others produced suppressing fire. Incredibly, all the SEALs reached the perimeter fence, which was topped with barbed wire, and only three were wounded, one of whom was Erskine – shot very painfully in the elbow.

The fence was breached with fortuitously available wire cutters. The PRA were cautious in their pursuit and that gave the Americans valuable time. The SEALs entered an area of thick vegetation, crossed a river and made their way to Beausejour beach. The team shed their weapons and most of their equipment. They entered the sea in pairs and swam parallel to the shore. One wonders how Erskine, in great pain and with only one arm, could swim. He did, and led his men out of the water and up steep cliffs.[6]

Three swimmers were despatched to commandeer a local fishing boat, but although they found some, the SEALs were unable to free the boats from their mooring lines. USN A-7 aircraft strafed the radio station, and during one pass, their fire came perilously close to the concealed SEALs. Erskine then led his team to a rocky peninsula from where they could jump straight into the sea.

The party split into three groups, and notwithstanding the three wounded men, they swam out to sea. This was on the absurd basis that, by some miracle, the USN would find them. One group came upon an untended boat. They climbed aboard and cut the anchor line but were unable to move the boat; they eventually discovered that it had a second anchor.[7]

It would seem that miracles do sometimes happen and when the USS *Caron*, a destroyer of the *Independence* group, patrolling offshore, saw the strobe lights attached to the SEALs' equipment, it moved to investigate and eventually recovered ten members of the team. The two still missing were seen but they were too close to the shore and an army helicopter was called to extricate them. The whole team was united on *Caron* at 0135 hrs on 26 October. It had been quite a long and arduous day. Later, Lieutenant Erskine was awarded a well-deserved Silver Star.[8]

* * *

The Beausejour operation and been a disaster and it was amazing that, given the ordnance directed at them, none of the SEALs had been killed. The assault on Richmond Hill Prison was, if anything, an even greater failure.

The plan was that the eight helicopters would fly to a traffic roundabout in the centre of St George's and here they would form into two groups and embark on their separate missions.

It came as a shock to Lucas when, as the pilot in one of the eight Black Hawks, he saw his objective, Richmond Hill Prison. He found that it was not where he expected it to be and nothing like the building in his briefing. The prison was located on the spine of a high ridge, with steeply sloping sides covered with scrub. The building had formidable walls about 20 feet (6m) high. These were surmounted by coils of barbed wire. Clearly, this was likely to be a tough nut to crack. An added surprise was that the helicopters came under immediate and sustained AA fire. This fire came not only from the prison, but also from Fort Frederick, sitting astride the same ridge. Fort Frederick was about 150 feet (46m) higher than the prison and it dominated the scene.

The AA gunners were presented with easy targets as the Black Hawks approached their objective. They were close to and sometimes below the gunners, who started to inflict damage on the airborne force. Had the assault been in darkness as per the long-lost original plan, the visually aimed Second World War-era AA guns would have been inadequate. However, in broad daylight, at short range the Cuban-trained Grenadian gunners with their two four-barrel 12.7mm guns and their two twin-barrel 33mm guns were able to produce a veritable hail of well-directed fire.[9] The Black Hawks urgently needed support from Spectre gunships, but none had been allocated to this mission, which was running well over an hour late. The only available gunships were busy supporting the landing at Point Salines.

The USS *Independence* was offshore and carried two squadrons, the 15th and 57th Attack Squadrons. The pilots had been briefed but, at that briefing, there were no representatives of the soldiers they would be called upon to support. In a later report it was stated, 'The navy pilots went into combat the first day with absolutely no knowledge of, or co-ordination with, the rangers and special forces operations.'[10]

Lucas searched for a landing site but could see nothing suitable nearby as he flew into a maelstrom of fire in which every PRA soldier played a part. The aircraft was being hit consistently with small arms fire and the crew and passengers suffered bullet wounds. The wounds bled, there was no immediate escape, and although the two gunners sprayed the ground, the energetic manoeuvring of the aircraft made the defensive fire ineffective. Lucas was then hit in the right arm. All eight helicopters pulled away and they regrouped over the sea. At this point, the two allocated to the rescue of the Governor General detached themselves and made for their prescribed target.

The degree of AA fire had been unexpected but 'the aircraft were standing up to the hammering better than the men'.[11] The remaining six helicopters were ordered to make another attempt, but the plan had not altered to accommodate the circumstances and this ill-considered order broke the important rule, 'Never reinforce failure'.

The result of the second attempt was entirely predictable as it was merely a replication of the first. Lucas was still at his controls and flying in fourth position. During his approach, a hail of fire crashed through his windscreen and killed him instantly. His co-pilot, Chief Warrant Officer 2 Paul Price, took over the controls, but the helicopter was badly damaged and started to emit black smoke. The SEAL passengers, some wounded and unable to contribute, were unnerved. Price struggled to keep his charge in the air. One of the other helicopters stayed alongside and the other three scattered.

Price realised that with his aircraft on fire, having lost fuel and with several men wounded, he was unlikely to be able to reach any of the many ships just off the Grenadian coast. He headed for Point Salines, where there was a safe LZ with Rangers on the ground. He did not make it and the Black Hawk inverted and crashed into thick woodland in the grounds of the Calabash Hotel at Amber Belair, about 3 miles (5km) south of St George's. The landing was very hard, the aircraft rolled over twice and the fire spread. Lucas was the only fatality but most of the survivors were wounded.

The assault on the prison had been planned to take place in darkness with the aim of freeing Grenadian political prisoners. It had been a curious, even inexplicable, priority, but it was now broad daylight and there was no element of surprise. As the helicopters moved in for their second attempt, they were attractive targets for the AA guns and every Cuban or Grenadian with an AK-47. The airborne commander of the assault was Major Larry Sloan, who sought to direct the operation from the navigator's seat from one of his Black Hawks. Within moments, he was wounded in the shoulder and his pilot was hit in the leg.[12]

The plan had been for Bravo Squadron's Delta soldiers to 'fast rope' from two of the aircraft into the prison courtyard. But it could be seen that the prison gates were open, and the place was deserted. This called for a rapid rethink and Sloan abandoned the assault. He radioed his decision and got grateful affirmation from all his subordinates. It was just as the six Black Hawks turned away that Lucas was hit and his helicopter very badly damaged.

All the other five aircraft had been the recipients of enemy fire, not least the one leading. In this helicopter, Major William Boykin was carrying a PRC-66 radio in a backpack. The radio was hit and it disintegrated, driving shards of metal and plastic into Boykin. He was very seriously wounded, and his injuries were clearly life-threatening. His comrades injected him with morphine and bound his wounds. The pilot of the helicopter was wounded, as were two Delta soldiers. Later, fifty-four bullet holes were found in this one aircraft.

Boykin needed immediate medical attention and the pilot flew out to sea to find a ship – any ship – that would accept him. The other four Black Hawks, all with wounded aboard, followed. The army pilots were not trained to make landings on ships. Chief Warrant Officer Bramel was wounded and piloting a Black Hawk. He arrived above *Guam* and, when his intentions became clear, he was waved off energetically by flight deck personnel. Bramel landed and the state of his aircraft and the copious blood quickly changed attitudes.

Chief Warrant Officer 3 Bill Flannery was flying the aircraft with the severely wounded Boykin. The aircraft was so damaged that its landing was little more than a controlled crash. The rotors continued to turn, and Flannery's controls could no longer turn off the engine. The photograph in the plate section of the Black Hawk after it had crashed onto USS *Guam* illustrates the solution to the problem.

Several Black Hawks landed on USS *Moosbrugger* – a destroyer designated as a search and rescue ship. There were eight wounded in one helicopter alone. The assault on Richmond Hill Prison had been a fruitless, painful and failed operation.

The unwounded Delta soldiers were mustered and reallocated to the less damaged Black Hawks and directed to seize the high ground just north of the Point Salines airstrip in support of the Rangers' parachute insertion.

Notes

1. Adkin, Major M., *Urgent Fury: The Battle for Grenada* (London, Leo Cooper, 1989), p. 216.
2. Kukielski, P., *The US Invasion of Grenada: Legacy of a Flawed Victory* (Jefferson, North Carolina, McFarland & Co., 2019), p. 54.
3. Durant, M.J., Hartov, S. and Johnson, R.L., *The Night Stalkers: Top Secret Missions of the U.S. Army's Special Operations Aviation Regiment* (New York, G.P. Putnam's Sons), p. 14.
4. In an interview with Philip Kukielski in May 2003. Quoted in Kukielski's book, p. 56.
5. Kukielski, p. 58.
6. Ibid., p. 59.
7. Ibid.
8. cawarstudies.wordpress.com.
9. Kukielski, p. 61.
10. Adkin, p. 188.
11. Ibid., p. 189.
12. Durant *et al.*, p. 22.

Chapter 13

82nd Airborne Division

The 82nd Airborne Division had been designated to be an occupation force and its only combat role was anticipated to be the 'mopping-up' of remnants of the enemy. Initially, only two battalions of the 325th regiment, 1,200 men, were committed.

The airborne soldiers were to use the Point Salines Airport as their entry point; the runway at Pearls was far too short to accommodate C-141s. Notwithstanding the selection of Point Salines, there was no confirmation that that airstrip was secure. The planners had not taken this possibility into account and so, late in the day, Major General Trobaugh, the divisional commander, decided that his troops would make a parachute insertion. This decision had the knock-on effect of restricting the size of the force and its scale of equipment. The LZ at Point Salines was narrow and with hazardous water on three sides.

The first of nineteen C-141 troop and resupply aircraft took off from Pope Air Force Base for the five-hour flight, an hour later than scheduled. The 82nd would arrive nine hours after H-hour and after the arrival of the Caribbean element of the coalition.

The Caribbean force, 300 West Indian soldiers and policemen, did arrive before the 82nd. The force was composed of a Jamaican infantry company, a strong platoon of fifty from Barbados. Antigua and Barbuda provided a squad apiece, and Dominica, St Lucia and St Kitts squads of armed civil policemen. Over the next twenty-four hours, additional support dribbled in. These 'coalition' personnel had no idea what to expect and had not been briefed on their responsibilities. The senior US planners had not included the CPKF in the planning process. Brigadier Lewis did not even know the name of the operation in which he and his men were to participate.

Admiral Wesley McDonald later admitted, in his report to the Chairman of the Joint Chiefs, 'During preliminary and final planning, the control of the Caribbean Peacekeeping Force was not co-ordinated with CJTF 120 [Metcalf], creating early confusion on the planning for inserting the CPKF.'[1]

This all served to negate the concept of the united coalition hoped for by President Reagan. It revealed the military unimportance of the CPKF in the operation. Its presence was, in effect, no more than a political gesture and an exercise in public relations.

It was the intention that Brigadier Lewis, Chief of Staff of the Barbados Defence Force and Regional Security Co-ordinator, was to be co-located with Metcalf on USS *Guam*. This would leave day-to-day command of the CPKF to Colonel Ken Barnes. This simple arrangement went awry. While Lewis waited at Point Salines for a helicopter ride to *Guam* to meet with Metcalf, the Admiral and his aircraft were waiting at Barbados Airport. It was another communications glitch. As a result, it was not until the following day that Lewis reached *Guam* and could start his, as yet unspecified, work.

Lewis realised that this whole exercise was a can of worms and he had to make the best of it. He established his headquarters in a house about 100 yards (90m) west of the airport terminal, previously used by engineers working on the airport. He took possession of the Cuban camp facilities and agreed with Major General George Crist, a Marine, and Major General Scholtes that his force would take over the security of prisoners from 2nd/75th Ranger Battalion with immediate effect.

This important but purely administrative task was addressed with gusto. By the end of the day, about 250 prisoners had been collected, and arrangements made to house and feed them. Cuban doctors and nurses were pressed into service to attend to the wounded.

* * *

While Lewis was coping with these unsatisfactory arrangements, early on 25 October, the 82nd was on its way to the Spice Island. Each trooper aircraft carried 120 men and during their flight to Grenada, these men were the unhappy recipients of four separate orders to take off and put on their parachutes. It was only twenty minutes before their arrival above the island that they received the message that it would be safe to land. It was 1405 hrs when the first airborne soldiers hastily exited their aircraft, some before it had stopped rolling, and it was to the sound of small arms fire at the eastern end of the runway.

The arrival of Trobaugh made him the most senior officer on the island and, inadvertently, 'further muddled an already complex command structure and introduced a new level of confusion that took hours to sort out'.[2] Trobaugh was in command of Task Force 121 but, in parallel, Scholtes was commanding Task Force 123. Task Force 124 was also involved and led by Captain Carl Erie, USN. (See diagram overleaf.) It took the formation of a 'special communications team on *Guam* to resolve the issue'.[3]

Scholtes and Trobaugh met and the JSOC commander briefed his compatriot on the state of play. The original optimistic plan was for all the JSOC troops to return to the USA as soon as they had accomplished their tasks. Unfortunately, only the hills closest to the runway were occupied, only a third of the medical

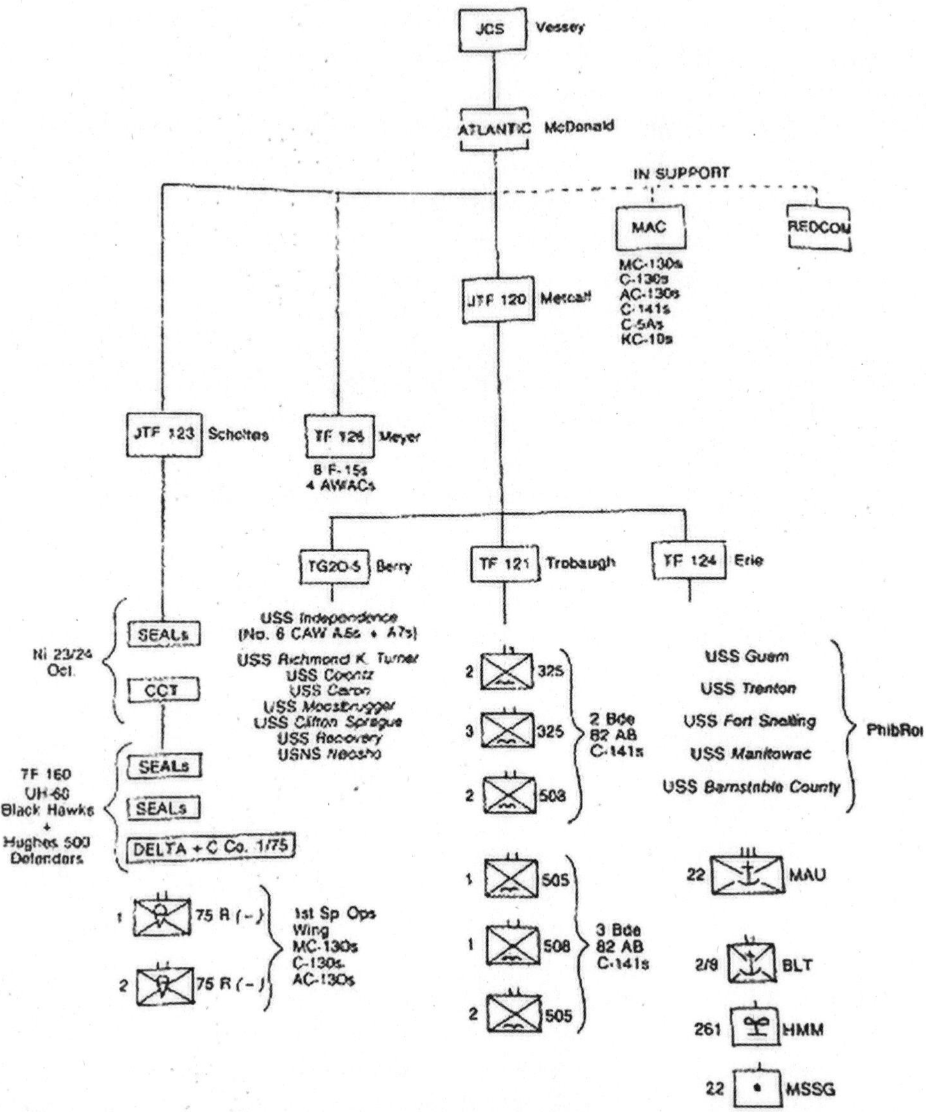

The Chain of Command. This diagram shows the convoluted command arrangements in which Admiral Metcalf did not have direct command over the SEALs, DELTA or Ranger formations. However, he did command the 22 MAU and 82nd Airborne Division. (*Adkin*)

students were secure, the Governor General was surrounded and the attacks on the prison had failed (see Chapter 14). The two generals were not in accord. Scholtes was reluctant to hand over responsibility for the airfield and he wanted to remain on the island until all his SEALs were safely mustered. The generals agreed to set up separate headquarters in the airport's unfinished terminal building.

Trobaugh now faced a significant logistic problem. The airport runway was incomplete and only about two-thirds of the surface was paved to commercial standards. The western end was only rough gravel bound with oil.[4] The airstrip, although well below the requirements of the US Army, offered the only facility for trooping and resupply aircraft. The narrow runway only provided sufficient space for an aircraft to turn at the eastern extremity. The unloading of aircraft was restricted to the apron around the terminal and then only one at a time. Later, a post-operation briefing was told:

> One of the most important decisions made during the deployment was the decision by the 2nd Brigade commander to remove a truck from his assault echelon and replace it with a 6,000lb [2,721kg] capacity, rough terrain fork-lift … for days this vehicle was the only piece of equipment capable of off-loading and moving heavy palletized loads from transport aircraft.[5]

This vital of piece of equipment was not, however, the panacea to all of Trobaugh's concerns. The physical limitations of Point Salines' airstrip determined that the 82nd, embarked on C-141 transport aircraft, could only land at twenty-minute intervals – given no breakdowns and no enemy interference. Darkness was an additional issue, as the airport had no lighting.

The eastern end of the airport came under fire, and it was later confirmed that the PRA, acting on the vehement urging of the Cuban ambassador, proposed to launch Grenada's Motorised Company against the invaders. This Grenadian unit was something of an elite by Grenadian standards. It was made up of fully committed, well-trained, professional soldiers. Twenty-four men, led by Warrant Officer Stephen McEwan, were mounted in three armoured personnel carriers. The aim of the attack was for the APCs to gain access to the airport and with their heavy, turret-mounted machine guns cripple an American C-141 and block the runway. The planning for this attack was painfully flawed. To be effective and achieve their mission, the three APCs needed a screen of infantry and some sort of covering fire – perhaps from mortars, as the Grenadians had no artillery. It also needed the benefit of surprise, but that was a forlorn hope as they were spotted by a Ranger patrol that been sent to look for survivors of an earlier ambush.

The Ranger patrol was led by Lieutenant Sydney Farrar and, as they neared the site of the ambush, they could hear the sound made by the three BTR-60s. Farrar radioed to his company commander that the three vehicles were 'moving toward me'. He readied his men and they prepared to engage the armoured enemy with their LAW (man portable, unguided, 66 mm) anti-tank weapon. When fire was opened, two of the APCs were hit but not disabled, and all three sped on towards the eastern end of the runway, where the two Ranger battalions were positioned.

On the arrival of the APC-borne Grenadian force at Point Salines, it drew fire from both battalions. The fusillade was effective: the first APC halted. Then, inexplicably, it reversed into the second. The two vehicles were stationary and drenched in fire, not least by 90mm recoilless rifles. The crews abandoned the two immobilised and badly damaged vehicles. Two Grenadians died on the spot and others fell as they fled. The third APC sought to escape but its fate was sealed when it attracted the lethal attention of a Spectre gunship. A round from the aircraft's 105mm gun turned the APC on its side. The attack had been a courageous but hopeless affair.

Farrar was now free to carry out his original reconnaissance mission.[6] His patrol found a towed XU-23 anti-aircraft gun abandoned in the road. It had probably been towed by one of the now destroyed APCs. At the approach of the patrol, an enemy soldier emerged from cover and fired on Farrar, who was hit by the burst of three rounds. The indications are that these Grenadians had survived the abortive APC attack and were still hostile – very hostile. A firefight erupted over the prone and badly wounded Farrar. Two soldiers pulled Farrar off the road and were later decorated for their courage. The minor battle was settled when A-6 Intruder aircraft participated and bombed the Grenadian position.

The failed attack on the airport nevertheless had a significant effect on American attitudes. Trobaugh and Schwarzkopf were old friends and each commanded divisions in XVIII Corps. Trobaugh was the senior of the two and he was convinced that he needed a stronger force to complete his tasks. He had served in Vietnam and was accustomed to the use of massive force in any operation. He explained in a later interview, 'I just don't like the idea of going in light where it might be a fair fight … I want to overwhelm the guys, that's all there is to it.'

Trobaugh's argument did not persuade Schwarzkopf but, nevertheless, Trobaugh sent a significant message back to his divisional headquarters in Fort Bragg, saying, 'Keep sending battalions until I tell you to stop.' The URGENT FURY force was already vastly superior to its adversary and Trobaugh's instruction led to six of his battalions being deployed to Grenada and added to the absurd overkill situation.

As it happens, the attack just recently and comprehensively defeated was effectively the end of the war. The arrival of yet more troops placed an intolerable burden on the very stretched logistic system. The Rangers were not equipped for other than a very short stay on the island. They were now short of food and fresh water. The hot weather and myriad flies and biting insects made Grenada a disagreeable place to be. The future insertion of about another 2,500 soldiers was not only heavy handed but it was also unnecessary and disruptive.

Trobaugh appealed to Admiral Metcalf and asked for the Rangers to be put under his command, albeit temporarily for the defence of the airport and until the bulk of his men had arrived. Predictably, Scholtes objected strongly but he was overruled at about 1900 hrs. It was not until the next morning that the commanders of the two Ranger battalions became aware that they had a new boss and their early return to the USA was shelved. Suffice it to say that it was not until 0245 hrs on 26 October that the first two battalions were complete and taking up defensive positions.

The 82nd deployed in light order, it brought with it no vehicles and all equipment had to be manhandled. An immediate issue was that all the division's long-range radio equipment was vehicle mounted and so communication was, yet again, an issue for URGENT FURY. The 2nd/505th addressed the vehicle issue robustly and promptly requisitioned about thirty civilian vehicles. However, although this did improve mobility, the soldiers were still heavily laden. It was very hot. Progress on foot was slow, but little wonder, as each man was carrying up to 110lb (50kg).

The 82nd Division moved out of its defensive positions around the airstrip just before dawn on 26 October. Its first objective was a Cuban facility, just north of Calliste, called 'Little Havana' by the Grenadians. In outline, the plan was for Bravo Company to move from the area of the tank farm and to assault from the west at around 0630 hrs; thereafter it would move on to the Grande Anse campus. In that initial attack, supporting fire would be provided by Alpha Company, with Charlie Company held in reserve.

Captain Michael Ritz, commanding Bravo Company, prudently set out to reconnoitre the Cuban position under the cover of darkness accompanied by his three platoon commanders and a sergeant.[7] They did not carry a radio. The recce patrol pushed forward, as Ritz wanted to view the objective from the last hill on a ridgeline. He sent two of the platoon leaders back to join their men and he went on with Lieutenant Stephen Seager and Sergeant Terry Guinn. Their movement through the undergrowth alerted the defenders and, in the gathering light, the three men bumped a Cuban position and drew fire.

Ritz was killed at once. Guinn was also shot but fell on the 'friendly' side of the hill. Seager engaged the Cuban position, was thought to have caused casualties, and then withdrew to the Bravo Company position. Here, the first sergeant had assumed command and he moved Seager's platoon towards the source of the fire.[8] An unsuccessful attack was mounted but Sergeant Guinn was recovered.

The plan changed, and before a ground attack, Little Havana was to be reduced by artillery and an airstrike by A-7s. Bravo Company, without Ritz, was now under the command of a platoon leader appointed by Lieutenant Colonel Jack Hamilton, the battalion commander. The air attack was devastating; it tore holes in the cinderblock buildings and caused havoc among the defenders. It was later reported by Lieutenant Selina Garcia, a translator, and the only female Cuban officer in Grenada, now caring for her wounded men, that Castro sent a message to his beleaguered force urging them to fight to the last man.[9]

The conditions inside the Cuban compound were dire and the survivors favoured surrender, but Colonel Pedro Tortolo and Lieutenant Colonel Orlando Matamoros, who had been sent by Castro only two days before to bolster the PRA and the PRG, decided to make a break for it. Matamoros said later:

> When the sun came up, they concentrated their fire, throwing mortars, planes, canon and machine guns against us. I was wounded by the fourth mortar shell. Tortolo wanted to know what the matter was with me. I shouted that I had been hit in the waist, but was OK. He asked if I could crawl over to where he was and I said no, but we couldn't hold the position, and that we should leave the compound and go to the hill behind the offices to be protected from a direct hit.[10]

Carlos Diaz, a Cuban diplomat, had been accompanying his two military colleagues when they were engulfed in this battle. He was one of the sixteen Cuban fatalities, and did not live to see Tortolo, Matamoros and a small group make their way up the steep slope of the Morne Rouge hill. Selina Garcia recalled, 'We walked along the crest of the hills, avoiding all paths so as not to be seen, and stopping every so often to rest. We went on that way until we got to a place where we could see the northern and southern coasts of Point Salines and the valley where the airport was.'

At this point, the party was within close proximity to the Russian embassy, and sanctuary. Far behind the small party of escapers, the denizens of the wrecked Cuban compound surrendered. A platoon moved in to effect the surrender of eighty-six Cubans. Three men made a successful run for it and followed in the tracks of Tortolo.

This had been a very minor affair, and it ended the only combat in which the 82nd was engaged. The battle casualties were minimal, with one killed (Ritz) and ten wounded. There was a second US fatality when an enemy recoilless rifle exploded as Staff Sergeant Garry Epps tried to unload it.

Charlie Company passed through Bravo and pressed on to a position close to the village of Frequente. It was from Frequente that, on D-Day, the Rangers had drawn fire. Charlie Company was commanded by Captain Mark Rocke, a last-minute replacement from the 2nd Battalion, who knew none of his soldiers. In Frequente village, Charlie Company came upon the Grenadian Army's logistic base. It was a significant facility housed in six warehouses; there was, in addition, a vast armoury filled with a miscellany of weapons, an ammunition store and a large garage.[11] Later, an inventory of this complex revealed that there were 6,322 rifles – sufficient to equip six infantry battalions. The store also contained 65 82mm mortars, 13 anti-aircraft batteries, 15 recoilless rifles, 11 machine guns, 68 rocket-propelled grenade launchers and 5,000,000 rounds of ammunition. This entire complex was guarded by a solitary soldier, who was most anxious to surrender.

The magnitude of these war stocks throws a light on the mindset of the now long-dead Maurice Bishop. How he proposed to recruit, train, accommodate and fund a sizeable army was never explained. Presumably, the potential enemy was the USA, in which case he would have also needed an air force and a navy.

Rocke moved his company into a defensive position along a ridge and when he was talking to his CO, Hamilton, they saw in the distance about 1,000 yards (915m) away an 82nd reconnaissance patrol in six vehicles on its way to collect the remains of four men killed the previous day.[12] This estimate of 1,000 yards tests credibility, despite Rocke providing it in an interview after the event.

The retrieval was an unpleasant but necessary task, and when completed the group of airborne soldiers was ambushed as it retraced its steps. Rocke's recce platoon provided supporting fire from jeep-mounted machine guns, as did his mortar men. The ambush failed and four of the instigators were killed. Incredibly, there were no American casualties. The dead were initially identified as Cubans but as the action took place after the engagement at Little Havana and the survivors were making their escape, the likelihood is that the dead were Grenadians, not least because their Soviet-manufactured BRDM-2 Scout car was in use by the Grenadian Motorised Company.

This brief firefight in the afternoon of 26 October was to be the last unit action of the operation. Henceforth, casualties were the result of either accidents or 'blue on blue' incidents. As the day wore on, by early afternoon the intense heat – about 90°F – combined with the burden of flak jackets and very heavy packs, took its toll on Charlie Company and five men became heat casualties.

Notes

1. McDonald, Admiral W., in his *After-action Report* to JCS, January 1984.
2. Kukielski, P., *The US Invasion of Grenada: Legacy of a Flawed Victory* (Jefferson, North Carolina, McFarland & Co., 2019), p. 116.
3. Adkin, Major M., *Urgent Fury: The Battle for Grenada* (London, Leo Cooper, 1989), p. 221.

4. Raines, E.F., *The Rucksack War: US Army Operational Logistics in Grenada 1983* (Washington, DC, Center of Military History, 2010), p. 264.
5. Fraché, Colonel L.D.H., 'Grenada Lessons Learned' (briefing at Fort Leavenworth, KS, 14 February 1984). Quoted by Kukielski, p. 117.
6. 'New Grenada Raider Threat', SOCNET.com.
7. Raines, p. 339.
8. Ibid., pp. 339, 341.
9. Adkin, p. 262.
10. Ibid.
11. Pirnie, R.B., *Operation Urgent Fury: The United States Army in Joint Operation* (US Army Center of Military History, 1986), p. 221.
12. Maraccini, M.J., 'Task Force 2/325 Operation Urgent Fury' (from a study conducted at Fort Benning, GA, 1988), p. 9.

Chapter 14

The Governor General and Fort Frederick

On 25 October 1983, Sir Paul Scoon, the Governor General, embodied all that was left of Grenadian government. He had no political function, but he represented the head of state, Queen Elizabeth II. He may only have been a symbol. However, he was a very important symbol.

Reagan may well have trampled over British sensibilities, but he did recognise that Scoon and his safety were of paramount importance if he was to sanitise the US invasion of an allied state. So far, URGENT FURY had not gone well for US Special Forces. They had taken multiple casualties, seven dead, and probably of the order of thirty wounded. Their next mission was to rescue and secure the Governor General, who was apparently in Government House.

After the murder of Bishop and his acolytes, and the imposition of a curfew with its 'shoot-on-sight' policy, the provisions did not apply to Scoon and his staff. Scoon was not under any restraint and on 22 October, he received a telephone call from Queen Elizabeth's Assistant Private Secretary, Robert Fellows. During this call, Scoon commented that he and his wife, Lady Esmai, were under no threat and were 'in good form'.[1] Up to this point, Scoon had been a compliant spectator to the anarchy in the Spice Island but his position changed on the arrival of three envoys: Montgomery, from the UK, and the Americans, Flohr and Kurze (see page 55).

Montgomery took the chance to speak with several long-time British residents, and their shared, very negative opinions of the Coard regime influenced his subsequent report to London. In this, he said that the likelihood was that the revolutionary government would succumb to fractional bickering. Then anarchy, or Bishop's surviving supporters, would ally themselves with other dissidents to confront the fledgling government in a general strike. He concluded that the fate of the island was 'in the hands of a clutch of inexperienced political opportunists dressed up as soldiers'.[2]

During the conversation between Montgomery and Scoon, the Governor General made it clear that he feared for his life were he to directly challenge the ruling junta by seeking external support. However, he said that if there were to be an intervention, he 'would do what was required of him'. He went on to say:

> If a military operation to achieve (law and order) were to be undertaken by our sister states – if necessary, with the assistance of the United States – I would give such initiative my fullest support.[3]

Scoon also agreed to meet with Linda Flohr, who was later revealed to be an agent of the CIA. It is speculated that she told Scoon of the intended invasion and of the arrangements made to safeguard him and his staff. After the event, a House of Commons inquiry established that Scoon had been appraised of the forthcoming invasion by an unnamed emissary – it can only have been Flohr.

Scoon was obliged to retain contact with the regime, and on 24 October, General Austin, the nominal head of government, called upon him. Austin advised that ships of the US Navy had been sighted offshore, and that an invasion was anticipated in the near future. He added that President Forbes Burnham of Guyana had heard, from Caribbean diplomatic sources, of American intentions.[4]

On 25 October, one of the highest military priorities for the USA was the wellbeing of Sir Paul Scoon. Two Black Hawks, filled with SEALs, arrived in the area of Government House but had difficulty in identifying the building. They attracted robust AA fire from four guns at Fort Rupert, two at D'Arbeau, from several APCs and from any PRA soldier who could bring his weapon to bear. The defensive fire was so intense that both helicopters turned away and flew out to sea. Here they delivered their wounded to *Guam* and prepared for a second attempt.[5]

The second attempt was an initial success. The soldiers in the first Black Hawk 'fast roped' onto steeply sloping ground. They were about 25 yards (23m) from the house, which was on the other side of a stone wall. The second helicopter decanted its passengers onto the tennis court. Some sporadic and poorly directed fire welcomed the invaders, but they occupied Government House without casualties.

The leader of the operation was Lieutenant Wellington Leonard, and he had with him twenty-one men – two Black Hawks' worth. The second Black Hawk, severely damaged by the intense fire, flew away bearing not only the commander of the operation, Captain Gormly, but also Leonard's principal radio. Gormly was hastened unwillingly to *Guam* and here he sought to encourage an army pilot to take him back to his men.[6] In the event, all he could do was get a flight to JSOC headquarters at Point Salines. From here, he was able to contact Leonard, but the radio available to him had limited range and battery life.[7] Leonard had a similarly limited radio.

The SEALs gained access to Government House and, armed with a photograph of Sir Paul, Lieutenant Leonard was able to identify the man he had come to liberate. Leonard's orders were to remain at Government House until relieved by ground forces. The anticipated timescale is unknown, but it was expected to be brief as the SEALs, at the radio station, were waiting for Scoon. It is now evident that there was no joined-up planning in this operation as the Government House SEAL contingent had no sense of urgency – one wonders if they realised that they were part of a wider canvas.

Soon after Leonard had met Scoon, three men approached the house. They were armed and when challenged raised their weapons; it was a foolish thing to do as immediately, two machine guns and a dozen automatic rifles responded. One of the three dead men was cut in half by the weight of fire. The morning wore on and the Grenadian Police Chief telephoned Scoon. He asked how many Americans were with him and Scoon replied that he had never seen so many guns in his life.[8]

It is a military fact of life that, after any attack, assault or invasion, the attacker will be subject to an immediate counterattack. This was illustrated at the radio station, and it was now to be reprised at Government House. At about 1000 hrs, PRA infantry soldiers were advancing on the house from the north-west, and making their way through a wooded area that provided a measure of cover. At the same time, an APC approached the house on the road to the south-east. The SEAL cordon around Government House was outnumbered and ill-equipped to deal with an APC or to engage in a full-scale defensive battle. They had no heavy weapons and urgently needed aerial support.

Leonard used his limited-range radio to contact Gormly at JSOC. 'Gormly's radio operator passed the message to an Army Delta Force radio operator sitting close by. That radio operator communicated with the gunships using a Vietnam-era back-up radio the army and air force had, but the SEALS did not.'[9]

By happy chance, a USAF Spectre gunship, piloted by Major Michael Couvillon, heard the call and at 1015 hrs, he arrived above the scene. Couvillon beat back the advancing infantry with his 20mm and 40mm weapons and he was soon joined by a second Spectre, piloted by Lieutenant Colonel David Simms. These two formidable weapon platforms, expertly handled, eliminated the immediate threat to Leonard and his men.

Couvillon flew off to Puerto Rico to refuel, leaving Simms to watch over Government House and its denizens. During the afternoon, two Grenadian APCs travelling along the road from the south-east approached Government House. Simms engaged both vehicles. One was badly damaged and abandoned; the other beat a hasty retreat.[10]

A measure of the inadequate communication arrangements throughout URGENT FURY was that, during the Spectre/APC skirmish, Leonard telephoned Fort Bragg to seek support. Leonard used a 'calling card' to pay for his call from the Governor General's phone.[11] The JSOC headquarters at Point

Salines was deluded to think that it was directing support to Leonard and his men. The reality, according to Lieutenant Colonel David Simms, USAF, in a post-war interview, was that the co-ordination was done directly with Fort Bragg.

The party in Government House was protected by a cordon of SEALs who were deployed about 25 yards (23m) from the house. The SEALs were in a situation for which they were not equipped. They were armed only with rifles and pistols. Their prime defence was the team of six gunships, which kept up a continuous presence.

Meanwhile, a very frustrated Captain Gormly and his superior, Major General Scholtes, asked Admiral Metcalf to hasten ground troops to Government House to ameliorate a situation that could become a disaster. Incredibly and unbelievably, Metcalf had not been briefed on any JSOC missions. Their deployment around the island was all news to him. The explanation, if there be one, was that the original, seriously flawed plan had assumed that all JSOC tasks would be accomplished, before ground troops were committed. Metcalf observed later:

> The rescue of the Governor General had not been included in any of my earlier instructions. But it soon became apparent, through talks with State Department representatives, that his rescue was of paramount importance. In a political sense, the success of the entire operation hung on the rescue of the Governor General.[12]

* * *

It is quite extraordinary and inexplicable that the overall commander of Operation URGENT FURY was unaware of the activities of JSOC troops and that he had not been appraised of the criticality of Scoon's safety. Metcalf was a three-star officer at the top of the command chain and as such, he had complete responsibility for every aspect of the operation. By halfway through the first day of URGENT FURY, it was clear that communication was inadequate, at best, and culpably so at the higher planning level.

The American soldiers who were committed to President Reagan's exercise in regime change were well trained, superbly equipped (apart from radios) and fully committed. They were high-grade troops who, when called upon to do so, acted professionally and courageously. They deserved high-grade leadership, but they did not get it. A wise man once said, 'There are no bad soldiers – only bad officers', and that is applicable in this case. The senior officers who planned the invasion were not 'bad' but they were very naïve.

The relatively junior officers at battalion level acquitted themselves well, but they were hamstrung by the 'plans' imposed upon them. Scholtes was judged to be an expert in the deployment of Special Forces. Nevertheless, he sent SEALs to the radio station, the prison and Government House in piecemeal, uncoordinated attacks, expecting/hoping that they would be relived, in short order, by ground troops. If there was any sort of joined-up plan, the orders to Erskine and Leonard did not reflect it.

* * *

Metcalf was understandably irritated by the autonomy of the Special Forces and was later quoted as saying, 'In many ways, they weren't the solution to anything. These Special operations are independent. They go in and do things in their own way. Then mainline forces are asked to bail them out. That's what happened.'[13]

Metcalf's view was endorsed by General Edward Meyer, a former US Army Chief of Staff, who said, sagely, 'A lot of things went wrong in Grenada because the Special Forces' plan was overlaid by the conventional forces' plan.'[14]

Notwithstanding the parlous situation at Government House, and in another curious order of priority, Metcalf was invited to direct his focus on Fort Frederick. This was thought to be the PRA headquarters, and which had contributed so much firepower in deterring the attack on the nearby prison.

The fort was about 200 years old and solidly constructed of stone. It employed in its defence two ZU-23s (see page 23) and the garrison's small arms. The Fort was not alone, and supporting fire was provided from other ZU-23s within line of sight of the fort.

Metcalf had at his ready disposal the awesome firepower of his fixed-wing aircraft. However, he was limited by the 'rules of engagement' imposed upon him. These included the phrase that he 'cause minimum damage and casualties'. Metcalf was limited in what he could do, and interpreted the rules to mean 'Do not use one more bullet, bomb or whatever that is necessary to accomplish the mission'.[15] This was very, very difficult to execute. He went on to aver that 'You take an armed force in there and you're not supposed to hurt anybody. That is absolutely against the principles in which you are trained.'[16]

Although Metcalf had the power, he could not use it, and so he determined that he would use helicopters and not the fighter jets available to him. Two unarmoured Cobra AH-1Ts, flown by Marine pilots Captain Pat Giguere and Captain Timothy Howard, were selected for the task. This was a very high-risk assignment, and the pilots were unaware of the AA defences they faced.

They attacked Fort Frederick together. The first made a pass at the target and his companion sought to attract the attention of the defenders. Giguere discharged a marker rocket that hit the roof of the fort; the co-pilot, Lieutenant Jeffrey Scharver, opened fire with 2.75-inch rockets and his 20mm Gatling gun.

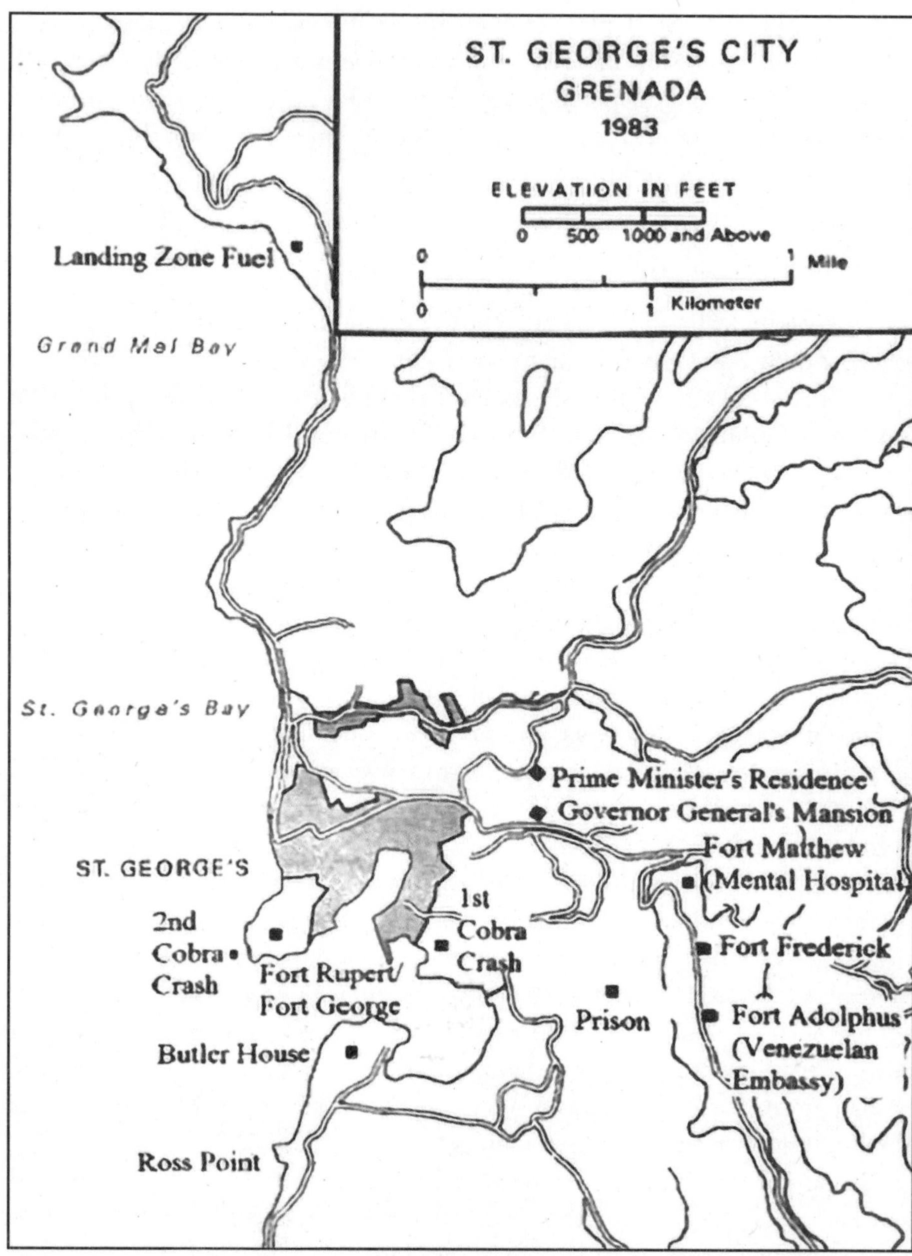

This map shows the small area that was fought over on 25 October and explains why AA fire from several sites was so effective. (*US Center of Military History*)

Then Howard lined up his target and released a wire-guided TOW anti-tank missile. This weapon is very effective, but the firer has to remain stable while the weapon makes its journey to the target. Howard was at his most vulnerable but, undaunted, he fired a second TOW.

USS *Clifton Sprague*.

Jacques Dyel du Parquet (1606–58),
Governor of Martinique,
1636–46 and 1647–58.

This view is of St George's, the capital of Grenada. The aspect is looking north-east from Fort Rupert. The arrow shows the approximate position of Government House, home of the Governor General in 1983.

Sir Eric Gairy, PC (1922–97), first Prime Minister of Grenada, 1974–9.

Maurice Bishop (1944–83), second Prime Minster of Grenada, 1979–83.

Sir Paul Scoon, GCMG, GCVO, OBE (1935–2013), Governor General of Grenada, 1978–92.

Selwyn Strachan.

Ronald Wilson Reagan (1911–2004), President of the United States of America, 1981–9.

Bernard (1944–) and Phyllis Coard (1943–2020).

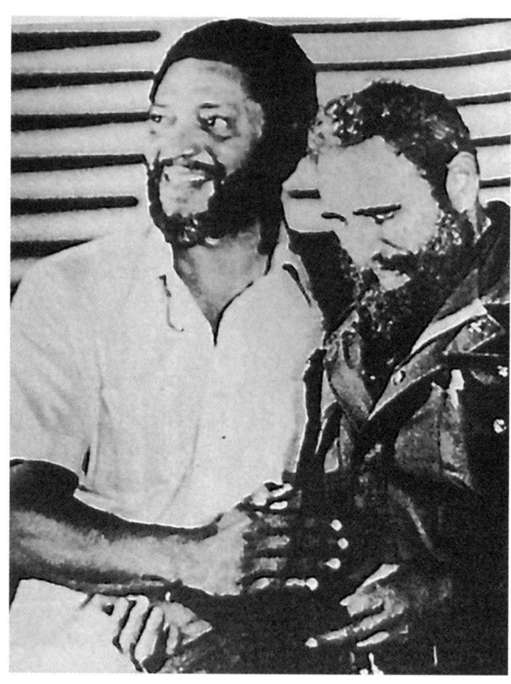

Maurice Bishop with Fidel Castro on 26 July 1983, celebrating the anniversary of the storming of Moncada Barracks in 1953. (*O'Shaughnessy*)

Admiral Wesley L. McDonald, USN, CINCLANT (1924–2009).

USS *Guam*, an *Iwo Jima*-class amphibious assault ship. She was of 19,217 tons and launched in 1964. She had a complement of 80 officers and 638 sailors. Vice Admiral Metcalf flew his flag in *Guam* during Operation URGENT FURY.

Major Mark Adkin, BDF. He was a witness to URGENT FURY and wrote an excellent book on the subject.

Bernard Coard – the instigator of the overthrow and murder of Bishop and seven others.

General Hudson Austin (1938–2022).

Major General Richard A. Scholtes, USA (1934–) Commander of US Special Forces in Grenada. (*US Army photograph*)

Vice Admiral Joseph R. Metcalf III (1927–2007), Commander of Joint Force 20 and Operation URGENT FURY. (*USN photograph*)

General H. Norman Schwarzkopf Jr. (1934–2012). Photographed later in life, when he had risen to the top of the US Army. (*US Army photograph*)

President Reagan, in pyjamas, conferring with George Schultz and Robert McFarlane early on 22 October 1983. (*Ronald Reagan Library*)

Mrs Margaret Thatcher, LG, OM, DST.J, PC, FRS, HON FRSC (1925–2013), Prime Minister of the UK, and Sir Geoffrey Howe, CH, PC, QC (1926–2015), Secretary of State for Foreign and Commonwealth Affairs.

Outside Bishop's house on the morning of 19 October 1983. The crowd, with placards aloft, is pushing past to rescue Bishop from house arrest. (Nation, *newspaper of Barbados*)

The airport at Pearls on 28 October 1983, with a USAF C-130 on the runway and two Marine CH-46 helicopters in front of the terminal. This facility was taken by 22 Marine Amphibious Unit on 25 October 1983. (*US National Archives*)

The incomplete airport at Point Salines, looking from west to east. The proximity of so much water and a strong wind made this a hazardous drop zone. (*US National Archives*)

Black Hawks of 160th Special Operations Aviation Regiment over Point Salines. (*US National Archives*)

Lord Palmerston (1784–1865).

Richmond Hill Prison. The scene of some of Bishop's ill-treatment of his political prisoners. In 1983, an American objective. The high walls and steep hillside made this a formidable target. (*US National Archives*)

The Radio Free Grenada station is the building bottom right. The transmitter is at the small white building, centre left. The thick undergrowth gave the SEALs welcome, but temporary, cover. (*US National Archives*)

A Russian ZU-23 23mm AA gun (left), manned by a crew of five, and (right) a Russian DShKM-4 12.7mm AA gun. These two weapons were very effective at close range, and they were a powerful deterrent to US aviators. (*US National Archives*)

Captain Keith Lucas (1957–83). Black Hawk pilot killed in action.

Major General Edward L. Trobaugh (1932–2024), Commander 82nd Airborne Division. (*US Army photograph*)

CW3 Bill Flannery's Black Hawk, carrying the wounded Major Boykin after it crashed onto USS *Guam*, and with its rotors out of control. The deck party drenched the engine in water to bring them to a halt. The aircraft had forty-eight bullet holes. (*US National Archives*)

On the hill behind the terminal buildings are the barracks housing the Cuban labour force. This bleak facility was commandeered by Brigadier Lewis and the CPKF on 25 October. (*US National Archives*)

This photograph illustrates the congestion at Point Salines Airport on the second day of Operation URGENT FURY. (*US National Archives*)

The two leading BTR-60s disabled at Point Salines Airport. (*US National Archives*)

The third APC destroyed by a Spectre gunship during the abortive attack on Point Salines Airport. (*US National Archives*)

The provision of potable water was a high logistic priority until civilian sources on the island had been identified and secured. (*US National Archives*)

Soldiers of the 82nd Airborne Division in one of the thirty commandeered civilian vehicles. (*US National Archives*)

Men of Bravo Company, 2nd Battalion, 505 PIR advance to contact. This photograph was probably taken on 26 October. (The Fayetteville Observer)

Staff Sergeant Dennis Tuggle of Bravo Company takes local advice. (The Fayetteville Observer)

Government House, Grenada. The building dates to 1780. It is now a ruin, and has been replaced by a modern residence.

Giguere's Cobra (bottom middle), just before it plunged into the sea. Major De Mars's CH-46 (top right) escapes with the wounded Captain Howard. (*Photo by AP*)

Denis, Baron Healey, CH, MBE, PC, FRSL (1917–2015), Secretary of Defence 1964–70, Chancellor of the Exchequer 1974–9, Deputy Leader of the Labour Party 1980–3.

Two CH-46 Sea Knights aboard USS *Guam*. These aircraft were allocated to 22 MAU and their deployment became a bone of contention when an opportunity arose to 'rescue' medical students. (*US National Archives*)

Students of St George's Medical School pictured after their 'rescue' from the Grand Anse campus. (*US National Archives*)

USAF AC-130. (*USAF Photograph*)

The formidable USN A-7.

This photograph of a Marine CH-46 Sea Knight is a favoured image of URGENT FURY but somewhat misleading. This aircraft was not shot down. Its pilot flew it into a palm tree during the 'rescue' of the medical students at Grand Anse Beach. The helicopter was beyond repair and was abandoned. Later it was strafed by an AC-130 to ensure that any of its classified construction details did not fall into unfriendly hands. (*US National Archives*)

The memorial to Maurice Bishop, who was instrumental in the building of the airport, now so important to the Grenadian economy.

On 3 November, the hostilities being over, CPKF was reinforced by a mixture of soldiers and policemen.

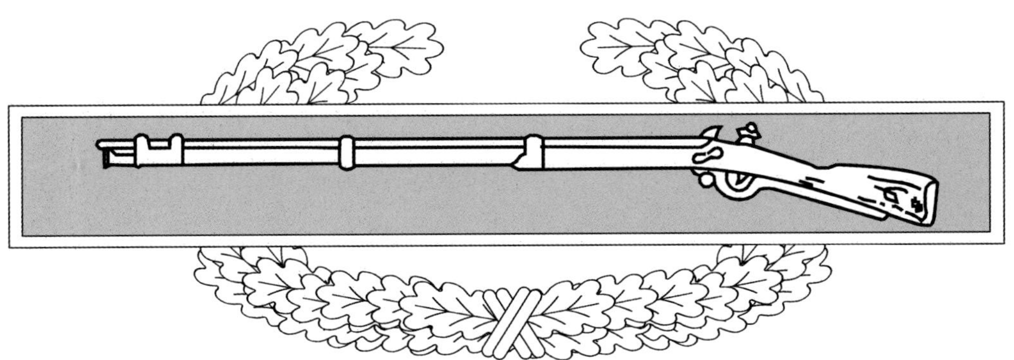

The Combat Infantry Badge.

Lieutenant General Leonard H. Perroots, USAF (1933–2017).

President Reagan entertains Oleg Gordievsky at the White House, July 1987.

American public opinion was influenced by this photograph of Jeff Geller, a medical student, pictured kissing the tarmac at Charleston Air Force Base after his repatriation. Geller had never been at risk. (*US National Archives*)

Herbert A. Blaize (1918–89), sixth Prime Minister of Grenada, 1984–9.

Colonel Theodore Roosevelt and his Rough Riders, pictured in 1898, after the capture of San Juan Hill during the Spanish–American War.

It was at 1327 hrs that Howard's aircraft was hit by three AA rounds. The effect was catastrophic. Howard was severely wounded; his right arm was all but severed, and his right leg was badly damaged. He tried to pass command of the aircraft to his co-pilot, Captain Jeb Seagle, but he was also wounded and unconscious. Howard, in a display of the most exemplary airmanship, whilst very badly incapacitated, landed the 5-ton Cobra. It was a hard landing. The canopy-removal mechanism activated, blowing out all the windows. The tail rotor broke off. Although the aircraft bounced on impact, it remained upright.

Seagle recovered consciousness and realised that Howard was very badly hurt. His femur was protruding from his leg, and he was bleeding profusely. Seagle dragged his comrade from the, now burning, wreck as small arms fire impacted around them. Howard ordered Seagle to leave him, and after the latter's protestations were rebutted, Seagle agreed to seek help.

The burning Cobra exploded and 'cooked off' the 2.75-inch rockets. Their random discharge served to keep the PRA at a distance. Giguere arrived above the scene and his firepower hastened the enemy withdrawal – albeit only temporarily. Giguere radioed for a medevac helicopter to lift out the two downed aviators.

A Marine CH-46E transport flown by Major Melvin DeMars and Lieutenant Lawrence King heard the call and responded at once, although they were fifteen minutes away. They made their prudent approach from the sea and rendezvoused with Giguere offshore. The Cobra pilot briefed the two Marines and advised them of AA defences around St George's harbour. There was, in addition, an active AA gun to the north at Fort Rupert defending a building known as Butler House. It may well have been this gun that had downed Howard and Seagle.

The agreed plan was that Giguere would seek to draw enemy fire while the larger aircraft would swoop in on the blazing wreck and rescue the two men. The Cobra flew over the harbour, at about 10 feet above the sea, and then made a strafing attack on Butler House. The Marine aircraft completed its very low approach and landed only about 30 yards (27m) from Howard. One of the crew, Gunnery Sergeant Kelly Neidigh, jumped out, weapon in hand, and shouted, 'I'm going to get him.' Get him he did, and Howard was dragged onto the Marine aircraft. However, there was no sign of Seagle. Giguere had run out of ammunition, but to cover the departure of the Marines he opted to bluff the enemy by making a strafing run. Then as both helicopters turned towards the sea, the Cobra was raked with fire. Both Giguere and Scharver were mortally wounded, their aircraft was clearly not under control, and it plunged into the sea at the entrance to the harbour. The rescue helicopter made its escape and Howard was soon in the hands of the surgeons. He survived.

Seagle had been killed before the rescue helicopter arrived. It was suggested, by witnesses on a Greek ship at anchor in the harbour, that he had waved his hat towards his enemies, which the spectators interpreted as a willingness to surrender. Nevertheless, Seagle was shot down. His body was eventually dumped on a beach near the crash site, from where it was recovered.[17]

After this action, Seagle was awarded a posthumous Navy Cross for his conduct in rescuing Howard and for drawing enemy attention on himself.[18] Howard, DeMars, Neidigh, Scharver and Giguere were all decorated with a Silver Star. King, the co-pilot of the rescue aircraft, received the Distinguished Flying Cross.

Admiral Metcalf was having a bad day. He had discovered that although he was nominally in command of the US forces invading Grenada there was another force, JSOC, fighting the same campaign in parallel. The Special Forces radio station operation had failed, as had the attack on the prison. The security of the Governor General had not been achieved – indeed, he remained beleaguered and at risk. Two of Metcalf's helicopters had been destroyed, several men had been killed, and to date, only the unopposed landing at Pearls and the sparsely opposed landing at Point Salines had been a success. One hundred and sixty-four of the American medical students had been 'liberated' but several hundred others were still unaccounted for. It was unwelcome news to Metcalf that there was another medical school campus, holding several hundred American citizens. Notwithstanding the fact that the safety of American citizens was one of the objects of the invasion, and the security of Sir Paul Scoon was another, Metcalf cast around for a new target.

Taking advice from Major General Schwarzkopf, Metcalf decided to bomb the well-defended Fort Frederick, utilising the A-7E Corsairs from USS *Independence*. There was confusion in identifying Forts Matthew and Frederick (see map on page 112); this confusion was not resolved before the fury of the USN was launched.

Fort Matthew was a mental hospital.

It was not marked as such but then it was never envisaged that it would be subject to attack from the air. However, one of its walls was decorated with a painted flag of the Grenadian Revolutionary Government and, earlier in the day, fire had come from AA guns just outside the walls.

The Corsairs attacked, dropped a 500lb (227kg) bomb, and killed between seventeen and twenty-one mental patients, depending on the source consulted.[19] Other patients roamed the streets and were at risk. However, radio traffic from Fort Frederick ceased.[20] Predictably, this egregious error of judgement was not advertised. Metcalf did not hear of it until 27 October, and it was four days after that, that the Pentagon confirmed the misdirected attack.

Metcalf and Schwarzkopf recognised that matters were not going well, and the admiral asked the general how he could relieve the pressure on the SEALs besieged at Government House. Schwarzkopf advised that opening another front would provide the enemy with a problem that might reduce the pressure at Government House. The result of this conference was that the only reserve force, two Marine companies, were to be landed at Grand Mal beach by sea and helicopter. It is presumed that landing, of perhaps one company of Marines, by helicopter at Government House was considered but rejected as being too risky. No evidence has been found of any debate about this alternative strategy.

A reconnaissance of the beach was conducted by a SEAL team and H-hour was set at 1630 hrs, 25 October. This operation was planned without the participation of Lieutenant Colonel Ray Smith, the Marines' commanding officer. At the time, Smith was engaged in leading operations on the eastern side of the Spice Island. It was not until 1400 hrs that he got wind of his battalion's new objective. Communications were poor and he heard the news from one of his platoon commanders standing on the upper deck of USS *Fort Snelling*, using a hand-held, limited-range radio. Communications on *Guam* were in disarray. Although Marine and Army units were equipped with the same backpack radios, they could not talk to each other because they used different voice encryption.

* * *

On *Guam*, a satellite radio system had been installed (Motorola URC-101) and this provided a command net – of sorts. A feature of this extraordinary system was that it was similar to a shared 'party line' telephone. In this case, the possible users numbered hundreds and any one of them could transmit, at will, on the single channel. *Guam*'s system deficiencies were matched by its inconvenience. The radio was mounted in the ship's radar room on the upper deck of the carrier's island structure. If anyone needed to communicate, they first had to climb up two decks to access the radio. Schwarzkopf recorded in his memoirs:

> We only had one single channel to talk … if it was operations, if it was intel, if it was administrative, if it was logistics, if it was sheer bullshit, it all went on the same line … General Trobaugh and I could be talking about something very critical, and all of a sudden we just get blown off the air by some guy who wants to send social security numbers.[21]

A further irritant was that radio contact was broken every time the ship altered course. This was a frequent occurrence, as the ship had to manoeuvre to provide the best conditions for aircraft operating on its deck. Each helm order caused the radio to lose its contact with the relay satellite. Then it was necessary for the radio antenna to be manipulated manually to re-establish contact. However, there was one unexpected benefit of the system. Because it was an open channel, any ship or unit so equipped could listen in on all the traffic. Metcalf commented later, 'So, all in all, despite its traditional disadvantages, the party line worked out well. Everyone involved in the mission decision-making knew the intended plans, and the pressures on the local command.'[22]

* * *

In a manner that epitomised URGENT FURY, Lieutenant Colonel Smith, the Marine commander of 2nd/8th, did not reach *Guam* until forty-five minutes before his designated H-hour. Smith recognised the absurdity of the situation and asked for a delay to give him time to co-ordinate the two separate company incursions, one by air, one by sea. A two-hour delay was agreed.

Smith decided to go to Pearls Airport on the east coast to ready his Fox Company for its airborne assault at Grand Mal Bay. There followed a succession of unfortunate events that bordered on farce. An air traffic mix-up saw Smith delivered to the wrong airport – Point Salines. He eventually reached his men at Pearls barely twenty minutes before the, now delayed, H-hour. Smith and his small staff aimed to join Golf Company, which was embarked on USS *Manitowoc.*

The light was fading and, unfortunately, the pilot could not make radio contact with, nor could he find, *Manitowoc.* Fuel was low and so he was obliged to land on the first ship he could find. This was USS *Trenton*, but she was inconveniently located. Smith transferred to another helicopter, and arrived at 2330 hrs back on *Guam*, from which he had started his peregrinations six hours earlier. Little wonder that Lieutenant Colonel Smith was more than a little discommoded. A Marine historian interviewed Smith, and when they discussed his odyssey of 25 October, the Colonel said, 'I was so frustrated and so pissed that I could hardly see.'[23]

At approximately the time Smith was about his business, intelligence sources suggested that a thrust by tanks and armoured vehicles was to be expected in the area of Pearls Airport. This was absurd; there were no tanks, and Grenadian roads in that area would not support such equipment – a detail ignored by the intelligence gatherers. This underscores the point that incorrect intelligence is as dangerous as no intelligence.

Golf Company came ashore at about 1900 hrs, supported by five tanks, and unopposed. The inadequacy of the roads was unchanged and the US tanks were little more than an encumbrance. However, the Golf Company commander, Captain Robert Dobson, had no means of communicating with his command chain nor with any USN ships just offshore. He and his men occupied a small crescent-shaped beach given the code name 'LZ Fuel' – because of the Shell Company fuel tank farm located at one end of the beach.

Grenadian troops started to fire illuminating mortar rounds as they sought to identify targets. Dobson was acutely aware that these very large containers, filled with volatile, indeed, explosive material, were a hazard. Golf Company had established a beachhead about 820 by 110 yards (750 by 100 metres). Nevertheless, Dobson moved two of his platoons to the coastal road and established blocking positions both north and south. A helicopter landing zone was marked with pulsing strobe lights.

Smith arrived at the scene at about 0100 hrs and the first day of Operation UGENT FURY was at an end. On the other side of the world, the operation was being debated once more in the British House of Commons.

Notes

1. Howe, Sir G., restricted telegram, 'Grenada' No. 291 to UK High Commissioner, Bridgetown, Barbados, 22 October 1983. (Margaret Thatcher Foundation Archives).
2. Montgomery, D., 'Grenada: General Impressions', confidential telegram No. 344 to UK Foreign and Commonwealth Office, 23 October 1983 (Margaret Thatcher Foundation Archives).
3. Scoon, Sir P., *Survival for Service: My Experiences as Governor General of Grenada* (Macmillan Caribbean, 2003), p. 67. Quoted by Kukielski, p. 73.
4. Ibid., p. 137.
5. Adkin, Major M., *Urgent Fury: The Battle for Grenada* (London, Leo Cooper, 1989), p. 184.
6. Gormly, R.A., *Combat Swimmer: Memoirs of a Navy SEAL* (New York, Penguin Group, 1998), p. 195.
7. Ibid., p. 197.
8. Fialka J.J., 'In Battle for Grenada, Commando Missions didn't go as Planned' (*Wall Street Journal*, 15 November 1983).
9. Kukielski, P., *The US Invasion of Grenada: Legacy of a Flawed Victory* (Jefferson, North Carolina, McFarland & Co., 2019), p. 94.
10. Couvillon, M.J., *Grenada Grinder: The Complete Story of AC-130H Spectre Gunships on Operation Urgent Fury* (Marietta, GA, Deeds Publishing, 2011), pp. 74–81.
11. These calling cards were in widespread use in the mid-1980s. They were issued to consumers by long-distance service providers such as ATT. They were embossed with a unique code. This allowed the possessor to make direct, reduced rate toll calls from touch-tone telephones anywhere in the world. Kukielski, p. 95.
12. Metcalf, J.P, 'Decision Making and the Grenada Rescue' (*Ambiguity and Command: Organisational Perspectives on Military Decision Making*, ed. Marsh, J.G., Marshfield, Mass, Pitman Publishing, 2006), p. 288.
13. Kukielski, p. 95.
14. Adkin, p. 167.
15. Metcalf, p. 281.
16. Strober, D.H. and Strober, G.S., *The Reagan Presidency: An Oral History of the Era* (Washington, DC, Brassey's Inc., 2003), p. 276.
17. Russell, L. and Mendez, M.A., *Grenada: Men-at-Arms 1983* (London, Osprey, 1985), p. 20.

18. Hall of Valor Project (*Military Times* https://valor.militarytimes.com/hero/4094, accessed 1 October 2018).
19. *Lessons learned as a Result of the U.S. Military Operations in Grenada* (US Congress, House Committee on Armed Services, 24 January 1984).
20. Schwarzkopf, in an interview on 15 December 1987.
21. Ibid., 21 November 1983.
22. Metcalf, p. 292.
23. Kukielski, p. 101.

Chapter 15

The British Position

After the first day of American operations in Grenada in which lives had already been lost, the British Foreign Secretary, Sir Geoffrey Howe, realised that he was going to face another eloquent and vigorous attack from his opposite number in the House of Commons. Howe's brief was to defend the indefensible, with the aim of protecting the mythical 'special relationship' between the UK and USA.

The Palace of Westminster was packed to witness the event, which started at 13.53pm when the Speaker, Mr Bernard Weatherill, called the House to order. Mr Denis Healey, the Deputy Leader of the Labour Opposition Party, 'opened the batting'.

Hansard recorded every word of those spoken that afternoon. What follows are mere extracts to give a flavour of the atmosphere in the House of Commons at the time. Healey started by saying:

> Let me start by quoting an editorial in *The Times* today—a paper that is not notorious for supporting the sort of views that I put forward. It says: 'There is no getting around the fact that the United States and its Caribbean allies have committed an act of aggression against Grenada. They are in breach of international law and the Charter of the United Nations.' [This is a reiteration of *The Times*'s view previously mentioned on page 88.]
>
> I hope that the Foreign Secretary will confirm that judgment when he speaks this afternoon, because international law is the only thing that stands between the world and anarchy. If Governments arrogate to themselves the right to change the Governments of other sovereign states, there can be no peace in this world in perhaps the most dangerous age which the human race has ever known.
>
> It is quite improper for hon. Members to condemn, as we have, the violation of international law by the Soviet Union in its attacks on Czechoslovakia and Afghanistan if we do not apply the same standards to the United States' attack on Grenada two days ago. The Security Council is meeting at this moment to consider the matter.

Healey went on to aver that, unless foreign troops were withdrawn from the Spice Island, there existed the prospect of guerrilla war for perhaps six months.

This prediction was based on views expressed earlier by the prime ministers of Barbados and Dominica. It was pure speculation and, in the event, not borne out. Nevertheless, he continued, saying:

> There can be no denial of the grave damage done to the unity of the Commonwealth by what has happened in the past few days. The Secretary-General made his opposition clear on the radio this morning. Next week the Prime Minister will be meeting her colleagues in New Delhi and there is no question but that this matter is likely to arise. Again, I ask the Foreign Secretary to confirm that in all those Commonwealth discussions the Government will stand for the principles of international law and make their condemnation of the invasion of Grenada plain for all to see.
>
> I come now to the impact of the invasion on relations between Britain and her most important ally, the United States. I fear that I must start by saying that information that has come to light in the past 24 hours makes it clear that the statements made by the Foreign Secretary on Monday and Tuesday of this week—I bow to the ruling that you made, Mr. Speaker, at the beginning of the debate not to use unparliamentary expressions—were imperfect, disingenuous and lacking in candour.
>
> The Organisation of Eastern Caribbean States issued a communique in which it made it clear that its member Governments met last Friday in Barbados and decided then to undertake what was described in the communique as 'a pre-emptive defensive strike' against an independent member of the Commonwealth—Grenada—and to seek assistance for this purpose from friendly countries both in the area and outside.

Healey then traced the passage of information between the USA and UK governments and challenged the veracity of a statement that 'no approach had been received from Commonwealth countries for assistance'. It is a very serious matter to suggest that a member has 'misled the House' and Healey went as close to that line as the Speaker would permit. He continued by saying:

> We now know, from what was said in Washington yesterday, that the United States began considering military intervention against Grenada as soon as the military coup took place on 13 October, a fortnight ago. Reports from Washington on British television yesterday declared that the CIA had been planning such an operation for months before a coup took place. Indeed, Mr. Bishop—over whose death the President of the United States wept crocodile tears in his statement on Monday—expressed, in an interview on British radio last August, his concern about the imminence of an invasion of Grenada organised by the United States … In any case, reports of a likely

> intervention by some east Caribbean countries and the United States were widely circulating throughout the Caribbean over the weekend. On Monday, Grenada radio reported in detail the proceedings of CARICOM, when some very important members of the Commonwealth—I mentioned some of them yesterday: Trinidad, the largest Commonwealth country close to Grenada, Belize, which is under threat from Guatemala, and the Bahamas—totally rejected that request.
>
> We know now, from reports from Washington yesterday, that the American national security council took a tentative decision to accept the OECS invitation on Sunday evening. Were Her Majesty's Government aware of this? Was the Foreign Secretary aware of it when he told us 24 hours later in this House, on Monday afternoon, that he had no reason to believe that America was contemplating such a step? Either Her Majesty's Government were deceived by their major ally, or Her Majesty's Government were deceiving the House.

Several members sought to speak and, as is the custom in the House, asked that Healey give way. Healey declined but Mr Churchill, the member for Davyhulme, persisted until the Speaker intervened and quietened him. Nevertheless, Healey was remorseless, and continued:

> I turn to the wider implication of what has happened for relations between Britain and the United States of America. The Prime Minister has made something of a cult of her special relationship with the American President at the expense of British interests, of her relations with our European partners and of our relations with the Commonwealth. Indeed, in her recent visit to the United States, she tried to outdo the American President in that astonishing outburst that was so rightly castigated by Lord Carrington a few days later as megaphone diplomacy. Nowhere has her servility to the American President been more evident than on the problems of central America and the Caribbean region. Contrary to all her undertakings at the European summit, she supported the use of force for the solution of the problems of central America although she had signed a communique, along with the other heads of Community Governments, specifically disavowing the use of force as a useful solution to the problems.
>
> The Prime Minister has been an obedient poodle to the American President. [Interruption.] The true state of the relationship was put with brutal clarity by Secretary of State Shultz yesterday. So much for the obligation to consult between allies, and so much for the relevance of joint decision on the use of cruise missiles placed in Britain. To make these points is not to be anti-American, because members of the American Congress make them with as much force as I do.

Healey then drew adverse conclusions upon the Prime Minister's relationship with President Reagan. He urged her to 'get off her knees' and assert the independence of the UK. He claimed that the foreign policy of the USA had broken the post-war diplomatic tradition in abandoning co-operation and consensus with allies in favour of a sort of global unilateralism. He expressed the opinion that the tendency of the United States to go it alone in every aspect of world affairs carried immense dangers for world peace. This drew appreciative cries of 'hear, hear' from some members.

The afternoon was well advanced when Sir Geoffrey Howe rose to respond. He started by saying that he 'welcomed this opportunity', at which there was laughter in the chamber. He then shared with the House the latest situation reports. Importantly, he was able to say that the Governor General was now in safe hands. He added:

> He may have an important role to play in the restoration of democracy in Grenada. He represents one of the few elements of constitutional continuity in Grenada. The American Administration are aware of that constitutional position and have, of course, undertaken to respect it.
>
> The Americans have now secured both the airports on the island, at Pearls and Salines, as well as the radio station and Fort Rupert. But fighting is apparently continuing at Port Frederick and elsewhere. Several United States service men have been killed. There are unconfirmed reports that 12 Cubans have been killed during the fighting. There is no firm information at present about the extent of other casualties. In addition, there are reports that a number of Soviet nationals may have been detained, and rumours that Mr. Bernard Coard, one of the leaders of last week's *coup d'état*, has sought sanctuary in the Soviet embassy. I am not in a position to confirm that. [Interruption]

Howe then summarised the events in Grenada that led to the invasion, but his timeline was at once refuted by Healey. The two protagonists argued over who said what to whom and when. Healey's job was to attack the Conservative government headed by Mrs Thatcher and he relished the role. There can be little doubt that HMG was not emerging from this political debacle with much merit. Mr Jack Straw, the member for Blackburn, interjected and asked, 'In view of what the Foreign Secretary has now said, which is very different from what he said yesterday, does he now condemn what the Americans have done?'

The Foreign Secretary ducked the question and replied:

> Not so, Sir. What I have just clearly said to the House is that this was an occasion when the United States, in company with a number of Commonwealth Caribbean countries, has taken one view and the United Kingdom, together

> with a number of other Caribbean Commonwealth countries, has taken another view. In those circumstances, it is no more for me to condemn the United States than it is for them to condemn us.

Healey was not going to let Howe get off this particular hook, and after a series of interruptions from those wishing to speak, Healey responded by saying:

> The United States has committed a breach of the United Nations charter in international law. The matter is now under discussion in the Security Council in the United Nations. Unless Her Majesty's Government wish to continue playing the role that I attributed to them, they must express a view on the violation of the charter. It is the obligation of the Foreign Secretary, representing Her Majesty's Government, to make his views plain and not to run away from the problem.

Sir Geoffrey, at his urbane best, and always one of the most courteous members of the House, answered smoothly that:

> The right hon. Gentleman is right to draw attention to the fact that the Security Council met last night at the request of Nicaragua, and will be meeting again today as a draft resolution has been tabled by Guyana, which would have the Security Council issue a strong condemnation of the action taken by the United States and the Caribbean countries acting with it, and which calls for the withdrawal of all troops involved. The right hon. Gentleman expressed his opinion that this country should support this resolution, and in advancing that argument, he sought to draw parallels with other circumstances that are irrelevant to this case ... The fact is that, in Afghanistan, troops have occupied the country. In Grenada, the intention of the United States and those who are acting with her is to move as quickly as possible towards the withdrawal of their troops and towards the holding of free elections. Would that the House could count on the prospect of free elections in Afghanistan—[Interruption.] ... What has happened in this case does not, and must not be allowed to weaken the essential fabric of our alliance with the United States. It does not, and must not be allowed to, cast any doubt on the firmness of our joint commitment to the North Atlantic Treaty Organisation and all that that means.

The elephant in the room, but as yet unmentioned, was the proposal that the USA might locate strategic missiles in the UK. The control of these missiles was a sensitive issue. The missiles were, emphatically, not for the defence of the UK. Dr Owen kicked the ball into play when he observed, 'I understand the Foreign Secretary's reluctance to damage Anglo-United States relations, and fully understand, too, his reluctance to use words such as "condemn" of our principal friend and ally, but I disagree with his judgment that this event does not mean that we should have dual key on cruise missiles.'

Howe had no option but, yet again, defend the *status quo.* He replied:

> The right hon. Member for Leeds, East [Healey] suggested that this week's events are relevant to decisions that might have to be taken about the use of nuclear weapons. There is no credible analogy between our exchanges with the Americans on Monday night and the consultations that would take place before any decision could be taken to fire American nuclear missiles from Britain. [HON. MEMBERS: 'How do you know?']
>
> There are quite specific understandings between the British and United States' governments on the use, by the Americans, of their nuclear weapons and bases in Britain. Those understandings have been jointly reviewed in the light of the planned deployment here of cruise missiles and we are satisfied that they are effective. As I say, these understandings are specific, as are the arrangements for implementing them. They mean that no nuclear weapon would be fired or launched from British territory without the British Prime Minister's agreement.

At its heart, the missiles and their location were dependent upon mutual trust. Given recent events, the question was, could the UK trust the USA to abide by the arrangements mutually agreed? The invasion of Grenada was now raising wider and potentially much greater issues. At the time, one of the most gifted members of the House was Mr Enoch Powell, who represented Down, South. He entered the fray and his speech, heavily edited in the interests of brevity, made the following points:

> Consultation and common decision mean, for the United States, that it will from time to time take such steps and such decisions as, in its judgment, it considers to be right in the interests of the United States, that it will permit representations to be made to it by its allies, but that in the end it will go its own way regardless.
>
> This has not been the first case from which we can learn that lesson. I disagree with the right hon. Member for Leeds, East [Healey] in thinking that this is at all a recent experience. It has been the pattern of behaviour of the United States over the past 20 or 30 years. During the Yom Kippur war in 1973, when the European members of the NATO Alliance said that they saw no reason for it, the United States put its forces on full nuclear alert. It did not listen to the views, and it did not concert its action with the views of its European allies.
>
> Again, hon. Members who were in the last Parliament will remember the humiliating experience of being driven to place upon the statute book

a sanctions Act against Iran. Yet hardly had the House recovered from the fatigue of sitting up all night to do so than it heard that, without consultation or information to those who were endeavouring to support it, the United States had engaged in a wild and unlawful attack on the territory of Iran itself.

This pattern of behaviour of the United States is perfectly consistent throughout; it is a pattern that can be accounted for by the policy and outlook of that country.

At the invitation of Her Majesty's Government, the United States is about to station on the soil of the United Kingdom nuclear weapons which, we are told, will be used only after consultation and by joint decision with Her Majesty's Government. *Anyone who, after the experience of the last few days and of recent years, imagines that the United States will defer to the views of the Government of this country if it considers it necessary to use those weapons is living in a dangerous fool's paradise. Anyone in office who entertains that illusion is in no position to serve the security of this country* [author's emphasis].

The United States is dominated by two mutually supporting delusions. The first is that it is within the power of any nation, let alone the United States, *to create what it calls freedom and democracy by external military force* [author's emphasis]—that it is within the USA's power to decide how the inhabitants of other countries should, in its [US] interests, be governed, and to bring that about, in the last resort, by military interposition.

It also believes that the world is involved in a Manichaean struggle between the powers of light and the powers of darkness and that the mantle of leading the powers of light has fallen on the United States. I do not think that the consequences of that delusion, a nationwide delusion held and expressed by Americans of every class and creed, can be better expressed than it was—significantly over 20 years ago—by the Washington correspondent of *The Times* during the Cuba crisis. He wrote: 'The President … in effect has assumed the supreme political authority that was always inherent in the American nuclear deterrent. The firm belief is that as the leaders of the Alliance, with control of most of the nuclear power available to the West, the Administration has a right and a duty to defend itself and its allies—even to the extent of bringing about a nuclear exchange. It is also firmly believed—and these last words are the most significant for what will happen unless the Government have wiser thoughts in the coming weeks—*'in the present situation that there will be no time for consultation; that a threat of war cannot be met by committee decisions'* [author's emphasis]. What we should have learnt, or been reminded of, in the last few days is that the only condition compatible with our national honour and independence for those weapons being stationed on our soil, if indeed

> they are to be so stationed, is that this country should hold the physical control and ultimate power of decision over their use.
>
> I commend to the Government and the House—and, greatly presuming, if I may, to our American allies—a remarkable and profound statement by, of all people, George Washington. He is reported as having said: 'The nation which indulges towards another a habitual hatred, or a habitual fondness is in some degree a slave. It is a slave to its animosity or to its affection, either of which is sufficient to lead it astray from its duty and its interest.'

There were two sides to this coin and the members of the House of Commons were not all of the same mind. Mr Julian Amery, Brighton, Pavilion, a Conservative member, reacted to Enoch Powell's remarks by redirecting fire from that aimed at the USA to HMG, of which he said, among other things:

> When there came a second military and bloodthirsty coup, the danger to the Caribbean was underlined, as was the danger to the United States. I think that my right hon. and learned friend, the Foreign Secretary, will agree that the majority of the Caribbeans—I have not added up all the islands—wanted some military intervention to take place. If the report in *The Guardian* is right, and if I understood my right hon. and learned friend aright, the Caribbeans wanted us to help them in the process of intervention. They wanted us to give a lead and the United States was prepared, in the circumstances, to take part.
>
> Here was an opportunity for Britain, as a leading Commonwealth power—I shall not say the leading power, because the Commonwealth is a community of equals, but Britain is a leading and founding member of the organisation—to give a lead. Here was our chance to send a Minister to co-ordinate the entire venture. Instead, we abdicated. *As a result of our relapse into pallid abstention, the Caribbeans turned to the United States for leadership and went ahead. We showed neither the courage to lead nor to oppose any form of leadership* [author's emphasis]. We should have taken, as the Opposition would have wished, a stand against intervention. We could, as I would have wished, have said, 'Let us join wholeheartedly in the intervention.' However, we did neither.

Mr Jeremy Corbyn, Islington South, contributed a typically strongly anti-American view in which he contrived to laud the New Jewel Movement in Grenada and to combine it with a measure of hostility towards the Conservative government. (Corbyn, who held very strong left-wing views, would, in 2019, lead the Labour Party to its most crushing electoral defeat since 1935.)

The consensus in the House on 26 October was that the American action was abhorred but that the supine and ineffective performance of HMG reflected no credit on any of the individuals involved – not least the Foreign Secretary.

At 6.39pm, the Foreign Secretary, Sir Geoffrey Howe, rose to wrap up what had been a robust, comprehensive and balanced debate. The House had a Conservative majority and the motion that 'this House do now adjourn' had been proposed by Denis Healey. It was important that HMG was not defeated and when the vote was taken, the motion was defeated by 336 'Noes' to 211 'Ayes'. In practical terms, the debate, and all that vented emotion, had changed nothing. In Grenada, the fighting went on.

Chapter 16

26 October 1983 Day 2 of Operations

The Governor General, Lady Scoon and their nine close personal staff had spent an uncomfortable and stressing night. They had had no sleep and no food. It was not what they had expected, and they were quite reasonably apprehensive as they were surrounded by hostiles.

Lieutenant Leonard, commanding the small SEAL team, had anticipated relief sometime during the previous day. He now expected a night attack and although all of his men were unwounded, they had expended a great deal of their ammunition. Leonard advised the Governor General that bringing in a helicopter to lift them out would be a very hazardous operation; they had no option but to wait for ground forces.

A review of the first day of American operations would point to the successful and almost bloodless seizure of both airports and the opening of the second front. These successes were offset by disappointment elsewhere. The original, robust *coup de main* was sound in concept, but it failed in execution when uncoordinated, early contact with the enemy did not achieve the supremacy expected. The reality was that none of the special operations planned for the first day was accomplished, and Atlantic Command acknowledged that some three months later.[1] Schwarzkopf commented later: 'What was supposed to be a highly unconventional situation that was going to be cleaned up in one day turned into a very conventional ground operation.'[2]

The operation at Beausejour, the radio station, enjoyed brief initial success but the anticipated broadcast by Scoon was not made because he was incarcerated in Government House, albeit with an armed escort. Two Marine Cobras and two Black Hawks had been destroyed, a further five Black Hawks were seriously damaged, three pilots had been lost and eighteen Delta Force commandos wounded. Only about 30 per cent of the American medical students were in safe hands. On *Guam*, the medical facilities were overwhelmed by the thirty-six wounded it had received.

* * *

It was just before dawn on 26 October that the leading troops of the second front, commanded by Lieutenant Colonel Ray Smith, started to move towards St George's, headed by Golf Company. This company was less a rearguard platoon that was to receive Fox Company when it arrived. Smith had been the recipient of intelligence that told him he was facing a combined Cuban and Grenadian force two battalions strong. That was entirely fallacious, and another example of the intelligence void in which American troops were operating.

For Golf Company it was, at most, just over a mile (2km) to the town. However, there was only one access road, and this clung to the shoreline. The narrow road had a very steep slope on the left and the sea on the right. There was no room for manoeuvre; a determined enemy could block the road and would be difficult to dislodge.

Smith had no other realistic alternative and so, in single file, his company advanced up the road, exercising great caution. There was no question of stealth because, behind the leading platoon, five M-60 tanks and thirteen amtracs (amphibious tractors) clanked loudly as they too followed the road.

On the outskirts of St George's, the small body of PRA defenders, commanded by 2nd Lieutenant Raeburn Nelson, recognised that they were outgunned and after loosing off a few ill-aimed rounds, they quietly decamped to somewhere safer. It emerged later that Golf Company and its armour had passed through a Grenadian ambush position. Prudently, the ambush was not sprung, as the ambushers were in awe of their opposition and they too had melted away.

Golf Company, having met no effective opposition, was then able to occupy Queen's Park, at about 0430 hrs on 26 October. Here Smith established his command post, and over the following few days, Queen's Park became the *de facto* Marine base in Grenada.

On the arrival of dawn, Smith sent Captain Dobson to secure Hospital Hill, which dominates St George's. Without any discernible opposition, Golf Company pushed on to the top of Mount Weldale, upon which were located the residences of the late Maurice Bishop, Mr and Mrs Bernard Coard, and Government House.

The Marines approached Government House up a steep slope and at 0730 hrs found that the besiegers had disappeared; there was no opposition. Another welcome surprise was that despite the persistent exchange of small arms fire there were no casualties. Lady Scoon gave to each of the SEALs who had protected her a small souvenir as a token of her gratitude.[3]

The rescue of the Governor General was an important success for URGENT FURY and reflected well on Schwarzkopf, whose strategy proved to be correct, and on Lieutenant Colonel Ray Smith, USMC, who had put it into practice.

The air attacks of the previous day had not only disrupted RMC activity but had degraded its morale. The command chain had broken down as communications failed. Lieutenant Colonel Ewart Layne and Major Basil Gahagan were incapable of passing coherent orders as the radio links closed.

Across the Spice Island, the PRA fell apart.

It lost any motivation to resist an overwhelming adversary. Early on 26 October, Austin and his closest staff agreed that their situation was hopeless. Their only viable option was to change into civilian clothes and hide. Their hideouts would have to be on the island because 'there was no possibility of escaping detection unless they could flee overseas'.[4] The RMC leaders abandoned Fort Frederick and concentrated on saving their skins. This collapse of the opposition was not detected by the American command chain and, quite correctly, it continued on the basis that it faced a viable and determined enemy.

This being the case, a helicopter evacuation of Sir Paul and Lady Scoon was judged to be hazardous and so, within a screen of Marines, they walked down the hill to Queen's Park, safe and sound. At about 0900 hrs, they were airlifted to USS *Guam*. Here they could shower, change clothes and enjoy a hot, freshly cooked breakfast. Scoon and Metcalf were each able to brief the other.

Scoon fretted that he should be with his countrymen and, accordingly, he was flown back to the island and landed at Point Salines Airport.[5] Later that day, at about 1600 hrs, Brigadier Rudyard Lewis, the senior coalition officer, visited Scoon. It was at this point that attempts were made to rewrite the history of the invasion.

Lewis offered to Scoon four letters, all pre-dated 24 October, and probably drafted by the CIA. The letters were addressed to President Reagan and the prime ministers of Barbados, Dominica and Jamaica. The text of these ill-judged letters is below. The example overleaf was directed to the prime minister of Barbados.

24 October 1983

Dear Prime Minister,

You are aware that there is a vacuum of authority in Grenada following the killing of the Prime Minister and the subsequent violations of human rights and bloodshed.

I am therefore seriously concerned over the lack of internal security in Grenada. Consequently, I am requesting your help to assist me in stabilizing this grave and dangerous situation. It is my desire that a peacekeeping force should be established in Grenada to facilitate a rapid return to peace and tranquillity and also a return to democratic rule.

In this connection I am also seeking assistance from the United States, from Jamaica and from the Organization of Eastern Caribbean States through its chairman the hon. Eugenia Charles [the prime minister of Dominica] in the spirit of the treaty establishing that Organization to which my country is signatory.

I have the honour to be,
Yours faithfully,
Paul Scoon
Governor General

Scoon was under pressure but, nevertheless, he signed all four letters and was, arguably, foolish to do so. The instigators of these pre-dated letters were ingenuous if they thought that they would stand any degree of scrutiny. Scoon was not a politician, nor a strategist. He was in an invidious position with no experience on which to draw. However, had Scoon signed similar letters on 24 October, when Coard held sway in Grenada, his own life would have been at risk.

That same evening, Lewis spoke by radio telephone to Buckingham Palace and in that call, he was able to give assurances that the Governor General was safe. Thereafter, Lewis and his token coalition force were employed guarding the increasing number of Cuban and Grenadian prisoners. The allocation of this mundane, hazard-free task to the Caribbean element of the force illustrated its standing in American eyes.

* * *

One objective of URGENT FURY still to be satisfied was the repatriation of the American medical students and this 'had been the principal pretext for the intervention as such it was repeatedly emphasised to the public that the situation in Grenada endangered their lives; therefore US forces were fully justified in going in to secure them. Seen from the US point of view it was a compelling argument, which convinced many Americans.'[6]

About 160 students were safely under US control but the balance was still at the Grand Anse campus and Metcalf came under pressure from Washington to reach them. More fallacious intelligence advised that, between Point Salines and Grand Anse, there was a major enemy force. This would make for a contested advance by the 82nd Airborne Division.

Major General Edward Trobaugh decided to commit his 2nd/325th Battalion, led by Lieutenant Colonel Jack Hamilton, to expand the small beachhead taken by the Rangers in the south-west corner of Grenada. Meanwhile, Schwarzkopf, embarked in *Guam*, spoke to Trobaugh, who was ashore, and asked him when he anticipated getting to Grand Anse. Trobaugh was not optimistic, and based on the intelligence, he replied, 'Probably won't be there for another day or two.'[7]

The existence and importance of the Grand Anse campus had been known to Metcalf and his staff since early on 25 October. But it eventually took thirty-three hours for US troops to reach the campus, only 1.5 miles (2,400m) from Point Salines. If the planners of URGENT FURY really thought that the students were at risk, then this delay was incomprehensible and inexplicable.

A lack of intelligence was a constant and significant feature of the intervention. However, in this specific case the American forces were aware of the location of the students, their buildings and the PRA deployment. This happy state of affairs was because telephone communications had been established with the campus and contact made with Mark Barettella, a radio ham operator. In the Pentagon, arrangements were quickly made for six radio hams in the USA to monitor Barettella's transmissions. At around 1000 hrs, Barettella advised that there were PRA troops in the campus area but not, at present, inside any of the buildings.

By happy chance, *Guam* had moved her position and was now laying off Grand Anse Beach, perhaps one of the most beautiful in the Caribbean. The beach was thronged with people, presumed to be students. It was at this point that Schwarzkopf demonstrated the lateral thinking and initiative that eventually propelled him to the top of the US Army. On the flight deck of *Guam* were twelve USMC helicopters – an asset that the General intended to put to use. He radioed Trobaugh and said, 'Look, if I can get you helicopters, how about an air mobile assault over on the beach and we'll pull them out of the way?'

Trobaugh swiftly agreed but asked that the Rangers, who had special training for this sort of operation, temporarily be placed under his command. Admiral Metcalf was enthused and said, 'Make it happen.'[8] There then followed an example of the bureaucratic mindset that sometimes infects large organisations. When Schwarzkopf summoned the Marine commander, he

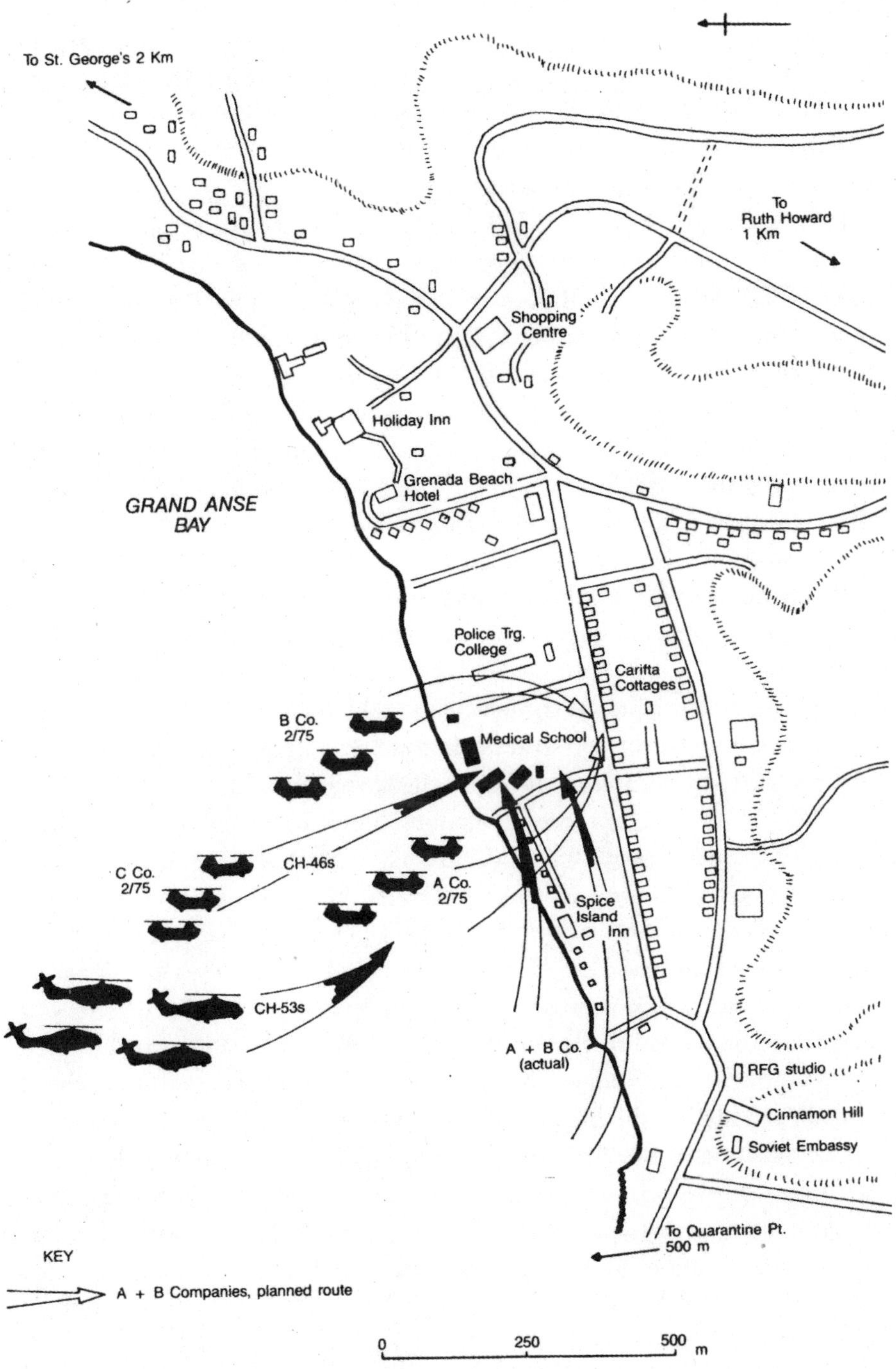

The student rescue operation, 1605 hrs, 26 October 1983. (*Adkin*)

ran into opposition The Marine colonel, almost certainly James Faulkner, stated bluntly, 'We don't fly Army soldiers in Marine helicopters.' Faulkner wanted his Marines to do the job, but he was not seeing the wood for the trees. It was not until Faulkner was given a direct order with the threat of court martial for non-compliance that the helicopters were made available, albeit after a very unpleasant scene.[9]

The mechanics of the rescue was in the hands of Lieutenant Colonel Grenville Amos, who commanded the helicopter squadron, and Lieutenant Colonel Ralph Hagler, who led the 2nd/75th Ranger Battalion. These two men were painfully aware of the trials of the earlier rescue Operation EAGLE CLAW, and the price to be paid for failure. They had no accurate intelligence on enemy forces, their strength or deployment, and had to rely on Barettella's observations. It the event, the rescue was to be conducted with massive force that involved airstrikes and naval gunfire.

A three-phase plan was devised. In phase one, a Ranger assault carried in CH-46 transports would establish a defensive cordon beyond the campus. This was a mere 2 miles (3.2km) from Point Salines. However, the only viable landing zone was the beach. The second phase, to be triggered when the campus was secure, would be the arrival of the Marine heavy lift CH-53D helicopters, which would move the students off the beach and take them to *Guam*. The third and final phase would be the retrieval of the Ranger battalion. The whole exercise was expected to be completed in about thirty minutes.

Hagler was to use his three companies, albeit each reduced to fifty men. Alpha Company in three CH-46 (Chinook) aircraft would lead and establish a beachhead. Bravo Company would follow and then the two companies would advance and cordon the campus. It was the function of Charlie Company, also in three CH-46s, to pack the students into four CH-53D Sea Stallions.

The bombardment started at 1500 hrs, and it involved A-7 Corsairs, which concentrated on the Police Training College. A Spectre gunship was to obliterate Carifta Cottages; the Rangers' mortar teams, army artillery, naval gunfire and two Cobras added to the blizzard of fire – none of which was necessary.

The evacuation worked very well, and the operation was completed in twenty-six minutes. However, it transpired that there were a further 200 students accommodated in houses between the two campuses. Many of these were on the Lance Aux Epines peninsula, about 5 miles (8km) south of Grand Anse. Most of these were not 'rescued' until the 28th or 29th. A further twenty-one individuals lived further away and were missed entirely.

Notes

1. Commander-in-Chief, US Atlantic Command, Operation URGENT FURY, 25 October–2 November (6 February 1984, Enclosure 2, Chronology).
2. Schwarzkopf, in an interview on 15 December 1987, quoted by Kukielski, p. 103.
3. Chalker, D.C. with Dockery, K., *One Perfect Op* (New York, Morrow, 2002), p. 172.
4. Adkin, Major M., *Urgent Fury: The Battle for Grenada* (London, Leo Cooper, 1989), p. 257.
5. Scoon, Sir P., *Survival for Service: My Experiences as Governor General of Grenada* (Macmillan Caribbean, 2003) p. 67. Quoted by Kukielski, p. 145.
6. Adkin, p. 263.
7. Schwarzkopf interview, 21 November 1983, quoted by Kukielski, p. 10.
8. Schwarzkopf, H.N. and Petre, P., *It Doesn't Take a Hero: General H. Norman Schwarzkopf, The Autobiography* (New York, Bantam Books, 1992), p. 254.
9. Jones, C.V., *Boys of 67: From Vietnam to Iraq. The Extraordinary Story of a Few Good Men* (Mechanicsburg, PA, Stackpole Books, 2006), p. 32.

Chapter 17

27 October
Day 3 – The Assault on Camp Calivigny

Metcalf probably enjoyed his breakfast on 27 October because he could reflect on several successes. The taking of Little Havana, whilst not an epic victory had nevertheless been with the minimal loss of two men killed and a handful wounded. Sir Paul Scoon was safe, and 230 civilians had been rescued. The PRA logistic base had produced massive booty.

There was every indication that native Grenadians were delighted at the American presence. The PRA had melted away; individuals had taken off their uniforms and were now seeking to integrate with the civilian population. Grenadian resistance was at an end, Coard and his henchmen had disappeared.

However, Metcalf and his superiors in Washington, anticipating more robust Cuban aggression, seemed not to realise that the 'war' was over. The minimal casualties, the hundreds of prisoners, the attitude of most Grenadians, the taking of the RMC headquarters at Fort Frederick and the uncontested rescue of the students should, in combination, have led to a winding down of URGENT FURY. However, there was a perceived need to occupy ground – most of which was unpopulated.

At around midday on 27 October, Metcalf received an order from Atlantic Command, in Norfolk, Virginia, to assault Camp Calivigny, a PRA barracks about 3 miles (5km) from Point Salines. On the basis of even more fallacious intelligence, it had been identified as an important objective. The camp had been built by the Cubans on a bleak, deserted, scrub-covered peninsula. On the very few available maps, it was shown as Egmont. Like all barracks across the world, it was fenced, and was equipped with an assault course, a water tower, accommodation and feeding facilities. The camp was the training base for the PRA and was constructed to house an infantry battalion but, in 1983, it was occupied by a single company. In Washington, the view was that the camp was a key Cuban training facility from which communism was distributed throughout the Caribbean. Metcalf was a three-star officer; any order given him must have emanated from a four-star – of whom there were not many in his command chain.

On receipt of the instruction, Schwarzkopf was angered and he told Metcalf, 'That's the stupidest goddam order I've ever heard.'[1] Metcalf went back to

Atlantic Command seeking verification of the order. The reply from Norfolk was brief and crisp. It said, 'The JCS has ordered you to take Calivigny barracks before dark.'[2]

Metcalf gave the mission to Trobaugh, whose 82nd Division was making very slow progress – they were not likely to meet the deadline and so, once again, Trobaugh decided to use the Rangers who were temporarily under his command. These men, who had accomplished their tasks, were waiting for passage back to the United States; this new mission was an unwelcome surprise. There is no doubt that Rangers were the best suited to the task as heliborne incursions were their speciality. Time was very short, and only two of the nine Task Force 160s' Black Hawks were still airworthy. The airlift was reassigned to the 82nd Aviation Battalion. The pilots of these aircraft were much less experienced than the 160 pilots.

The location of Camp Calivigny was interesting. It was remote and could only be approached by way of a long, unsurfaced track from the village of the same name. For the Grenadian soldiers it had little to commend it, as there was seldom opportunity for 'beer and skittles'. The plateau upon which the camp was built was close to the sea, but at the top of 150ft (45m) cliffs. Access from the sea was onto a small beach that also gave entry to the rifle range. The camp was not a defended location; it was a domestic facility.

The original operational plan had been for the Rangers to take the camp on D-Day, and so they were well briefed on the objective. However, Trobaugh had abandoned that objective on his arrival (see page 83). Forty-eight hours later, and although to the men on the ground the camp was of no apparent strategic or tactical importance, there was at least one who thought it most definitely was. Hence the order to Metcalf to mount a battalion attack. Trobaugh selected Hagler's 2nd/75th for the task. One Ranger, Daniel Bolger, wrote later:

> Calivigny looked uninviting for a bold, overwhelming stroke. Although labelled a raid, this air assault was not suited for Rangers, but rather was a job for a lot of line infantry with significant supporting fire. Given the tiny landing zones, *any* helicopter attack into the narrow streets of the Calivigny barracks compound begged for defeat in detail as the force dribbled in. Not surprisingly, it was considered a 'suicide mission' when briefed to the 2nd Battalion of the 75th Infantry which tried to execute it.[3]

Bolger and his comrades were told that their objective was well defended by 600 Grenadian troops and 300 or more Cubans, led by up to 60 Russian and Cuban advisors. In addition, 'there were six AA-guns defending the place'.[4] H-hour for this operation was set for 1630 hrs following a thirty-minute bombardment. The aim was to raze the camp and, when that was accomplished, the Rangers would attack from UH-60 Black Hawks. It was a painfully simple and unsophisticated plan, which substituted unrivalled firepower for guile.

It was arrant, military nonsense to pit a handful of Rangers in a heliborne assault against 900 entrenched enemy. A numerical superiority of at least 3:1 was required but, even then, significant casualties would be an inevitable result. Schwarzkopf and Metcalf were well aware of this and so it is evident that they had dismissed the intelligence for the claptrap it clearly was.

The participants were given only an hour to fine-tune their role and the only planning tools available were aerial photographs. These were of good quality, and they showed the layout of the camp, but did not provide any information on defences and the AA guns could not be seen.

Colonel Scott, a brigade commander in the 82nd, assumed overall command and he would be airborne in a UH-1. Sensibly, he delegated tactical control to Hagler, who would attack with his three rifle companies, supplemented by seventy men of Charlie Company of 1st/75th. This force would deploy in four company waves, each of four Black Hawks. The approach would be very low over the sea but end with a steep climb above the cliffs. The Black Hawks would land in the middle of the camp. Alpha and Charlie companies of 2nd/75th were to land at the southern edge of the camp and Charlie Company of 1st/75 was to be held in reserve.

The bombardment by aircraft, army artillery and naval gunfire from USS *Moosbrugger* would be the biggest but, as it happens, not the best of the campaign. Three batteries of M-102, 105mm howitzers, at Point Salines 8,750 yards (8,000m) from the target would deliver crushing devastation. In the air, AC-130s and A-7s would contribute shellfire and bombs.[5]

The plan started to unravel from the beginning. The artillery at Point Salines fired 500 rounds at Calivigny from its seventeen howitzers; only one round hit the island of Grenada. The other 499 fell hundreds of yards short into the sea, to the consternation of the local marine life.[6]

This was an egregious example of abject gunnery, exceeded only by that at Fort Sumter in April 1861.[7] It emerged later that 'the Airborne Gunners had mis-plotted their own position by 765 yards (700m), their co-ordinates for camp Calivigny were inaccurate and that they had left their artillery circles [compasses on tripods] behind in Fort Bragg'.[8]

USS *Moosbrugger* fired one round before the firing deadline, as the USN protocol did not allow fire by surface ships when aircraft were close to the target. Trobaugh was incensed until he was told that Metcalf had applied the usual protocol.

The razing of the camp was now in the hands of the USN A-7s and the USAF A-130 Spectres. Many of the insubstantial camp buildings were demolished, and in the process, two large capacity oil drums were set alight. These burned furiously, emitting clouds of black smoke. There was no return fire but one building exploded – probably an ammunition store.

The bombardment had not been half as destructive as planned, but the way was now clear for the Ranger assault. The first two Black Hawks landed and debouched their Ranger passengers. However, it all went horribly wrong when the third, piloted by Chief Warrant Officer Wayne Sinibaldi, suffered explosive damage to its tail boom. The aircraft was about 15 feet off the ground at the time and Sinibaldi completely lost control.[9]

The cause of the damage remains unclear. There is speculation that the contents of the ammunition store mentioned earlier might have 'cooked off' or it was perhaps misaimed friendly fire from another Black Hawk or, most unlikely, small arms fire from a small group of Grenadians on a distant ridge. Whatever the cause, the effect was catastrophic.

The Black Hawk plunged to the ground and landed so heavily that it bounced towards the second Black Hawk. Their rotors entwined and, on both aircraft, they started to disintegrate into lethal debris. Witness to this unfolding disaster was Black Hawk number four, which turned away to avoid the wreckage below. However, it was unable to find a flat LZ and landed, very heavily, in a ditch. The passengers of three Black Hawks were on the ground but already some were badly injured by the debris from the two entwined helicopters. One of these was Sergeant William Sears, who had been hit with something on his right shin. He fell and called for help. A medic, Kenneth Lannon, responded at once.

The pilot of the fourth helicopter decided to adjust his position and vacate the ditch. However, he was unaware of the damage his heavy landing had done to his aircraft. On landing, his rotor blades had flexed and cut the drive shaft to the tail rotor. From his seat, the pilot had no instrument warning of a malfunction. Suffering from very serious damage, the Black Hawk did not respond readily to the controls, but it did lift sufficiently to leave the ditch, its engine screaming in protest. At the same time as Lannon was treating Sears's wound, the fourth helicopter careered towards them. Sears pushed the medic away and told him to run, and Sears started to crawl to safety. The out-of-control Black Hawk drove into the two wrecked aircraft, killing Lannon.

With rotors still turning on all three Black Hawks, lethal pieces of rotor flew into the ranks of 2nd/75th. Two more Rangers, Sergeant Eric Slater and Specialist 4 Philip Grenier, were killed and a further three Rangers were injured. The uninjured Rangers got on with the job they had been sent to do and cleared the buildings in the compound. First Lieutenant Raymond Thomas commented, 'We didn't find anything worth shooting at.'[10]

The camp was empty, abandoned – there was no enemy to fight.

Just like the Battle of Fort Sumter, the Battle of Camp Calivigny had been a major military non-event. There were no 600 Grenadian troops, and the 300 Cubans did not exist either. This operation had been a debacle, bordering farce, from the beginning.

The intelligence was patently nonsense, the artillery bombardment was utterly inept, and the naval gunfire did not happen. The helicopter crashes were an unhappy combination of accidents, but the USA had spent a great deal of treasure attacking an empty barracks and, in the process, caused the death of three soldiers, the wounding of fifteen others and the loss of three aircraft. How fortunate for the Rangers that they were not faced by a resolute adversary.

There was an upside and that was the resolution and courage of the American Rangers who put their lives at risk, notwithstanding the absurd odds they were told to face. Sergeant Stephen Trujillo, a medic, from the only undamaged aircraft, was sent to deal with the casualties. When he reached the scene, an explosion blew him over and burned him. He heard shouts and extricated 1st Lieutenant William Eskridge from deep mud below a burning Black Hawk. He treated the officer as best he could, but Eskridge had lost his right leg and was wounded in his left. Sears was found, near death, but the attention of Trujillo and Sergeant Gerry Holt among others was critical. Sears survived but was paralyzed for the rest of his life. Trujillo was awarded a Silver Star, Holt a Bronze Star and Lannon a similar medal (awarded posthumously), all with a Combat V to mark their valour.

Many of the wounded were taken to *Guam* and Schwarzkopf visited them, when the needless suffering enraged him. When, much later, he wrote his memoirs, he said, 'There had been no military reason we had to take the Calivigny barracks. I wondered which son of a bitch had ordered the attack.'

The general was quite right. The official history noted that no record of the JCS ordering the attack could be found.[11] Schwarzkopf, among others, speculated that the order had been instigated in McDonald's headquarters in Norfolk. There was also not a shred of evidence that the initial helicopter crash was caused by ground fire. Schwarzkopf described Calivigny as a 'dry hole'. The official history covered this debacle in just forty-two words. They were:

> VADM Metcalf's ships delivered salvoes of naval gunfire and launched sorties of Corsairs. Army UH-160 Black Hawk helicopters then landed the Ranger battalions at the barracks compound area; three helicopters were damaged [destroyed, actually], but the Rangers took control of the barracks by 2100.[12]

* * *

One of the aims on 27 October was the joining of Army and Marine units at a point south of St George's; the taking of the prison at Richmond Hill would be part of that process. Lieutenant Colonel Ray Smith's Marines were allocated to that task. This had been a tough nut to crack on D-Day but by now the defenders were seeing the writing writ large upon the wall and they abandoned their posts. They offered Smith no resistance. The prison was the temporary residence of several hundred criminals and 100 political detainees.[13] The absence of the guards had led to prisoners breaking out of confinement. The Marines released the remaining occupants, one of whom was Alister Hughes, a Grenadian journalist, arrested after the murder of Bishop.

In the late afternoon of 27 October, the leading platoon of the 3rd/325th approached the road junction at Ruth Howard Road/Sugar Mill. They had only advanced about 1,100 yards (1km) since early morning and so extreme caution had been their watchwords. After an uneventful day, they came under sniper fire. Usually, a trained sniper always gets a kill with his first shot. In this case, he fired several shots that went over a jeep carrying a component of the Air Naval Gunfire Liaison Company (ANGLICO) that happened to be on the road. They had been having a bad day because they had not been provided with the radio codes, call signs and frequencies that would allow them to communicate with interested parties on *Guam*.

The unnamed chief warrant officer commanding this group was able to identify the house – white with a red roof – from which the fire had come. Bravo Company of the 307 Engineer Battalion had also identified the same house as the site of the sniper.

Colonel Stephen Silvasy, the commander of the 2nd Brigade of the 82nd Division, had established his forty-four-man headquarters in the area and his three radio operators were located inside a tin-roofed structure on a hill. These three radiomen, acting as a team, controlled naval, artillery and air support for both Rangers and 82nd Division.

Meanwhile, the chief could not call down fire on this house because he could not communicate with anyone about anything! However, he did take the chance to talk to Captain William Stephen, the air liaison officer of Lieutenant Colonel George Crocker's 1st/505th Battalion, which was nearby, to the south of Ruth Howard Road. It was agreed that the chief was best placed to control supporting fire and with Stephen's equipment, he tried to call in a Spectre gunship, but there were none available.

The chief did make contact with the flight leader of four A-7s who had just finished blasting the barracks at Calivigny. It seemed to be a straightforward mission. The target white house with the red roof was just north of a drive-in cinema. In the normal course of events, an air strike would require the authorisation of a battalion commander – in this case, Lieutenant Colonel John Raines, commanding 3rd/325th. However, the chief was not in contact with either Raines or Silvasy and was unaware of their positions relative to the white house.

The A-7s' leader made several practice runs over the target. It was at this point that it all went horribly wrong.

The Corsairs, by mistake, strafed Silvasy's command post and radio shack. The 20mm cannon shells ripped through the flimsy building. The occupants were either wounded or terrified, or both.

The chief warrant officer realised the mistake and called off any further strikes on that target but directed a flight of A-6 Intruders to the original target. The misdirected strafing had caused at least seventeen casualties and as they waited for evacuation, the wounded lay under a tropical downpour. Two men lost both legs, one of whom died later. It had been a disaster – the lone sniper was forgotten; perhaps the Intruders killed him.

Lieutenant Colonel George Crocker had witnessed the 'blue on blue' incident at a distance and, after the aircraft had left, he went in search of the person responsible. He came across the Marine chief warrant officer and said, 'Do you know that the airstrike just hit the 2nd Brigade?' 'Yes,' acknowledged the Marine, who was clearly filled with remorse. At the enquiry that followed, the pilots were exonerated but the Marine was found to be culpable. His punishment, if any, is not recorded.

* * *

During 27 October, the 82nd and the Marines gathered a mixed bag of 595 American civilians; in addition, there were uncounted British and Canadians. The American medical students, never at risk, nevertheless reacted very emotionally, laughing, kissing and hugging their liberators. The evacuation of these people started on Friday, 28 October. That same day, the Rangers were also repatriated.

The progress of the 82nd was giving cause for concern and criticism. It emerged that Scholtes, with his extensive Vietnam experience, insisted that during his division's advance, his men conducted thorough searches for concealed combatants and arms caches. He wanted to ensure that he had eliminated all the elements needed for a revival of anarchy. Trobaugh was also the victim of the fallacious intelligence estimates of enemy strength and, in reality, the 82nd were searching for something that was not a threat. The 82nd and the Marines were closing on each other and Trobaugh was alert to the potential for another 'blue on blue'.

The tropical heat and limited fresh water combined to make life unpleasant for the airborne soldiers. Their rucksacks were too heavy, and their uniforms were intended for wear in a temperate climate. Unlike the Marines, they did not have Vietnam-era hot weather uniforms. Heat-related casualties became more frequent and Hamilton, in 2nd Battalion, ordered the shedding of the 20lb (9kg) flak jackets.

St George's was a silent city as American forces moved in. There was no traffic, and no one walked the streets. The PRA was noticeable by its very absence. Bishop's two most important installations were Butler House and Fort Rupert. Both had been recipients of well-directed American air power, although Butler House did yield a mass of classified documents. These were parcelled up and despatched to the USA for analysis.

When the leading platoon entered Fort Rupert, it had clearly been abandoned save for the sole occupant, a dead PRA soldier. All the buildings were in ruins. This had been the scene of the murder of Bishop and others, but the walls, pitted by the executioners' bullets, were now showing evidence of American weaponry.

Metcalf, unimpressed by the 82nd, decided to move the boundary line between the Marines and the Airborne. The new inter-force boundary was to run from Ross Point in the west to Requin Bay in the east. Once again, communications failed. Smith did not hear of the change until late on the 27th whilst the 82nd were unaware until the following day, when the two components linked up. The new arrangements were not promulgated below brigade level and as the two formations converged, so did the possibility of a 'blue on blue' incident. The soldiers of the 82nd were told that they were in a free-fire zone, and they did not know of the nearby presence of Marines. This situation, the result of abject communication and incompetence, could so easily have been catastrophic.

At Point Salines, the 1st/508th had just arrived and Lieutenant Hugh Shaw was given responsibility for the security of the airhead. Notwithstanding the cessation of hostilities, two further battalions, in accordance with Trobaugh's instructions, were heading for Grenada. The units on the ground were advancing at a snail's pace – about 1,100 yards (1km) per day.

This very slow progress had to have a reason. Communications between Trobaugh and Metcalf were sporadic at best, although Trobaugh had the means to fly out and share his concerns with the commander. It is suggested that, imbued with vastly inaccurate intelligence, Trobaugh, like many others, could not believe that the day was won. An overwhelming victory had been accomplished but the victors were blissfully unaware of their success.

Three years later, a team of researchers at the Walter Reed Army Institute of Research submitted a paper to *The Military Review*, the professional journal of the US Army. The paper examined the overloading of the infantry in Grenada.

The team had interviewed representatives from seven of the nine battalions, many just after the end of operations. The conclusions came as no surprise as one battalion 'had twenty-nine heat casualties in one day, another battalion had to treat forty-eight and a third used up the entire supply of intravenous solution on heat cases'.[14]

The reasons were blindingly obvious. The men had no vehicular support, they were not acclimatised, were carrying too much weight (up to 110lb), and were wearing unsuitable polyester clothing while trying to cross rugged country. Why they were so grotesquely overloaded is the question, and the answer is, once more, the abject intelligence gap.

The planners did not have accurate information on whom they were going to fight, or where or for how long. Because of this ignorance, they sought to accommodate every likely contingency, and carried all the equipment to meet those contingencies. The report commented that in the planning phase and during the early operations, the reinforcement plan – if there be one – was not known.

Notes

1. Schwarzkopf, in an interview, 15 December 1987. Quoted by Kukielski, p. 126.
2. Cole, R.H., *Operation Urgent Fury: The Planning and Execution of Joint Operations in Grenada 1983* (US Joint Chiefs of Staff, Washington, DC, Joint History Office, 1997), p. 53. Schwarzkopf, *Hero*, p. 256.
3. Bolger, D.P., *Special Operations and the Grenada Campaign* (USA, Carlisle, PA, US Army War College, 1988), p. 57.
4. Speakes, T., a helicopter co-pilot. Quoted by Adkin, p. 280.
5. Adkin incorrectly named USS *Caron* as being the Navy presence (p. 281) in this operation.
6. Atkinson, R., *The Long Gray Line* (Boston, Houghton Mifflin, 1989), p. 488.
7. The Battle of Fort Sumter was a major military non-event. The Confederate Army fired 3,341 artillery rounds at the fort and received about 1,000 in reply. The only casualty on both sides was a non-combatant mule minding its own business. Keegan, J., *The American Civil War* (London, Vintage, 2010), p. 34.
8. Adkin, Major M., *Urgent Fury: The Battle for Grenada* (London, Leo Cooper, 1989), p. 283.
9. Sinibaldi, W., in an interview by an unidentified individual on 14 December 1983. The transcript is archived in the Army Centre of Military History in Washington, DC.
10. Adkin, p. 277.
11. Cole, p. 76.
12. Cole, p. 53.
13. O'Shaughnessy, H., *Grenada: Revolution, Invasion and Aftermath* (London, Sphere Books, 1984), p. 93.
14. Adkin, p. 290.

Chapter 18

28–31 October
Final Operations – Mopping-Up

Trobaugh's orders for 28 October were given without the benefit of radio contact, with the Marines only 1,000 yards (915m) away. On that fourth day, it was anticipated that the important south-west corner of the island would be cleared of residual opposition. Despite the complete absence of any aggressive Grenadian actions, it was speculated that soon there would be guerrilla operations in the rugged hills of the island. In fact, the people who might initiate such activity were devoting themselves to self-preservation.

Austin, James and Layne all recognised that there was likely to be a day when their behaviour would be judged and, anxious to avoid any form of retribution, they moved out of Fort Frederick. For them, refuge in Guyana was an attractive option, where President Forbes Burnham was of like mind. He had been supportive in the past, sending defence training teams to Grenada and hosting visits from Austin. It was Burnham who had telephoned a warning of impending invasion. The difficulty facing the fugitives was that they lacked the means of getting anywhere near Guyana. They desperately needed a boat, and someone to sail it.

The three most senior PRA officers had cobbled together US$7,000 with which to pay for their passage. Money alone would not suffice, and so they armed themselves with Makarov pistols, an AK-47 and grenades. Austin had a friend called Gerhard Jonas; he was an East German Communist and an advisor to the PRG on security matters. Jonas had lived on the island for several years and settled on the peninsula of Westerhall Point, where he was well connected.

Jonas was unenthused at being involved but he was nevertheless able to identify an unoccupied bungalow with a very convenient private jetty about halfway down the peninsula. The three men decided to hide out there until a boat could be found for them. Jonas was to be their agent.

Two officers of the Caribbean Peacekeeping Force realised that an escape by sea was the only option available for the deposed members of the PRG. The obvious place to seek a boat was from Spice Island Charters, who maintained a marina at the north-western corner of Lance aux Epines. Major Hartland and Lieutenant Commander Tomlin, having discussed the matter with Major

General Crist and Brigadier Lewis, were provided with a vehicle and a single US soldier as an escort.

The owners of the Marina were helpful and directed the three men to the house of one Dod Gorman nearby. At the house, they found a crowd of about thirty-five people, most of whom were American medical students whose very existence was unknown to the US forces. The students, mistakenly, presumed that the two officers and their escort had come to 'rescue' them.

Mr John Kelly (later CMG, LVO, MBE), the Second Secretary of the British High Commission in Grenada, was present. He was the permanent Representative of the Foreign and Commonwealth Office. The couple had had amiable relations with Bishop and had made every effort to establish a soundly based relationship with the Marxist, unelected dictator of Grenada.

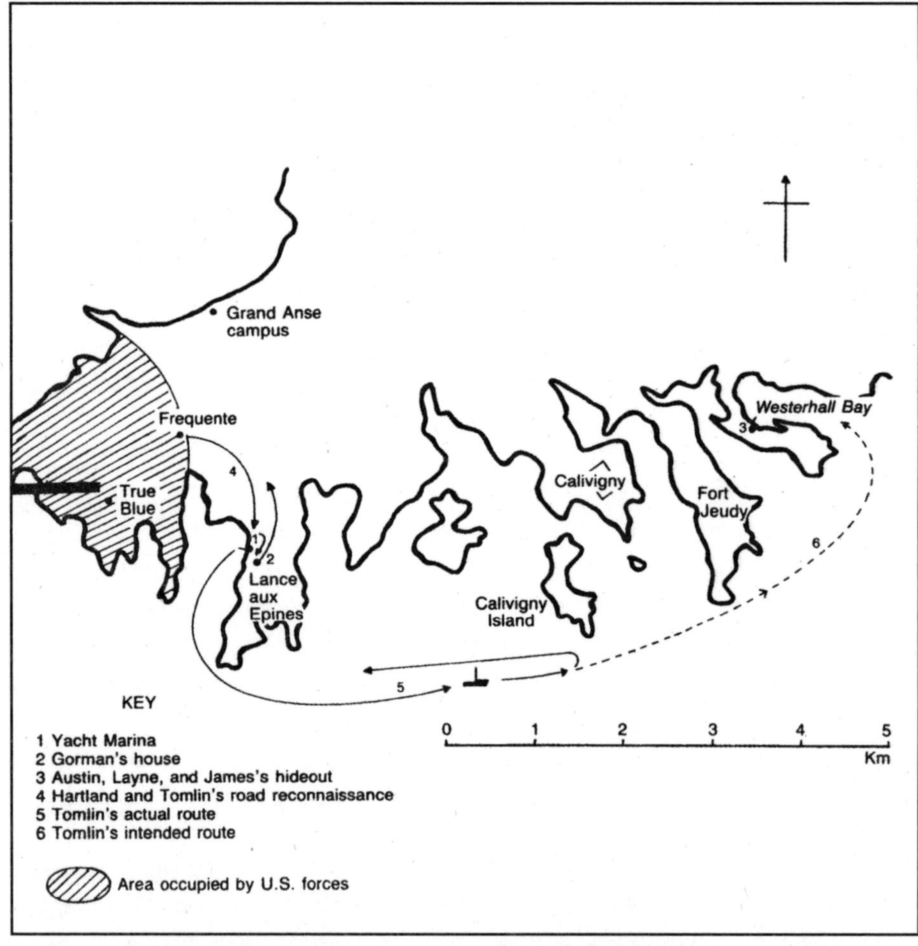

This map illustrates the rugged and sparsely inhabited coastline of south-west Grenada and the abortive first attempt to arrest Austin, James and Layne. (*Adkin*)

Kelly went so far as to grow a beard, shaped as that of Bishop. This was hastily removed when Coard seized control. There is no evidence of Kelly taking any proactive action during the turbulent period 10–25 October 1983. He was not at Scoon's side and, if he gave any advice to the Governor General, it went unrecorded. Nevertheless, he was made a member of the Most Excellent Order of The British Empire (MBE) in 1984 for his service in Grenada. (The citation for this award could not be found.)

It was Mrs Kelly who pointed out to Hartland and Tomlin a European man who, she claimed, would know where Austin and his colleagues were to be found. The man was Jonas, who prevaricated for about two hours, pretending to be drunk and not speaking English. The two officers persisted and eventually Jonas threw in his hand and admitted that he was intent on hiring a yacht to take Austin, Layne and James to Guyana. He added that they were at Westerhall. Jonas appreciated that his being associated with the trio was likely to have unpleasant consequences, so he turned his coat and agreed to assist in the capture of the fugitives.

Tomlin took Jonas to Brigadier Lewis and the three of them constructed a highly convoluted plan to apprehend Austin, James and Layne. The planning for URGENT FURY does not stand scrutiny and the arrangement to capture three fugitives is of little importance in the much wider scheme of things. However, it was sufficiently bizarre that it justifies a brief mention. Adkin's account cannot be bettered. He wrote,

> A yacht would be hired and sailed around Westerhall by Tomlin with Jonas, plus three or four US soldiers concealed below. On arrival, Jonas would go ashore in a small boat to persuade Austin that all was well, and they could start their voyage to Guyana.
>
> Jonas was to get them to wrap up their weapons in plastic sheets against the water and put them in the bottom of the boat. He would then row them towards the yacht, but about halfway he would lose an oar and then jump overboard to retrieve it. This would be the signal for the soldiers and Tomlin to throw stun grenades and cover the fugitives, calling upon them to surrender. If they declined, they would be shot.[1]

The plan was accepted by Lewis and Crist, but the agreement of Trobaugh was also required. Initially, the commander of the 82nd was unenthused and doubted that the plan would work. He asked any of his personal staff would like to take part in 'this crazy scheme'. His *aide de camp*, Captain Robert Hoidahl, was first to volunteer, and a lieutenant and two senior NCOs completed the team.

The party assembled at the marina, having made contact with *Guam* from the Gorman house. The object was to explain the reason for a yacht sailing out of Prickly Bay and to avoid a 'blue on blue' incident. The yacht owner was very co-operative and gave the party use of his vessel; his girlfriend assured them that the yacht was fully fuelled.

At 1700 hrs, just as the debacle at Camp Calivigny was unfolding, the yacht set sail. There was a strong wind blowing and a heavy swell. In combination, they made the 7-mile (11km) voyage an unhappy prospect. Tomlin was at the helm as he set out to round Prickly Point and bypass Calivigny Island and Fort Jeudy Point. The hope was that once the yacht turned north into Westerhall Bay the sea would be calmer. Tomlin managed to maintain a speed of around 7 knots and all was well until, at about the halfway point, the engine stopped: the yacht had run out of fuel.

So much for the earlier assurances. This was now a hazardous situation as the yacht, at the mercy of the wind, was blown towards the rocks. Tomlin was the only sailor and he managed to get his lubberly crew to hoist the sails. The wind speed increased, and Tomlin cut his losses and headed back towards the marina. They arrived safely, but exhausted and wiser.

The next morning, Tomlin proposed to try again. However, Jonas correctly felt that he had to give Austin some reassurance that all was well, and a boat was being sourced. He was given a pass that would get him through American roadblocks. He reported back that Austin, Layne and James were still at the house, and content that their flight from Grenada was in good hands.

One might speculate that with over 7,000 heavily armed, highly trained professional troops, ample helicopters and powered landing craft the apprehension of these three frightened men should have presented no problem to the military might of the USA.

Notwithstanding the wealth of American assets, Tomlin busied himself collecting diesel fuel. He met briefly with Metcalf, who had come ashore to speak to Trobaugh. A little later, Trobaugh cancelled the operation on the basis that it was 'too dangerous' and withdrew his men.

The three lightly armed fugitives were perceived to present such strong opposition that the 82nd Division would not take them on. This seems to be highly unlikely, but Adkin, who made the assertion almost contemporaneously, was a witness to these events.

There is a strong element of credence because a Special Forces Team was summoned for the task. It arrived on 29 October, when Tomlin briefed the team members at the Point Salines Terminal. There was a delay as the team leader said he needed the authorisation of his JSOC headquarters. This was presumably the same headquarters that had sent them. Tomlin returned to check on progress, to be told that JSOC also considered the operation to be 'too dangerous', and it was cancelled for the second time. The CIA whisked Jonas away.

After five full days waiting for their boat, Austin *et al.* were captured by soldiers of the 82nd without a shot being fired. Perhaps Trobaugh had rescinded his earlier order or perhaps, over time, the 'mopping up' had just happened to reach Westerhall Point as American troops were fanning out across the island seeking to uncover arms caches and widening the area under their control.[2]

Elsewhere, the rounding up of members of the RMC was assisted by Grenadians who were only too anxious to help. Bernard Coard and his wife Phyllis had holed up in an anonymous private house to the east of St George's. On the morning of 29 October, and acting on local intelligence, Marines surrounded the house. They invited the Coards to surrender; as an inducement, they pointed to an anti-tank weapon at the hideaway. The pair emerged and Coard kept repeating, 'I'm not responsible. I'm not responsible.'[3]

The Coards, Austin, Layne and James were all flown out to *Guam* and were placed in cells. Some eight days later, they were taken to Richmond Hill Prison to await their trial for murder.

It was on 28 October that the leading platoon of 2nd/325th, moving cautiously along the road that hugged the cost from Grand Anse to St George's, came upon a roadblock, which was initially presumed to be mounted and defended by the PRA. However, the occupants of the roadblock were Marines of Fox Company. The link-up between TF 121 and TF 124 had been made.

Trobaugh's order to 'send more battalions' was still extant and the 2nd/505th arrived, followed soon after by 2nd/508th. Trobaugh now had an embarrassment of riches – two brigades, each of three battalions – to cement the American possession of Grenada. Four days after the initial landing, when Crocker's 1st/505th occupied the Lance Aux Epines peninsula, it found about 200 American citizens patiently waiting to be 'rescued'. They were duly transported back to the USA, where they were included in the 662 US Citizens and 82 foreigners evacuated. Later, a further twenty-one, who had somehow been overlooked, stayed in Grenada.[4]

A Grenadian advised the Americans that Bishop had been buried at Calivigny and guided a party to the spot. The camp had been razed by the earlier air strikes. Apart from a handful of personal effects, nothing remained of Bishop and his colleagues, except badly burned bones, some tissue and remnants of clothing, possibly of Creft's.

A curious fact was that in the pit in which the corpses had been incinerated by Abdullah, it was reported that there was no trace of any heads or hands. Adkin was sceptical. He suggested that as the exhumation was conducted by Americans, with no other nationals present, the probability was that the remains had been flown to the USA to prevent the grave becoming a national shrine. Quite why the USA would care about such an eventuality, he did not explain. In fact, Bishop's memorial is at Point Salines, which was named 'Maurice Bishop Airport' in 2009.

The painfully slow progress of the 82nd Division quickened slightly as it pushed on into the Mount Hartman Estate and the Calivigny area. A small party reached the village of Crochu. The suggestion that the M-60 tanks be used to head the advance was discarded when it was realised that none of the bridges on the minor roads would bear their weight. Instead, 2nd/508th, mounted in loaned Grenadian trucks, moved swiftly and uncovered a PRA supply dump. Five trucks, brimming with ammunition, were neatly parked nearby. As the airborne soldiers passed through small villages they were greeted by enthusiastic and welcoming crowds. The 11-mile (18km) advance to Crochu in the south-east of the island, about 7½ miles (12km) south of Grenville, was the longest in the whole operation. It was completely uncontested.

General Vessey and Admiral McDonald arrived in Grenada. Vessey had been unimpressed by the performance of the 82nd Division and its leader, Major General Trobaugh. He, not unreasonably, thought that this elite formation taking the better part of four days to advance 3 miles (5km) against minor opposition was dilatory. General Vesey reportedly called Major General Trobaugh and said, 'We have two companies of Marines running all over the island and thousands of Army troops doing nothing. What the hell is going on?'[5]

It is a characteristic of airborne soldiers of all nations that they exhibit drive, aggression and a sense of urgency. It is what makes them an elite force. That had not applied in Grenada, where the pace of the advance had been determined by their overly cautious leader.

Vessey urged Trobaugh to inject some urgency. Having identified Grand Etang in mid-island as a PRA base, still unsecured, Trobaugh selected Hamilton's 2nd/325th to take the position. It was a military picnic. A delightful drive, no opposition, but on arrival the camp was empty save an abandoned APC.

The very small island of Carriacou, north of Grenada, was taken by Marines on 31 October in a very friendly 'invasion' when the PRA was, again, noticeably absent. Two days later, the Marines sailed for the Mediterranean and their duties in Beirut.

In Grenada, the prisoners, both Grenadian and Cuban, were being guarded and confined by the Caribbean Peacekeeping Force. Vessey was displeased to see the prisoners sitting out in the glare of the sun and insisted that they be provided with shade.

There could be no doubt that the USA had achieved its aims. It had repatriated its citizens resident in Grenada, it had eliminated a communist regime, reduced the Cuban influence in the Caribbean and emphasised its overwhelming power economically, politically and militarily. However, along the way it had embarrassed a long-term and supportive ally and, by a wide majority, had been condemned by the United Nations as acting illegally. The US Government was, as ever, indifferent to the sensitivities of those with whom it did share a view.

The Vietnam Syndrome had been overcome by the demonstration of apparent military prowess. National morale in the USA was lifted and President Reagan's personal standing was enhanced. The rapid removal of American armed forces from Grenada after 4 November enjoyed general approval.

Grenadians viewed the invaders of their island as liberators and had welcomed their presence. The members of the short-lived Revolutionary Military Council would now face retribution for the killing that it had instigated. However, justice could not be served in Grenada, as its judicial system was not functioning – nor had it for several years.

In the Pentagon, objective analysis of URGENT FURY had revealed serious, fundamental flaws in the operation that would take some years to correct. This issue is addressed in Chapters 20 and 25.

Notes

1. Adkin, Major M., *Urgent Fury: The Battle for Grenada* (London, Leo Cooper, 1989), p. 296.
2. Pirnie, B.R., *Operation Urgent Fury: The United States Army in Joint Operations* (Washington, DC, US Army Center of Military History, 1986), pp. 166–7.
3. Jenkins, L., 'Search and Destroy Patrols Under Way' (*Washington Post*, 30 October 1983).
4. Adkin, p. 305.
5. Atkinson, R., *The Long Gray Line* (New York, Henry Holt & Company, 2010), p. 485.

Chapter 19

The Cost

The vast American sledgehammer had cracked the miniscule Grenadian/Cuban nut. But there had been a price to pay. The Cubans had suffered 24 killed, 59 wounded and 602 taken prisoner. Only two of the dead and eight of the wounded were professional soldiers the others were all armed labourers. The surviving Cubans were repatriated from 4 November. Cuba had 784 of its citizens in Grenada at the outbreak of hostilities and of these, 44 were women.

Grenadian military losses were forty-five killed. There were, in addition, 'at least' twenty-four civilian deaths.[1] That twenty-four includes the seventeen patients killed in the bombing of the mental hospital. The number of Grenadian wounded is imprecise, although the JCS study by Cole suggested a figure of 358. This was lumping military and civilian together. Of these, sixty civilians were sufficiently injured that, of necessity, they were flown to American military hospitals for treatment.[2]

American forces lost 19 killed and initially announced that 115 had been wounded. At that point, the credibility of the Department of Defense came into doubt as it awarded 152 Purple Hearts.[3] Of these, many were accidental injuries rather that combat wounds, and at least sixteen were the result of the strafing of Silvasy's command post (see chapter note 3).

For reasons never satisfactorily explained, the Pentagon was evasive about its casualties. The presumption is that it sought to conceal damage inflicted on Special Forces, although quite why that should be an issue long after the operation is inexplicable.

In 1987, an Indian Army officer wrote a paper in which he compared the combined Cuban/Grenadian casualty number with that of the US forces.[4] He was not alone and subsequently, Cole, in 1997, and Raines, in 2008, followed his lead. Tiwathia suggested that the casualties in this conflict were unusually balanced at 1:4 in favour of the Americans. This was notable because the norm was for the attacker to suffer double the casualties of the defender. Here the ratio was completely unprecedented and further so when there was an under-reporting of Special Forces casualties. Tiwathia concluded that the imbalance was a reflection of the American reliance on its overwhelming firepower, especially in aircraft.

One might judge this to be significantly to the credit of the USA. If it had dominating firepower and its use would preserve American lives, why not use it? However, that prodigious firepower came at a price. The cost of URGENT FURY was cited as $134.4 million.[5] That included $22 million for helicopter replacements but not the salary of the soldiers, sailors, marines and airmen. That $134.4 million in 1984 equates to $267.025 million in 2024. In 1984, $134.4 million was equivalent to $1 million for every square mile of Grenadian territory, or $224,000 for very American evacuated.

Money was never a consideration for President Reagan or any of his planning team, and, post-conflict:

> The United States is planning to spend an additional $30 million on Grenada – $15 million in economic assistance primarily for the new government on the island and $15 million to support the peacekeeping force made up of units from the six East Caribbean countries that took part in the invasion last month.[6]

There were, however, other less tangible costs. Internationally, the USA was perceived to have acted illegally. The Caribbean Community (CARICOM) response to the outcome of URGENT FURY was mixed. Some, especially those who had participated, were content, but the remainder were incensed at the breaching of Grenada's sovereignty. The relationship of the USA and UK had been dented but not broken – in very large measure as Mrs Thatcher and her government acquiesced weakly to the American *fait accompli*.

Cuba and Fidel Castro had emerged from URGENT FURY humiliated, and were, without question, the major loser in this Caribbean crisis. 'In the space of a few short weeks an expensive four-year investment in the cultivation of Communism on Grenada had literally and figuratively been blown away by the United States.'[7]

Spain acted as an intermediary and arranged the return of Cuban dead and the survivors. The first tranche of sixty Cubans, fifty-seven of whom were wounded, travelled, on 2 November, to Havana in a chartered Swiss aircraft. They were accompanied by a medical team. Only eight of the wounded were regular soldiers but Castro greeted each of the sixty as heroes.

The impact of this reversal in Cuban fortunes in Cuba was evident in the National Day of Mourning marked on 14 November in Havana's Plaza de la Revolution. The coffins of the twenty-four dead were displayed at the event, which included a ninety-minute speech by Castro that was broadcast on National TV.

Castro explained to his people how the burgeoning relationship that Cuba had with Grenada had come to a sticky end. He laid the blame at the door of Coard and his sixteen associates and said, 'In our view, Coard's group effectively destroyed the revolution and opened the door to imperialist aggression.' Castro, warmed by his own rhetoric, went on to describe the RMC as 'the Pol Pot group', 'hyenas' and, a little later, as 'extremists drunk on political theory'. Bishop was lauded as being a 'noble, modest and unselfish leader' whose only fault was his 'excessive tolerance and trust'.

Castro then laid into President Reagan and, apart from alleging that Bishop's assassination was but a pretext for his illegal action, he accused the President of telling nineteen lies, which he enumerated, to the entertainment of the crowd. Castro's listing of nineteen lies came very close to the truth. He said that Reagan had asserted that:

1. Cuba was involved in the *coup d'état* and Bishop's death.
2. The US students were in danger of being taken as hostages.
3. The invasion's main objective was that of protecting the lives of US citizens.
4. The invasion was a multinational operation carried out at the request of Mr Scoon and the east Caribbean countries.
5. Cuba was thinking of invading and occupying Grenada.
6. Grenada was becoming an important Soviet-Cuban military base.
7. The airport that was under construction was not for civilian purposes, but for military use.
8. The weapons that were in Grenada would be used for exporting subversion and terrorism.
9. The Cubans fired first.
10. There were more than 1,000 Cubans on Grenada.
11. The majority of the Cubans were not builders but professional soldiers.
12. The invading forces were careful not to destroy anything or cause civilian casualties.
13. The US troops would only remain in Grenada for one week.
14. Rocket silos were being built on Grenada.
15. The 'Vietnam Heroico' was transporting specialized weaponry.
16. Cuba was warned about the invasion.
17. Five hundred Cubans were fighting in the mountains.
18. Cuba had given orders to carry out reprisals against US citizens.
19. The press was excluded for their own protection.[8]

The Cuban military did not go unscathed and neither did its diplomatic representatives. The ambassador, Julian Rizo Torres, was blamed for not detecting the Grenadian leadership struggle earlier and demoted.[9] Colonel Pedro Comas Tortolo faced a court martial.

Castro had tried to avoid armed action against the USA and had given very specific orders to that effect. However, he expected Cubans to give a good account of themselves if attacked. Subsequently, a number of Cuban soldiers were also tried by court martial.

Notes

1. Cole, R.H., *Operation Urgent Fury: The Planning and Execution of Joint Operations in Grenada 1983* (US Joint Chiefs of Staff, Washington, DC, Joint History Office, 1997), p. 3.
2. 'US Hospitals Treating Grenadian Wounded' (*New York Times*, 5 February 1984).
3. In 1932, to mark the bicentennial of Washington's birth, General Douglas MacArthur initiated an effort to revive the medal. It was designed to commemorate bravery, but also recognised soldiers with wounds. Later, during the Second World War, the medal was changed into a recognition of combat injuries and deaths. Over time, the military has further modified the award. For example, US soldiers wounded in acts of terrorism now qualify for the Purple Heart, as do soldiers injured in friendly fire.

   An individual soldier can apply for a Purple Heart, but usually a commander submits the names of those who have met all criteria for the award. Today, the military has awarded an estimated 1.7 million Purple Hearts to soldiers, sailors, marines and airmen.

   Unlike other military awards, the Purple Heart is an entitlement – it does not depend upon the recommendation of a superior officer. Instead, the military gives it to those troops that meet basic criteria. In general, the wound must have occurred during hostilities, and it must have required treatment that was documented by a medical officer.
4. Tiwathia, V., *The Grenada War: Anatomy of a Low-intensity Conflict* (New Delhi, Lancer International, 1987).
5. 'Auditing an invasion' (*Time*, 23 July 1984).
6. *Washington Post*, 24 November 1983.
7. Kukielski, P., *The US Invasion of Grenada: Legacy of a Flawed Victory* (Jefferson, North Carolina, McFarland & Co., 2019), p. 196.
8. Speech by Fidel Castro in Havana, 14 November 1983.
9. Castro, F., Elliot, J.M. and Dymally, M.M., *Nothing can Stop the Course of History* (New York, Pathfinder Press, 1988), p. 153.

Chapter 20

Aftermath – The Truth

On 28 October, the Department of Defense in Washington gave a news conference. At this event, the press was told that there were 1,100 Cubans who had been fighting in Grenada. Admiral McDonald sweetened the pill by saying that 638 of them were prisoners, and when asked about the remainder, he said:

> I think that they're going back into the hills. They're fighting a delaying action or they're taking us on to defend the military areas that they have been assigned to. As those places are being overrun – I would say with restraint of force – they are disappearing into the mountains.

McDonald was regurgitating what he had been told, and it was nonsense. The reality was that hostilities ceased on 27 October. Macdonald continued:

> When it appeared that the US intervention was likely, Cubans took control of the island. All evidence indicates the entire Point Salines facility was Cuban controlled and sealed off from Grenadians … Impersonating as construction workers, Cuban soldiers' resistance was well organized with fire being well aimed and directed. Assessments indicate that they were well-trained professional soldiers. Documents indicated that there were at least 1,100 on the island.

This statement was grossly misleading and the first indication of a deliberate misinformation policy. What evidence was there to indicate the degree of Cuban control? Similarly, there was no corroboration of the presence of 1,100 Cubans. Perhaps the Cubans had exaggerated their numbers to a gullible audience? Perhaps the figure of 1,100 was just plucked from the air? Macdonald vastly overemphasised the quality of Cuban/Grenadian resistance. If the Cuban fire was 'well aimed and directed', it would have been expected that American casualties would have reflected that degree of enemy expertise. Clearly, the intelligence staff made error after error and commanders, unknowingly, accepted false intelligence as it was presented to them – it was all that was on offer.

The military aims were accomplished, effectively, within the first forty-eight hours. The 'war' was won, but the public relations war had still to be concluded. In 1983, the American public was still affected by the Vietnam Syndrome (as mentioned in Chapter 4). There can be no doubt that the extensive media coverage of that war had been graphic, almost entirely negative, and it had played a part in the defeat of the USA as the military operations lost public sympathy. The leadership of the American armed forces in 1983 had all served in the Vietnam War and their view of the media was shaped by that experience.

The Reagan government had embarked on a campaign of post-operation disinformation. It played down the strength of the invading force, emphasised the part played by Cuban soldiers and again exaggerated the numbers of Cubans present in Grenada to 1,600. This was hastily reduced on 29 October when, 'the Cuban Government refuted the numbers and went as far as specifying the job descriptions of all the 784 Cuban personnel resident on the island'.[1]

When the Pentagon had approved the plans for Operation URGENT FURY, it made no provision for the media, in any of its forms, to witness military activity in Grenada. Indeed, positive steps were taken to ensure that reporters were barred from access to the Spice Island for the duration of the incursion.

'Metcalf's epic battle with the media over Grenada in 1983 was not the result of any written directive from Washington.'[2] The admiral suggested that 'the "No Press Policy" just happened … a logical extension of the tight security that covered the early planning'. That was indeed the case because as early as 21 October, General Vessey had:

> stressed the importance of communications security. He directed that all coordination be limited to secure teleconferences and SPECAT messages. In the Pentagon, Lieutenant General T.G. Prillaman directed the Joint Chiefs of Staff response cell to transfer all Grenadian message traffic from General Service (GENSER) channels to SPECAT channels. However, these precautions were too late, for CBS had already learned of the diversion of the warships to Grenada and would break the story on the news later that evening.
>
> The stringent limits placed on message distribution to the commanders and key personnel prevented further leaks. But they also excluded from preliminary planning and preparation the Strategic Air Command (SAC), the National Security Agency (NSA), and the Defense Mapping Agency. It also excluded four Joint Staff organizations.[3]

The *New York Times* published a headline on 27 October that read, 'US Bars Coverage of Grenada Action: News Groups Protest'. The censorship gave rise to vehement and vociferous representations by the three US TV news channels as well as the American Newspaper Publishers Association.

Metcalf commented in 1991, saying, 'While Grenada was skirmish in terms of warfare, it may also have been the information warfare "mother of battles".'

Back on 21 October, when President Reagan signed the National Security Decision Directive, it required the Defense Secretary and the Joint Chiefs of

Staff to take 'all possible measures ... to preserve the secrecy of these activities and reduce the possibility of a pre-emptive action by the Soviets/Cubans'. The other, but unstated, reason for secrecy was that Reagan wanted to avoid public and congressional opposition. The President was painfully aware of the oft-mentioned Vietnam Syndrome, and in his memoirs, he said, 'I suspected that if we told the leaders of Congress about the operation even under terms of strictest confidentiality, there would be some who would leak it to the press ... we didn't ask anybody, we just did it.'[4]

Prior to the invasion, Vessey and MacDonald had discussed the secrecy/press issue. They agreed that the press would be allowed access to the theatre after the Special Forces had departed from Grenada and that would probably be 'at the tail end of the first day ... or at least on the second day'. A major issue that prevented transparency was the very existence of a Joint Special Operations Command. This organisation was under wraps, and Vessey was anxious that its equipment training or tactics should not be revealed. There was fear that in some quarters, the JSOC might be perceived to be 'a tool for quickly invading third world countries'.[5] This was, of course, just what it was, and Grenada had been the test bed.

Most nations have Special Forces of some kind. They vary in number and effectiveness. The UK has the SAS and SBS. The world knows about them, they have been the subject of multiple books. They set the benchmark for Special Forces and their lethality is seemingly unaffected by their positive public image. Their operations are secret, but their existence is not, and never has been.

From about 21 October, the international press interpreted the diversion of USN ships as being significant and speculated that Grenada was their current focus. An intervention to evacuate American citizens was thought to be a plausible reason for the diversion. Bill Plante, the CBS representative in the White House Press Corps, questioned Larry Speakes, the government spokesman, about the possibility of an invasion.

Unfortunately, Speakes was not entrusted with any information on the subject of Grenada, and he could only offer to find out. His highest priority that weekend was the killing of 241 Americans in the Beirut bombing. A measure of the secrecy surrounding URGENT FURY is that, long after the event, Speakes wrote, 'I had suspected that we might send troops into Grenada at some point to rescue the American medical students, but I had no inkling that was imminent, nor did I have any idea that we might launch a full-scale invasion of the island.'[6]

Ignorance of the forthcoming operation was widespread. However, Rear Admiral John Poindexter, USN, the Deputy Director of the National Security Council, was one of those well aware of the operational planning. He answered to James Baker III, the President's Chief of Staff. Poindexter, guided by Baker, made it his business to quell any speculation and his instruction to the White House spokesman was, 'Preposterous. Knock it down hard.'[7]

This advice from such a senior and well-connected source should have been sufficient to kill the story stone-dead, but unknown to the denizens of the White House, *Newsweek* sent its copy for the 31 October edition to the printers on 23 October. This carried an article on the Windward Islands and included a lengthy article on Grenada – not least, the grisly details of Bishop's assassination.

Speakes became conscious of unusual activity in the White House on 24 October. That he was not invited to attend a meeting that the President was having with Congressional leaders sent him the clear message that something was afoot. He raised the issue with James Baker. The Chief of Staff was guarded and merely told Speakes to be in the office at 5.45am the next morning.

In the Caribbean, Reagan's policy of secrecy 'buttered few parsnips', and hints and nods from OECS and CARICOM representatives were sufficient to motivate seven journalists to set out from Bridgetown, Barbados, to St George's, Grenada. The seven represented, among others, the *Miami Herald*, the *Washington Post*, *Newsday*, *The Guardian* and *Time*. One of the others was Hugh O'Shaughnessy, who later wrote a book on the subject. He was less concerned about the military operation and focused on the political. He is a prime source for this book and one of the very few neutral observers of URGENT FURY.

O'Shaughnessy and his colleagues did not have an easy passage to Grenada. The first leg was by air, in a chartered aircraft from Barbados to St Vincent, the nearest island to Grenada. Here they found a man willing to take them in his boat the 10 miles (16km) to Carriacou. This tiny island was not beset by officialdom and the passage through immigration and customs was swift and unimpeded. 'The reception from Edwin Stiell, the administrator of Carriacou and Milton Coy, the political education officer, was cordial, and after a lobster dinner at the Silver Beach Hotel, conversation about the crisis lasted well into the night.'[8]

The next morning, the journalists heard Radio Free Grenada announcing that the invasion was under way, and it called upon militia and medical personnel to report for duty.

The journalists found a second, willing boatman. He owned a boat named for the Norse god of war. The final 34 miles (55km) of the journey took five uncomfortable hours over a rough sea in *Odin C*. As the small boat approached the Spice Island, two A-7s flew around it, with *Odin*'s passengers waving, hoping to indicate they were 'friendly'. It was at this point that Alfred, the boatman, became less enthused with his mission. He wanted payment up front, and before he put his passengers ashore. They demurred, there was a debate, but eventually, *Odin C* slipped into St George's harbour, and Alfred was duly paid. O'Shaughnessy wrote later:

> Though none of us realised it at the time we had narrowly missed death. Ten weeks after the event I learnt that a soldier of the PRA had the *Odin C* in the sights of his rocket launcher and, as we glided closer to the Carenage, was ready to fire a missile that was fully capable of sinking the boat and killing all the occupants. He decided not to fire after a colleague identified Alfred, our skipper, as a loyal Grenadian.[9]

Just after the party got ashore, four PRA soldiers arrived and interrogated them as to their business. Passports were checked and the journalists were ordered to stay in the fire station. 'It was most friendly detention,' as one of the journalists commented.

The press appealed to the soldiers to assist them in filing copy to their editors. 'The Grenadian soldiers appeared to be as anxious for us to put out the news as we were,' recorded Don Bohning.[10] Here they remained until the following day.

Then, four of the journalists, representatives of the *Miami Herald*, *Washington Post*, *The Guardian* and *Newsday*, bluffed their way onto a helicopter that Metcalf had sent to pick up members of Scoon's entourage. It seemed like an opportunity not to be missed, and they flew away to spend a frustrating twenty-four hours on the ship, where they were denied access to telecommunications. Their arrival on *Guam* was reported to the Pentagon, which swiftly endorsed its 'no press' policy – Metcalf was admonished for allowing the press onto his ship.[11]

They flew back to discover that they had missed the US occupation of St George's. On the island, and in their absence, Grenadian soldiers continued to try to help, but they were unable to find the keys to an office with telex or a functioning telephone line. At this point, the gentlemen of the press were escorted to the St James Hotel, where the proprietor was told that they were 'guests of the revolution'. Kukielski commented acidly, 'It's ironic that, at this point the leaders of the Marxist military coup, which had expelled international reporters, were more accommodating to uncensored first-hand reports by Anglo-American journalists than anyone in charge of the Pentagon or the White House.'[12]

Over the next few days, other journalists sneaked into other parts of the island but US forces went to great pains to prevent any eyewitness coverage of the operation. 'The measures had been ordered by Caspar Weinberger, the Defense Secretary.'[13]

During the first three days of Operation URGENT FURY, USCINCLANT banned reporters from Grenada for operational reasons. Faced with cries of 'censorship' from the media and some members of Congress, General Vessey directed USCINCLANT to land reporters in Grenada, starting on 28 October. Vessey would later comment, 'The huge mistake at the National level was failing to find a way to take some press along.'[14]

Weinberger's spokesman later sought to justify this non-cooperation with the press by arguing that secrecy was necessary for surprise, and that furthermore, the military could not be held responsible for the safety of journalists. This was nonsense, as in previous wars, the US press had had full access and took responsibility for its own safety.

In Grenadian waters, a vessel that was chartered in Barbados and carrying a TV crew from the ABC network was intercepted. A US aircraft dropped a buoy in front of them with the message that they should return to Barbados. Then the A-7 made a series of mock strafing passes over the boat, opening its bomb doors to emphasise the earlier message. They turned their boat around. Another group managed to land at the non-functioning Pearls Airport. They were held there briefly and then ordered to return from whence they had come. O'Shaughnessy observed:

> When the first journalists, US citizens all fifteen of them, were allowed to go to Grenada they went under heavily armed guard late on Thursday (27 October). Twenty-four followed on Friday (28 October) but none was allowed to move out of the vicinity of Point Salines. Despite the fact that US aircraft were maintaining a virtual shuttle service between Barbados and Grenada, no space was allocated to non-US journalists until the fighting was over. Even after the fighting was finished the US sought to control the flow of information from Grenada.[15]

On Saturday, 30 October, Metcalf warned a group of reporters against acting independently. Allegedly, he said to them, 'Any of you guys coming on press boats? Well, I know how to stop those press boats. We've been shooting at them. We haven't sunk any yet, but who are we to know who's on them?'

This exchange appears in O'Shaughnessy's book (page 203), although there is no source quoted. First, the thought of US aircraft shooting at small civilian vessels seems highly improbable, and secondly, Metcalf was a very experienced officer and these intemperate words, if said, will have been accompanied with a smile to indicate that he was joking – 'pulling their legs', to use a British idiom.

The first few US journalists to be ferried in from Barbados were shown by the US forces the enormous stocks of weapons and ammunition discovered during the mopping-up phase. This arsenal was according to a preliminary count submitted to Congress by General George Crist, USMC, and the small arms found on Grenada included:

> 158 submachine guns, 68 grenade launchers, 1,241 AK-47 rifles, 1,330 model 52 rifles, 1,035 Mosin-Nagant carbines, 506 old Enfield rifles, 87 miscellaneous small-bore rifles/carbines, 8 gas riot guns, 48 pistols, 304 shotguns, 15 air rifles, and 5 flare pistols. Other weapons included 5 12.7 quad machine guns, 3 PKT tank machine guns, 23 model PLK heavy machine guns, 16 23 mm antiaircraft

guns, 20 82 mm mortars, 7 RPG 7 grenade launchers, and 9 75mm recoilless rifles. Nine armored amphibious vehicles were also found there. Thus, there were about 5,000 individual infantry weapons on the island, along with some crew-operated weapons and ammunition sufficient to last two battalions for more than 45 days.[16]

The US banned British journalists from using the RAF Hercules, which had transported David Montgomery, Deputy High Commissioner, to the island. This inexplicable decision did nothing to repair US/UK relations.

The numbers killed in the accidental bombing of the mental hospital varied just afterwards. For example, a hospital worker, speaking on 2 November, eight days after the incident, and when digging through the ruin continued, said that thirty people had died in the raid; the publicly acknowledged death toll is seventeen.

The press did not always cover itself in glory and an egregious example is that of *Newsweek*, published on 7 November 1983. The news famine had left a gap and so the magazine, bereft of news, substituted 'creatively'. It conjured up a 'special report' under the headline 'The Battle for Grenada'. The article started by saying:

> American troops take charge on the island, but face surprisingly stiff opposition. In order to minimise civilian casualties, the American commanders decided against a full-scale ground assault. Instead, they deployed small units backed by heavy air power.

At this point, it moved from fact to fantasy, and continued:

> Inside St George's they fought a tough battle for Fort Rupert, where a week before troops loyal to the rebel junta executed Prime Minister Maurice Bishop. From behind the limestone walls of the French-built 18th century fortress, Cuban and Grenadian defenders showered small arms on the US attack squads. Grenadian soldiers fired their AK-47s straight up at dive-bombing US jets and helicopters … Eventually the American attack reduced Fort Rupert to a smouldering shell with only one wall left standing.

The reality was that Fort Rupert fell without a shot being fired on the morning of 27 October. No Cubans were seen to be defending the fort and none fighting in St George's. The fort's walls were intact and quite undamaged. The article was particularly inventive when it asserted:

> The intervention forces also readied to storm Carriacou, a tiny island north of Grenada. Officers had delayed the action until they could get a better fix on the strength of the Grenadian and Cuban forces there. US intelligence had

> picked up radio signals from Carriacou, and also had evidence of sophisticated Cuban bunkers on the island.

Newsweek had accepted without question the US Government's assertions that the Cubans on Grenada were a formidable force and likely to resort to guerrilla tactics in the mountains after the fall of Point Salines. It committed itself further by endorsing the myth that had been created around the unfinished new airport. The magazine pronounced:

> strategically the assault cost Castro a well-placed refuelling depot on the air route between Cuba and his troops in Africa. And it denied his Soviet sponsor a potentially valuable harbor convenient to western oil lanes.

Newsweek was, and is, a well-respected publication and hitherto quick to criticise the machinations of the Reagan government. Previously it had produced a well-researched expose of the US support of the counterrevolutionaries operating from Honduras against the Sandinista government of Nicaragua. The reputation of the magazine was sufficiently solid to give credence to whatever it said. The effect was for lesser publications to treat *Newsweek* as a trusted source, and so the misinformation spread.[17]

A voice of dissent in the Caribbean, unconvinced by either *Newsweek* or US propaganda, was that of Rickey Singh, who edited the *Caribbean Contact*, based in Barbados. The publication was the mouthpiece of the Caribbean Council of Churches (CCC). He wrote an article for *The Nation* in which he condemned the invasion of Grenada in uncompromising terms. He described it as 'a dark day in the history of the Commonwealth Caribbean … a dangerous precedent has been set that could have far-reaching implications for the future peace and security of the entire Caribbean.'

For his forthright view, Singh was served with a deportation order signed on 2 November by Adams, the Prime Minister. Singh's work permit still had twenty months to run and he had five children in Barbadian schools. In the face of strong political pressure, the CCC softened its line, but Singh was still expelled.

There was further misinformation when the Pentagon published a list of medals to be awarded to participants in URGENT FURY. It revealed that although there had been only 125 'reportable' US wounded, it appears that the 32 SEAL, Task Force 160 and Delta wounded were excluded. They would raise the wounded to about 157. The issue is further complicated by the 219 Purple Heart medals that were awarded.

Reagan and the Pentagon had embarked on a policy to mislead the American people, but it was being ineptly managed. Reporting from Washington, Geoffrey Smith wrote:

> There is a burning sense of indignation, the strength of which takes even me as a journalist by surprise. It is clearly causing the Administration a good deal of anxiety ... The outraged are ... the most politically influential members of the news media of the country. If this colours the whole attitude to the Reagan Administration, it could be a serious matter for the President and his colleagues.[18]

Smith's view may have been valid at the time, but 'a week is a long time in politics', and Reagan was hoping to be re-elected in 1985. His campaign started just three months after URGENT FURY. The President expected to benefit from the wave of goodwill that he had accrued by his crushing victory over a dangerous communist enemy. He was correct and, in November 1984, he was re-elected for a second term.

Notes

1. Castro, F., Elliot, J.M. and Dymally, M.M., *Nothing can Stop the Course of History* (New York, Pathfinder Press, 1988), p. 204.
2. Kukielski, P., *The US Invasion of Grenada: Legacy of a Flawed Victory* (Jefferson, North Carolina, McFarland & Co., 2019), p. 134.
3. Cole, R.H., *Operation Urgent Fury: The Planning and Execution of Joint Operations in Grenada 1983* (US Joint Chiefs of Staff, Washington, DC, Joint History Office, 1997), p. 19.
4. Reagan, R., *An American Life* (New York, Simon & Schuster, 1990), p. 451.
5. Vessey, in an interview with Ronald Cole, the official historian, 1997.
6. Speakes, L. and Pack, R., *Speaking Out: The Reagan Presidency from Inside the White House* (New York, Scribner, 1988), pp. 150–3.
7. Kukielski, p. 236.
8. O'Shaughnessy, H., *Grenada: Revolution, Invasion and Aftermath* (London, Sphere Books, 1984), p. 199.
9. Ibid., p. 201.
10. Bohning, D., 'Lots of Story but No way to File it' (*Washington Post*, 28 October 1983).
11. Metcalf, Admiral J., 'Decision Making and the Grenada Rescue' (Marshfield Mass, Pitman Publishing, *Ambiguity and Command: Organizational Perspectives on Military Decision Making*, ed., Marsh, J.G.), p. 57.
12. Kukielski, p. 137.
13. O'Shaughnessy, p. 202.
14. President Ronald Reagan's interview by reporters at the White House on 25 October 1983. Quoted by Cole, p. 4.
15. Ibid., p. 203.
16. Bell, W., 'The American Invasion of Grenada: A Note on False Prophecy' (*The Yale Review*, Vol. 75, No. 4, 1986), pp. 564–86.
17. O'Shaughnessy, p. 214.
18. Smith, G. (*The Times*, November 1983). Quoted by O'Shaughnessy, p. 211.

Chapter 21

On Medals

Successful soldiers of all nations can expect little reward for their efforts. Some are promoted, but the vast majority are not. The most they can hope for is a small and morale-boosting medal. The volume of medals issued varies from country to country. The North Koreans deck their soldiers, who do not fight anyone, in an array of medals and badges. They are covered from shoulder to the waist in decorations of various shapes and sizes. To a European, they may look absurd but there is no 'right' or 'wrong'. It all depends upon the culture of the country concerned.

If North Korea is at one end of the medal scale, the UK and Commonwealth countries are at the other end. They are frugal in the extreme. Campaign medals are only awarded to those who spend time in an active war zone, usually twenty-eight days. Decorations are scarce and, when awarded, the subject of great pleasure to the recipient and those around him/her. The value of a medal/ decoration is dependent upon the difficulty in winning it.

On the medal scale, the USA is closer to North Korea than the UK, and Major (later General) Colin Powell, who served in Vietnam, commented on a change of command ceremony during in that war, saying:

> the departing CO was awarded three Silver Stars, the nation's third highest medal for valor, plus a clutch of other medals after a tour lasting six months … his troops had to stand there and listen to an overheated description of a fairly typical performance.
>
> Awards were piled on to a point where writing a justifying citation became a minor art form. The departing battalion commander's 'package', a Silver Star, a Legion of Merit and an Air Medal, just for logging helicopter time became almost standard issue … these wholesale awards diminished the achievements of real heroes – privates or colonels – who had performed extraordinary acts of valor … a corrosive careerism had infected our army, and I was part of it.[1]

General Powell's observations on medal inflation were not made until long after URGENT FURY. In the ten years after the Vietnam War, nothing had changed, and the medal awards for this operation exceeded previous levels.

In a few short weeks after the operation, the US Army issued 8,500 medals; later additions raised that to 9,802.[2]

Nineteen US servicemen were killed in Grenada, ten were caused by accidents. Notwithstanding the unfortunate nine, each a mother's son, URGENT FURY barely qualifies as a skirmish. The US Army deployed two understrength Ranger, six Airborne and four battalions from the Marine Amphibious Unit (MAU). Only two companies of the 82nd Division (2nd/325th) were involved in serious fighting but, nevertheless, 812 Bronze Stars were awarded and 59 of these came with the V device denoting valour. The criteria for a Bronze Star is: for heroic or meritorious achievement of service with operations against an opposing armed force.

The Army Commendation Medal is probably the least prestigious of the suite of medals available. The criteria are: distinctive meritorious achievement and service, acts of courage involving no voluntary risk of life, or meritorious performance of duty. There were 5,079 recipients. Adkin observed cynically, that to win this medal, 'all you had to do was turn up'.[3]

In total, 2,946 individuals were given the Army Achievement Medal for 'meritorious service in a non-combat area', like Washington.

A prestigious badge with strict criteria is the Combat Infantry Badge (CIB) (see plate section).

For award of the CIB, a soldier must meet the following three requirements: a) be an infantryman satisfactorily performing infantry duties; b) be assigned to an infantry unit during such time as the unit is engaged in active ground combat; c) actively participate in such ground combat. Of these sought-after badges, 3,100 were distributed to members of 82nd Division, whilst the Rangers collected 430.

The US Armed Forces have a system of unit awards. These are known as 'Streamers'. It is a cloth item that is attached to the unit's flag as a battle honour. 'GRENADA 1983' on a streamer was awarded to sixty-four separate units.

The USAF had its share of medals and it made 3,076 awards, including 272 Bronze Stars, 841 Air Medals, 1,649 Air Force Commendation Medals and 311 Air Force Achievement Medals. The USN was less generous in its rewards. It did, however, give a unit commendation to Task Force 124. The Secretary of the Navy signed the citation, which in part read:

> For conspicuous gallantry and intrepid action against a heavily armed rebel force threatening the personal safety of American citizens and the established government of Grenada … Through calculated forethought and incisive action by the officers and men of Task Force 124 … The lives of hundreds of American citizens were saved, rebel forces were subdued, and the Government of Grenada restored.

The total medal count in all their forms for URGENT FURY was estimated to be between 30,000 and 35,000. Everyone, it seems, got something to treasure.

Notes

1. Powell, C.L., *A Soldier's Way* (London, Hutchinson, 1995), p. 146.
2. These figures exclude the Armed Forces Expeditionary Medal, which was given to all participants in whatever capacity they had served during the period 23 October to 21 November – nineteen days after the last shots were exchanged. The number of those distributed was more than 14,000, and Adkin (p. 321) suggests, 'probably nearer to 20,000'. The Expeditionary Medal was in addition.
3. Adkin, Major M., *Urgent Fury: The Battle for Grenada* (London, Leo Cooper, 1989), p. 322.

Chapter 22

Reckless Rhetoric

The events in Grenada in 1983 cannot, and should not, be viewed as standing in splendid isolation, in some sort of political desert. They were, in fact, just a part of a very much wider and complex international tapestry.

The rhetoric of Ronald Reagan coupled with a major NATO exercise in the Caribbean, which was initiated on 7 November 1983, arguably brought the planet to the very threshold of nuclear Armageddon.

Reagan had just amply demonstrated his willingness to take military action to further his aims. He was continually very robust in expressing his unvarnished hatred for communism in all its forms. He chose to present himself as a determined adversary to the Warsaw Pact – and in the Kremlin, they believed him. Reagan was naïve in the extreme: he seemingly did not give any deep consideration to the effect of his words and the likely reaction to them.

As far back as May 1981, in a closed-session meeting of senior KGB officers and Soviet leaders, Leonid Brezhnev and Yuri Andropov, the two leading members of the Russian Government, made it clear that, in their view, all the signs showed that the USA was making ready for a nuclear attack on Russia.[1]

This assumption was the result of American naval and air incursions, which, over a period, had tested Russian defences around the globe. Recent NATO exercises had further emphasised American attitudes and, in combination, they sent a worrying message. As a direct consequence, the Soviet leadership decided to launch Operation RYaN.

> RYaN (Russian: РЯН) was a Russian acronym for 'nuclear missile attack' (Ракетно Ядерное *Нападение, Raketno Yadernoe Napadenie*); Operation RYaN was the largest, most comprehensive, peacetime intelligence-gathering operation in Soviet history. Agents abroad were charged with monitoring the figures who would decide to launch a nuclear attack, the service and technical personnel who would implement the attack, and the facilities from which the attack would originate. It is possible that the goal of Operation RYaN was to discover the first *intent* of a nuclear attack and then pre-empt it.[2]

The British had a high-level agent in place in the KGB and Oleg Gordievsky, who was witness to the atmosphere in the Kremlin, commented that the situation was brought about by 'the potentially lethal combination of Reaganite rhetoric and Soviet paranoia'.

- Moscow's threat perceptions and Operation RYaN were influenced by memories of Hitler's 1941 attack on Russia and Operation BARBAROSSA.
- The Kremlin exploited the war scare for domestic political purposes, aggravating fears among the Soviet people.
- The KGB abandoned caution and eschewed proper tradecraft in collecting indications-and-warning intelligence and relied heavily on East German foreign and military intelligence to meet RYaN requirements.

Gordievsky advised his British handlers that Brezhnev and Andropov 'were very, very old-fashioned and easily influenced … by Communist dogmas'. They believed that the verbally aggressive Reagan had shown his colours when speaking in the UK's House of Commons. On this important occasion, he pronounced an ambition 'to leave Marxism-Leninism on the ash heap of history'.[3] Gordievsky's advice was that the Kremlin was responding to Reagan's strong words by making military preparations, not only to repel an attack but, significantly, to make a pre-emptive strike.

This judgement was endorsed by a second source, and Fischer, the CIA historian, concluded that a CIA source was, at least partially, corroborating Gordievsky's reporting. This source was a Czechoslovakian intelligence officer — who worked closely with the KGB on RYaN. He 'noted that his counterparts were obsessed with the historical parallel between 1941 and 1983. He believed this feeling was almost visceral, not intellectual, and deeply affected Soviet thinking.'[4]

The rhetoric of the Reagan administration reinforced the Kremlin's conviction that America was in an aggressive path to a lopsided nuclear war. Fischer revealed examples of American actions that fostered the Russian need for RYaN. He observed that the introduction of psychological operations (PSYOP) had fuelled Soviet apprehension. A definition of PSYOP is:

> The planned use of propaganda and other psychological actions having the primary purpose of influencing the opinions, emotions, attitudes, and behaviour of hostile foreign groups in such a way as to support the achievement of national objectives in war, having the primary purpose of influencing the opinions, emotions, attitudes, and behaviour of hostile foreign groups in such a way as to support the achievement of national objectives.

The United States had initiated psychological operations in early 1981 and they took the form of clandestine naval incursions into Soviet territorial waters in the far north and in the far east. This demonstrated not only the worldwide scope of the NATO naval forces but showed how close to major Soviet military installations they could approach unseen.

In 1981, eighty-three American, British, Norwegian and Canadian ships sailed through the 'Greenland–Iceland–United Kingdom Gap' (GIUK). This armada went undetected by Russian surveillance systems and reached the very sensitive Kola Peninsula.

Further and similar operations were conducted in the Barents Sea and the Baltic Ocean to irritate and discomfort the Russians. The US sent intelligence-gathering ships to the Crimean coast. It was dangerous, but US bombers

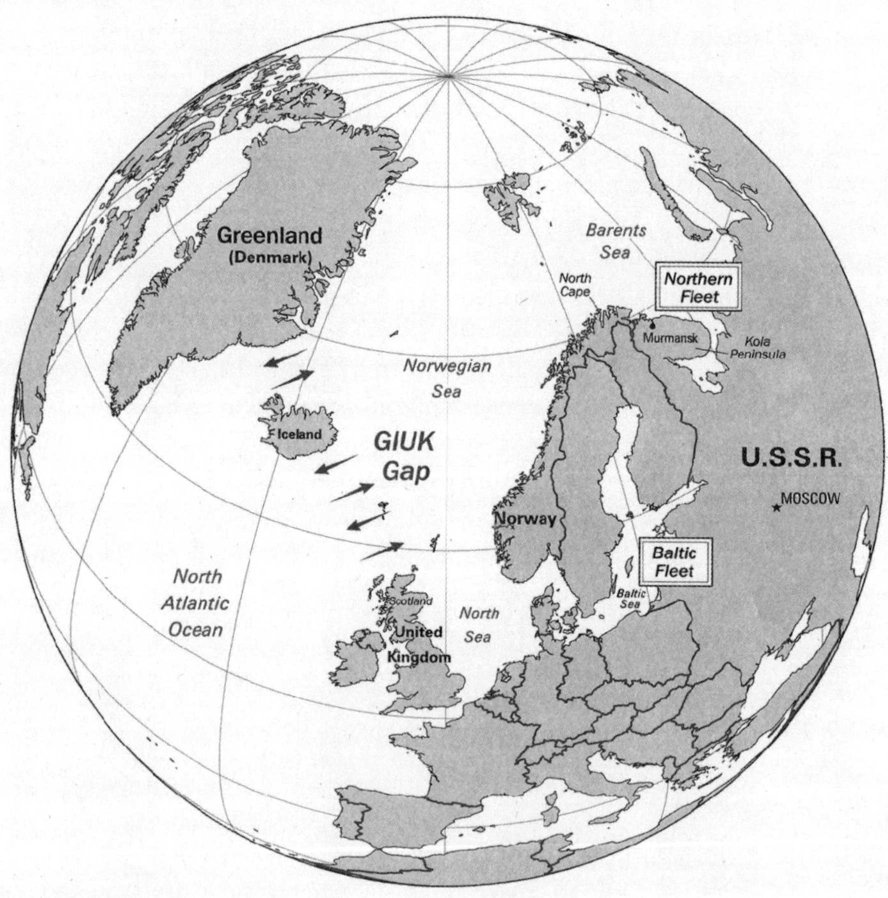

regularly flew towards Soviet air space, turning away at the last moment. All of these provocations were intended to show the capability of the USA to conduct nuclear war – if it had to. The effect on senior Soviet politicians and service officers was to unsettle them and instil doubt in their capacity to resist any American/NATO aggression.

It was against this background that the USA had invaded Grenada and by so doing, went some way to confirm the worst of Russian fears about American aggression. Then – with Grenada quelled and Marxism-Leninism on the island destroyed, NATO launched a major exercise.

On 7 November 1983, at about the same time that most US troops had vacated Grenada, NATO launched the exercise called ABLE ARCHER 83. The object of this exercise was to simulate the conditions of grave tension between NATO and the Warsaw Pact and to chart the process of escalation that could lead to a nuclear exchange. It was intended to practise the protocols that would lead to a simulated DEFCON 1 attack on Warsaw Pact countries.[5]

The exercise, of five days' duration, had the participation of all NATO commands throughout Western Europe. This participation was co-ordinated by the Supreme Headquarters Allied Powers Europe (SHAPE) in Belgium.

In order to enhance the exercise and to introduce realism into the play, several new ingredients were included, such as new coded communications, radio silence and the active participation of Western heads of government. This injection of realism alarmed the Soviets to the extent that they prepared their nuclear forces and brought them all to an alerted status. The Soviet 4th Air Army began loading nuclear bombs into their aircraft.[6]

The world owes a debt of gratitude to an officer of the USAF who recognised the unnecessarily dangerous atmosphere that ABLE ARCHER had created. Lieutenant General Leonard Perroots, USAF, advised NATO against responding to the Soviet measures. His advice was taken, the exercise was wound down and was concluded on 11 November.

There has emerged a broad, but not unanimous, consensus that November 1983 was one of the times when there was a realistic possibility of nuclear war. 'The declassification of related documents in 2021 supported this notion.'[7] Other scholars have disputed that the exercise almost led to nuclear war. One of these is Simon Miles and in 2020, he wrote refuting the past possibility of nuclear war.[8] However, Miles was writing over thirty years after the event, and he had not been sitting around the same table as Gordievsky.

On 10 October 1983, a month before ABLE ARCHER 83, President Reagan watched on TV a film about a small American town being destroyed in a nuclear attack. The film was called *The Day After*. It was a gripping and awful story. In his diary, the President wrote that the film 'left me greatly depressed'.[9] Later that month and while the invasion of Grenada was imminent, the President attended a briefing on nuclear war and, of course, its dire consequences. Reagan described the briefing in his own words: 'A most sobering experience with Caspar Weinberger and General Vessey in the Situation Room – a briefing on our complete plan in the event of a nuclear attack.'[10]

Notwithstanding the warnings from Gordievsky, of the fragility of the Soviet leadership, Grenada was invaded and soon after, ABLE ARCHER 83 was initiated.

The USA is the greatest contributor to the NATO alliance and without doubt, it is the President of the United States (POTUS) who, in practice, will decide if, and when, nuclear weapons are to be used by NATO. It is an awesome responsibility, for any man or woman, when he or she is obliged to hold the very existence of the human race in his hands. The hope is that the incumbent of that office will always be sufficiently gifted to meet the demands of the role.

In January 2025, the recently elected 47th President of the USA took office. He was elected by over 80 million Americans. The world can but watch to see how POTUS performs in an increasingly dangerous environment in which his actions and decisions have an impact far beyond American shores.

Notes

1. Macintyre, B., *The Spy and the Traitor* (London, Penguin, 2018), p. 179.
2. Fischer, B.B., 'A Cold War Conundrum: The 1983 Soviet War Scare – Phase II: A New Sense' (1997). This was an internal CIA study.
3. Reagan, President R.W., speaking in London to the House of Commons on 2 June 1982.
4. Fischer.
5. The DEFCON system is defined by the USA as: The defense readiness condition (DEFCON) is an alert state used by the Armed Forces of the USA. For security reasons, the US military does not announce a DEFCON level to the public. The DEFCON system was developed by the Joint Chiefs of Staff (JCS) and unified and special combatant commands. It prescribes five graduated levels of readiness (or states of alert) for the US military. It increases in severity from DEFCON 5 (least severe) to DEFCON 1 (most severe) to match varying military situations, with DEFCON 1 signalling the impending outbreak of nuclear warfare.
6. Oberdorfer, D., *From the Cold War to a New Era: The United States and the Soviet Union 1983–1991* (Baltimore, Johns Hopkins University Press, 1998), p. 66.
7. Kaplan, F., 'The World Came Much Closer to Nuclear War Than We Ever Realized' (*Slate Magazine*, 17 April 2022).
8. Miles, S., 'The War Scare That Wasn't: Able Archer 83 and the Myths of the Second Cold War' (*Journal of Cold War Studies*, 1 August 2020), pp. 86–118.
9. Reagan, R.W., *An American Life* (New York, Simon & Schuster, 1990).
10. Ibid., p. 585.

Chapter 23

Aftermath – What Happened Next?

The undoubted military success in Grenada was well received by the American people. This euphoria was fuelled by the emotional response of the medical students to their 'rescue'. Two independent public opinion polls were conducted on 26 and 27 October. One was a joint exercise between the *New York Times* and *CBS News*; the other was run by *Newsweek*. The results of both polls showed 50 per cent of American adults approved of the decision to send troops into Grenada. *Newsweek* commented: 'In 1980, the American People consciously chose a president who saw the world as a battle between good and evil and was willing to use force to protect what he perceived to be good. Last week Ronald Reagan kept those campaign promises.'

The people of the Eastern Caribbean were the subject of a poll conducted by *CBS News*. They talked to 304 people, of whom 91 per cent agreed that 'they were glad the United States troops came'.[1] This degree of approval was high, and it was only a little lower elsewhere in the Caribbean. It is worth noting that 25 October is now celebrated in Grenada as a day of National Thanksgiving and is a public holiday.

The weapons found in Frequente were inventoried and then shipped back to the USA, where examples were put on public display at Andrews Air Force Base. Documents captured at the same time proved that the weapons were the result of military arrangements between the Bishop government, Cuba, North Korea and Russia, and they had been delivered between April 1979 and August 1983. There was sufficient hardware to allow the expansion of the Grenadian Army to equip four regular and fourteen reserve battalion by 1985.[2] 'If implemented the force of between 7,200 and 10,000 soldiers would put roughly 10 per cent of the population in uniform, proportionately one of the largest military forces of any country in the world.'[3]

Reagan turned the weapons seizure to advantage when he claimed that 'we got there just in time … [preventing Grenada becoming] a major military bastion to export terror and undermine democracy.'[4] In 2008, a ten-page report compiled by the CIA and dated 30 October 1983 was declassified. It disproved Reagan's assumptions and concluded that the arms were intended solely for the defence of Grenada. There was no evidence of any intention to use them externally. The report proved to be very unpopular at the time, especially with William J. Casey, the Director of the CIA (1981–7). Casey viewed the work of his subordinates to be 'unimaginative'. They had presented the facts, but the facts, inconveniently, did not match Casey's political position, nor that of his master, the President.

There were unintended consequences to URGENT FURY. One of these was in Suriname, a former Dutch colony, and one of the smallest sovereign nations in the world. It is located on the northern edge of South America. This country was ruled by a military officer, one Lieutenant Colonel Dési Bouterse, and, hitherto, he had been flirting with Cuba. Now he announced, 'The leadership of the Suriname revolution is convinced that a repetition of developments in Grenada should be prevented here.'[5]

On that basis, and acting quickly, he gave the Cuban ambassador six days to leave and expelled twenty-five diplomats and a further sixty 'advisors'. This was not unlike the icing on the cake – and there was more to come.

In Nicaragua, the hard-left Sandinista government believed that it could read the writing on the wall, and it anticipated being the next American target. As an immediate defensive measure, it went to pains to assure the USA that it would not permit the Russians to establish a base on Nicaraguan soil.

The Sandinistas went further, and by Christmas 1983, had reduced by half the number of Cubans working in Nicaraguan schools. It hastened the exit of El Salvadorian rebels taking refuge in the country and, to further demonstrate its new liberality, it relaxed internal censorship.

However, these measures were insufficient, and the USA gave continued support to the Contra guerrillas, who were in violent conflict with the ruling Sandinistas. In effect, the USA supported the civil war and conducted covert military operations in Nicaragua. The CIA led attacks on Nicaraguan infrastructure. It is outside the bounds of this book to deal in any detail with the USA's engagement in Nicaragua, other than to say that it did not end well, and Reagan and his government were embarrassed.

In Grenada, democracy had to be rebuilt and central to the process was the Governor General Sir Paul Scoon. He said, very reasonably, 'It is important that within the shortest possible time we should live and work in a situation where security support takes the form of a police operation that will increasingly come under the command of a Grenadian or West Indian commissioner of police.'

He was insistent that the US troops leave as soon as possible. On 15 November, Scoon invoked his authority, representing Queen Elizabeth II, the Head of State, and he appointed a nine-member council to steer the country until a general election could be held. Those elections were held just over two weeks later, on 3 December. The result was a victory for the New National Party, led by Herbert Blaize, which won fourteen of the fifteen seats. Voter turnout was 86 per cent. Sir Eric Gairy had reappeared, and he threw his hat into the political ring. The voters firmly rejected him, and he shuffled off the political scene into well-deserved obscurity.

The last US combat troops left Grenada on 12 December, although about 300 remained. Of these, 150 were military policemen and an integral part of the Caribbean Peacekeeping Force.

After the dust had settled, support for the American invasion was limited to the participating Caribbean nations. The NATO allies of the USA held negative views. The UK had been humiliated, although Reagan tried to make amends by speaking to Margaret Thatcher on the telephone on 28 October. It is reported that his opening remark was, 'If I were there, Margaret, I'd throw my hat in the door before I came in.'[6] These two principals spoke for ten minutes, during which, Reagan argued his case to a chillingly cold prime minister. Thatcher cut the conversation short, and her attitude mirrored that to be found across Europe.

'A spokesman for the West German ruling coalition declared that their government would have advised against intervention "had we been consulted". France also said that it was not consulted on intervention and archly described the intervention as "a surprising action in relation to international law".'[7]

The 'war' was won. Although Grenada had been rid of its Marxist-Leninist dictators, the earlier inept economic management, the curfew, the regional trade embargo, the cessation of inter-island communication and the breakdown of effective civil service management of national affairs all combined to make Grenada an ailing economy. The island was in very bad order, and it would need help to get back on its feet.

The USA was its usual generous self. Its engineers fixed the damage to the island's infrastructure, repairing electrical facilities and constructing a sanitary landfill.[8] The immediate provision of food, water and medical supplies was valued at US$475,000. A further US$1.7 million contribution was made for infrastructure repair and improvement. US$15 million was injected to 'shore up the national budget, revive commercial lending and commerce and put Grenadians back to work'.[9] American munificence did not end there, and in April 1984, Reagan gained from Congress agreement for a two-year, US$40 million support package for the Spice Island. Much of this money was to be put towards the completion of the airport at Point Salines.

The airport opened on 28 October 1984 – it was to have a major and positive effect upon Grenada and its tourist industry. Admiral Metcalf, reminiscing later, remarked, 'The whole thing with Bishop was completely mismanaged; we should have built the airport for them ... it was short-sighted.'[10]

Grenada began to flourish, and Philip Kukielski summarised that success in his book, oft quoted here. He said:

> The quality of Grenada's democracy in 2019 was rated marginally superior to the United States according to a rating system by Freedom House, an independent American watchdog organization dedicated to the expansion of freedom and democracy. The organization rated the quality of American rights and civil liberties to be 86 on a scale of 100 in an annual rating of 209 countries and territories. Grenada by comparison got a score of 89. The United Kingdom rated 93 and Canada 99.[11]

All that lay in the future but, in early November 1983, the occupiers had got something of a problem with the eighteen men and one woman who had been responsible for the assassination of Bishop and his acolytes. That their acts had been criminal was not in dispute, but to whom did they answer? Certainly not the USA, although it had arrested and incarcerated them all, initially on USN ships. To deal with these people, an *ad hoc* court was formed from other Caribbean nations. The next chapter follows the unsatisfactory and severely biased 'legal' process.

Two years after the invasion, Queen Elizabeth II visited the island. At the time, she said:

> In the last few years, Grenada has been through momentous events, and you have emerged with tremendous credit. As your Queen, I want to take this opportunity of congratulating the people of Grenada on the way you have prepared for and carried through the recent parliamentary elections which underlined your commitment to democracy. It has been a notable achievement, and the world has watched with admiration.[12]

Notes

1. Clymer, A.C., 'Grenadians Welcomed Invasion Poll Finds' (*New York Times*, 6 November 1983).
2. Presidential address to the nation on 27 October 1983. 'Events in Lebanon and Grenada'.
3. *Grenada: A Preliminary Report* (US Department of State and Department of Defense, 16 December 1983), p. 20.
4. Presidential address, 27 October 1983.
5. 'Suriname Ousts Envoy and Halts Cuba Pacts' (*New York Times*, 27 October 1983).
6. White House, memorandum of telephone conversation, Reagan and Thatcher, secret transcript, 28 October 1983. Declassified and accessed on 17 July 2018 by Philip Kukielski. Quoted by him on p. 195.
7. Kukielski, P., *The US Invasion of Grenada: Legacy of a Flawed Victory* (Jefferson, North Carolina, McFarland & Co., 2019), p. 195.

8. Perkins, A.H., 'Operation Urgent Fury: An Engineer's View' (*The Military Engineer*, March–April 1984), pp. 86–90.
9. Kukielski, p. 219.
10. Strober, D.H. and Strober, G., *The Reagan Presidency: An Oral History of the Era* (Brassey's (US), 2015), p. 257.
11. Kukielski, p. 219.
12. Scoon, Sir P., *Survival for Service: My Experiences as Governor General of Grenada* (Macmillan Caribbean, 2003), p. 230.

Chapter 24

Aftermath – Retribution

The suppression of Marxist-Leninism on Grenada left several issues unresolved and the most pressing of these was how to deal with the murderers of Bishop and his acolytes. It is germane to provide a summary of the fate of the Revolutionary Military Council. There was a group of nineteen people alleged to be directly involved in the murder of Bishop and seven others. Those eventually indicted were:

Bernard Coard	Colville McBarnette
Phyllis Coard	Christopher Stroude
Hudson Austin	Lester Redhead
Ewart Layne	Calistus Bernard
Selwyn Strachan	John Ventour
Liam James	Cecil Prime
Leon Cornwall	Andy Mitchell
Dave Bartholomew	Vincent Joseph
Cosmos Richardson	Ian St Bernard
Fraser Nelson	

By 29 October, they were all in the custody of the USA. This was notwithstanding the fact that they were citizens of a separate sovereign state and not subject to the laws of the USA. Amnesty International took an interest in the manner in which this group was incarcerated and later tried. It published a report twenty years after the event, in October 2003, that was scathing about the judicial process that the accused had faced. Amnesty International commented: 'Many analysts believed the invasion may have had little to do with Bishop's death or Coard's accession to power but may have been motivated by the USA's desire to remove left-wing leaning governments in the region.'[1]

This was hardly an original thought and was no more than the worldwide consensus. The UN General Assembly Resolution 38/7 of 2 November 1983 had been passed by a vote of 108:9. The nine were the participants in the invasion plus Israel and El Salvador.

The murder of eight people was a heinous crime and the perpetrators richly deserved punishment. However, they also had every right to civilised treatment and a well-prepared defence at trial, before an unbiased judge. In practice, the accused got none of these.

Initially, all of the Grenada accused were held incommunicado on US naval vessels. They were confined in metal containers or wooden crates and subjected to lengthy interrogation. During their detention, the whereabouts of the group was kept secret and requests from lawyers, family members and others to see and talk with them were rejected. They were held, by the US, for periods of nine to twelve days before eventually being handed over to Grenadian and Caribbean Peacekeeping Force authorities at Richmond Hill Prison on or around 5 November 1983.

The nineteen were moved to Richmond Hill Prison – always a dreadful place. It had been filthy and badly run under the Bishop regime. Any residual semblance of discipline and good order had evaporated when it received its new inmates. The staff were scruffy, lacking complete uniforms. They had no pride in themselves and none in their jobs. They cooked over open fires and slept on dirty bunks. This appalling shambles was what confronted Lionel Maloney, a Barbadian prison officer, when he was appointed commissioner and invited to take charge of the prison.

Maloney was a strict disciplinarian and he hit the prison like a whirlwind. He put an instant stop to the prison guards deferring to the inmates and addressing them by their military rank. Maloney begged and borrowed to clean up his new domain and, in a surprisingly short time, he transformed the prison and the attitude of those in it, guards and prisoners alike.

Maloney was not popular, especially so with the nineteen. Their lawyers made every effort to have him removed but because he applied prison rules and stuck to those rules, he was inviolate. Coard and the others had been content with the management of the prison when it did not apply to them, but they did not take well to life under what had been their system. They resorted to allegations of torture and inhuman conditions.

Phyllis Coard had her own agenda, and in April 1984, she managed to smuggle out a letter to the British politician Dame Judith Hart. Hart, who held strong left-wing views, was president of the United Kingdom Committee for the Violations of Human Rights in Grenada. Although Coard hit the right target with a host of allegations, there is no evidence that Hart took any action. Coard's next step was to embark on a hunger strike in which her weight shrank from 168lb to 133lb. This weakened her and at one point, she collapsed. Soon after, she made a jail break but did not get beyond the prison walls.

The investigation into the killing of Bishop and the others was conducted by police officers from other Caribbean nations, including Barbados and Jamaica. During this process Bernard Coard and ten others again alleged that they were tortured, initially by American personnel and later at Richmond Hill Prison by police officers. Eleven of the accused – Redhead, Bernard, Mitchell, Richardson, Bartholomew, Layne, James, Strachan, Cornwall, McBarnette and Stroude – made confessions to the investigators. They not only confessed personally but also implicated others as being guilty of murder. The confessions were made although they were allegedly given warnings from the interviewing officers that 'You are not obliged to say anything unless you wish to do so but what you say may be put into writing and given in evidence.' Amnesty International commented:

> None of the nineteen were allowed to have legal representatives present as they were interrogated, despite many of them requesting lawyers. The United Nations Special Rapporteur on the independence of judges and lawyers has stated that 'it is desirable to have the presence of an attorney during police interrogation as an important safeguard to protect the rights of the accused. The absence of legal counsel gives rise to the potential for abuse.'[2]

Clearly, the denial of access to a lawyer was, and is, a serious breach of the accused rights under international law. Had the Grenadian authorities ensured this right was met, the confessions would have had more veracity in court.

The investigation was conducted by police officers from Barbados, and Inspector Watson, specifically, was alleged to have inflicted torture. The acting Director of Public Prosecutions, in a letter to the Commissioner of Barbadian Police on 3 July 1986, stated that the accusations of torture 'have been dismissed as being totally unsupported by the doctor whom the accused persons alleged attended them'. Lester Redhead gave compelling evidence when he said in court:

> I say that statement was taken under torture. I admit that the signature at the bottom of the statement is mine. I only signed the statement after being tortured for several hours by Barbadian police officers, Sergeant Ashford Jones and Courcey Holder … On or about 29 October 1983, I was captured by US invasion forces and taken to a prison [*sic*] of war camp at Port Saline. There I was subject to physiological torture. I was placed in a box 8 x 8 [feet] with a little door I had to lie down to crawl into. On first night that box was beaten for the entire night … A forklift actually lifted that box off the ground with me inside. I was only given one meal per day. …
>
> On 11 November 1983, I was taken … by Sergeant Ashford Jones and Courcey Holder among others … I was immediately handcuffed to a chair and left there for about 30 minutes with a Bajan police officer pointing a .38 pistol at my head … I told him [Sergeant Jones, who had entered the room] I would only do so [make a statement] in the presence of my lawyers. Having said that Courcey Holder immediately started to beat me in the head. …

> After this Sergeant Jones start [*sic*] reading from what I assumed was a statement in front of him asking me if I know anything about this. I told him to my knowledge I don't know anything about what he is speaking about. Having said that Courcey Holder started to beat me in the chest and stomach telling me to say that I know what Sergeant Jones was reading. This pattern continued for several hours. …
>
> After they completed writing that so called statement Sergeant Jones asked me to read the statement. I told him that as far as I was concerned, I did not give any statement. I refused to do so. Again, they started beating me. When I could not take the blows anymore, I had to give in and sign the statement. I was then taken back to Point Salines and put back in the box.

In October 1984, and during Phyllis Coard's hunger strike, a much more serious matter came to light. There was a plot to stage a mass breakout from Richmond Hill and this was being organised by Gerhard Jonas – the same man who had assisted in the capture of Austin *et al.* (see page 145). It seemed that Jonas had become a double agent and, in that role, was now determined to free his former comrades.

Jonas and a group of former PRA soldiers, armed from hidden caches, intended to launch their plan on the night of 3/4 October 1984. Prominent Grenadians, not least Sir Paul Scoon, were to be taken and used as bargaining chips. American students, now back at the Medical School, were to be ambushed as they bussed between campuses. The caves at Grand Etang or the now desolate Camp Calivigny was where the students were to be held. A list of targets for demolition was drawn up and high on the list were US helicopters parked on the Grand Anse playing fields. There was an assassination list and it included Commissioner Maloney and several other Barbadian police officers with responsibility in public order.

Several former members of the PRG, including St Bernard, Justin Roberts and Basil Gahagan, were central to the plot. These last three were out on bail, having been recently freed from prison, as there was insufficient evidence against them to justify their incarceration.

On the morning of 3 October, matters came to a head outside the Grenville courthouse, where a number of people, including Ewart Layne, Lester Redhead, James Cornwall and Tan Bartholomew, were present. An ex-PRA officer cadet called Ronnie Spooner threatened and then assaulted a corporal of the Jamaican Defence Force. It was an ugly incident, but Spooner was arrested and searched. The search revealed a letter addressed to Cornwall and the plot then quickly unravelled.

Jonas was expelled from Grenada and sent back to East Germany – he disappeared into obscurity and was never heard of or seen in Grenada again.[3]

The preparation for the trial of these men was a lengthy, convoluted and unsatisfactory process. It extended over two years and there was no consistency as different judges heard the arguments. During this period, charges against Ian St Bernard were dropped for lack of evidence. There were now eighteen facing trial and they challenged the legitimacy of the court. This challenge was rejected and the Court of Appeal, composed of three Grenadian judges, upheld that decision.

The pre-trail proceedings involved twelve defence lawyers and their corporate outrage at the competency of the court culminated on 11 April 1986, when the entire group announced that they were withdrawing from active participation in the trial.[4] The police conduct was problematic at best, but the judicial process was also deeply flawed. It was not until 10 May that the accused 'were tried before a tribunal created specifically for their case and before a judge who lacked both independence and impartiality'.[5] The USA funded, in part, the proceedings, which lasted until 4 December 1986. There were thirty-three persons in the original jury pool, and when *The Informer* questioned why the judge had summarily dismissed thirty of these, the editor of the newspaper was charged with contempt and jailed for two weeks.

The jury was then picked/nominated without any of the usual interrogation and probe for prejudice. None of the defending lawyers were permitted to be present during the selection of the jury. When, during preliminary hearings on 11 April 1986, the judge informed the defence lawyers that they were liable to be cited for contempt of court, it was alleged, by Amnesty International, that the jury cheered.

Defence lawyer Jacqueline Samuels-Brown swore on oath that:

> immediately after he [the judge] initiated contempt proceedings, there was widespread clapping by jurors, as well as jeering and booing. During the adjournment, the jurors continued to make hostile comments in relation to the accused and their Counsel … On this adjournment, the array of jurors hurled further hostile remarks, threats and jeers at the accused … [calling them] 'murderers' and 'criminals'.[6]

It was from this group that twelve persons were subsequently empanelled to sit in judgement on the facts in the case. The Amnesty International report quoted here is voluminous and detailed. That Bishop and seven others were murdered is not disputed and the consensus then, and now, is that Bernard Coard was the instigator and that he was supported to some degree by some of the other seventeen. At the conclusion of the trial, one man, Fraser Nelson, was acquitted. However, fourteen of the accused were found guilty of murder and sentenced to death by hanging.

The remaining three, Andy Mitchell, Vincent Joseph and Cosmos Richardson, were all soldiers in the People's Revolutionary Army and were found guilty of lesser crimes.

> Andy Mitchell was convicted of eight counts of manslaughter and Vincent Joseph and Cosmos Richardson were each convicted of eleven counts of manslaughter for taking part in the actual killings that occurred at Fort Rupert in October 1983. Mitchell was sentenced to fifteen years' incarceration for each count, with count two to be served consecutively, for a total of thirty years' imprisonment. Joseph and Richardson were sentenced to fifteen years' incarceration for each count, with counts two and nine to be served consecutively. For a total of forty-five years' imprisonment.[7]

The *Los Angeles Times* reported on the trial, saying:

> Fourteen people were convicted of murder Thursday and sentenced to hang for killing Prime Minister Maurice Bishop and 10 [*sic*] supporters in a coup that prompted the U.S.-led invasion of Grenada in 1983.
>
> Among the fourteen were the former deputy prime minister and his wife. Three other defendants were found guilty of a lesser charge of manslaughter and sentenced to prison terms ranging from 30 to 45 years, and one was acquitted of all charges.
>
> The 12-member jury in the seven-month trial delivered the verdict after the minimum three hours of deliberation. Acting Chief Justice Dennis Byron delivered the sentences to the hushed courtroom, which was packed with more than 100 spectators. All 17 defendants had pleaded innocent in the killings of Bishop and 10 followers on Oct. 19, 1983, during a coup by a radical faction of the prime minister's leftist New Jewel Movement.
>
> The United States, coordinating troops and police from Jamaica, Dominica, St Lucia, Antigua, St Vincent and Barbados, invaded the eastern Caribbean Island six days later and ousted the coup leaders.
>
> At the time, President Reagan said the goal of the invasion was to rescue American students at the St George's College of Medicine and restore democratic institutions. But the United States, already alarmed by Bishop's Marxist leanings and warm ties with Cuba and the Soviet Union, also wanted to stop a more extreme move to the left by the radical military faction that overthrew Bishop and his government.
>
> Twenty Grenadian police officers stood guard Thursday inside the whitewashed courtroom, and Prime Minister Herbert Blaize, elected in 1984, still thought it prudent to summon police reinforcements from neighboring islands as the day of the verdict approached.

The prosecution said ten defendants were members of a government central committee that issued orders to kill Bishop and his followers. The murders were carried out by a four-man firing squad led by Lt. Callistus Bernard, the prosecution maintained.

Found guilty were former Deputy Prime Minister Bernard Coard and Hudson Austin, a former general of the now-disbanded People's Revolutionary Army. Both testified they were close friends of Bishop and had no reason to kill him, but the prosecution portrayed them as leaders of the radical faction.

Also found guilty of murder were central committee members Phyllis Coard, Bernard Coard's wife; Leon Cornwall, Bishop's ambassador to Cuba; Selwyn Strachan, Minister of mobilization; Lt. Col. Ewart Layne; Cecil Prime; Liam James; John Ventour; Dave Bartholomew, and Kamau McBarnette.

The soldiers found guilty of murder were Lester Redhead, Colville McBarnette, Christopher Stroude and Callistus Bernard. Redhead was said to have slit Bishop's throat and cut off his ring finger. Soldiers Vincent Joseph and Cosmos Richardson were found guilty on 11 counts of manslaughter and each sentenced to 45 years of imprisonment, and Andy Mitchell was found guilty of eight counts of manslaughter and sentenced to 30 years.

Soldier Raeburn Nelson, who wept and expressed remorse over the incident during the trial, was found innocent. 'I feel very happy to be given a chance once again among the Grenadian people,' said Nelson, who became a born-again Christian while imprisoned.

Coard said they were convicted in a 'kangaroo court and show trial'. His wife shouted at Judge Byron, 'the world will condemn you'! Layne, who was the army officer of the day when Bishop was killed, said: 'My entire life has been dedicated to the revolution. I acted alone.'

The defendants were taken to lunch before the verdict was read and were brought back into the crowded courtroom in handcuffs. The men wore drab clothing, but Coard's wife wore a bright green dress, and her hair was swept back with a green band.

All the defendants had dismissed their attorneys during the trial and represented themselves. During the trial, prosecutor Karl Hudson-Phillips told the court that a proposal to allow Coard to share power with Bishop prompted the murders. The leadership of the New Jewel Movement, founded by Bishop before he took power in a 1979 coup, split over the proposal, Hudson-Phillips said.

The army finally was sent to kill Bishop, Education Minister Jacqueline Creft, Housing Minister Norris Bain, Foreign Minister Unison Whiteman and seven [*sic*] other people, the prosecutor said. The prosecution's star witness was Fabien Gabriel, a soldier given immunity in exchange for his testimony.

> Gabriel said he was present with six of the defendants when Bishop and the others were lined up against a wall at Ft. Rupert in downtown St George's.
>
> Those convicted Thursday have the right to appeal, but there was no immediate word on whether they plan to do so. The murder charges carry a mandatory penalty of death by hanging.

The conduct of the trial does not bear close examination and after several appeals, the UK Judicial Committee of the Privy Council (JCPC) met on 7 February 2007 to consider the matter. Established in 1833, this is the highest court of appeal for the Crown Dependencies, the British Overseas Territories and some Commonwealth countries. The Privy Council formerly acted as the court of last resort for the entire British Empire, other than for the United Kingdom itself.[8]

The JCPC ruled that the death sentences originally imposed in the cases were unconstitutional and that this also invalidated the process by which those sentences were pronounced. The sentences of each of the accused were later commuted to life imprisonment. In its ruling the JCPC stated, 'The question of the appellants' fate is so politically charged that it is hardly reasonable to expect any Government of Grenada … to take an objective view of the matter even after 23 years.' It ordered that the case should therefore be referred back to the Supreme Court of Grenada for a new sentencing determination, 'taking into account the progress made by the appellants during their time in prison'.

The consequence of the JCPC ruling was that the three who were serving imprisonment for manslaughter were immediately released. In 2009, the last seven prisoners were freed, having served twenty-six years in prison.

Coard was interviewed on his release, and he denied that he gave any orders to execute the eight political opponents but admitted to having faulty judgement in unspecified areas. He did concede that 'we were amateurs, we were arrogant and intolerant, and all our mistakes came home to roost'.[9]

Coard swore off politics for life and embarked on writing his memoirs – this project extended into a five-volume history that covered not only his life but also the political history of Grenada. The first three volumes were published by 2020.

Notes

1. Amnesty International Report, AMR 32/001/2003, p. 4.
2. 'Report of the Mission of the Special Rapporteur to the Commissioner of Police of Barbados United Kingdom' (UN Doc. E/CN.4/1998/39 add. 4, para 47, 5 March 1998).
3. Adkin, Major M., *Urgent Fury: The Battle for Grenada* (London, Leo Cooper, 1989), p. 329.

4. 'The Maurice Bishop Murder Trial' (*The Grenadian Newsletter*, 6 December 1986, Vol. 14, No. 19).
5. Amnesty International Report, p. 14.
6. Ibid., p. 17.
7. Ibid., p. 28.
8. Howell, P.A., *The Judicial Committee of the Privy Council, 1833–1876: Its Origins, Structure, and Development* (Cambridge, UK, Cambridge University Press, 1979).
9. 'Elated Coard: Speaks of Prison' (*Jamaica Gleaner*, 13 September 2009).

Chapter 25

The American Perspective

When the dust had settled there was understandable satisfaction in American political and military circles. Seemingly, URGENT FURY had accomplished all its declared and also its undeclared aims. The loss of life was minimal and the loss of equipment bearable.

There was an air of self-satisfaction. President Reagan announced that 'the Armed Forces are back and standing tall'. Admiral Metcalf pronounced that 'we blew them away'. The Army Chief of Staff General John Wickham described the operation as 'superb' and expressed confidence that the military was 'on the right track'.[1]

On 6 February 1984, just before the launch of ABLE ARCHER, Admiral McDonald's headquarters held a meeting to discuss the operation; the aim was to identify problems, lessons learnt, and to seek any remedial action necessary to resolve issues. McDonald duly signed off on the record of the meeting saying, 'The outcome of this military mission reaffirmed the outstanding professionalism, dedication and flexibility of all the forces involved in this effort.'[2]

A White House aide was asked if there was any downside to the recent operation and he replied, 'Hell no, none, zero! You can scream and shout and gnash your teeth all you want, but the folks out there like it. It was done right and done with despatch.'[3]

This, all-round ingenuous and corporate complacency was dangerous. The reality was that URGENT FURY had been a masterclass in military and political ineptitude. The operation was a hairsbreadth away from disaster, and the only matter that merited satisfaction was the consistent and undoubted courage of individual American servicemen.

One of the features of American military life is the liberal use of the word 'outstanding'. An officer's efficiency report will inevitably describe him as 'outstanding'. To do otherwise is to deny him promotion. In a society in which everyone and every activity is 'outstanding', it is difficult to discriminate between the mediocre, the good and the very good. Like the award of medals, this is a cultural thing; it is the American way. It works for them but usually self-criticism is not, from choice, their 'cup of tea'.

In this case, some common sense was applied and McDonald's report did acknowledge a few of the cruel facts of life. It did accept that air assets were not always properly controlled and in a statement of the blindingly obvious, noted that 'helicopters are highly vulnerable to well-aimed ground fire'. It was agreed that the deployment of the Caribbean Peacekeeping Force had been the cause of 'confusion'. Medical evacuation at night was seen to be an issue that required attention. This was because Black Hawk pilots were not trained to land on seaborne helicopter platforms and were accordingly denied permission to land. Despite the grudging acceptance that all had not been well, Adkin observed that was no public acknowledgement that 'it had taken so painfully long for nine elite battalions of US infantry backed up by overwhelming firepower, to defeat one weak battalion of third-rate Grenadians and another of half-trained civilians'.

A Marxist-Leninist regime had been swept away, American citizens had been 'rescued' and democracy re-established. However, all of this came at the cost of marked, negative international reaction. President Reagan was unconcerned, and on 3 November, at a press conference, he was asked 'why so many nations had opposed intervention'. He replied, 'One hundred nations in the United Nations have not agreed with us on just about everything that's come up before them where we've been involved, and it didn't upset my breakfast.'[4]

Reagan's flippancy was not enough to satisfy his critics and there were issues that required explanation or justification. Many of the most vociferous critics of Reagan's actions were themselves American. There was sufficient heat surrounding the invasion to cause the American Bar Association to commission a report on the matter.

This report was to be authored by four lawyers, each expert in international law. They started work on 3 December 1983. Their prime function was to make an assessment of the US Government's legal defence. They were swift and, by early 1984, they had produced a first draft of their report that they could share with State Department officials.[5]

The report did nothing to excuse their country's actions and concluded that the invasion was 'incompatible with the restraints on the use of force contained in the charters of the United Nations and the Organization of American States as confirmed at the Rio Treaty of 1947'.[6] Predictably, the State Department rejected the judgement, and by February 1984, its own in-house legal expert had mounted a spirited defence. In this defence, several sweeping assertions were made, such as that 'the intervention was essentially a three-legged stool that stood on a triad of well-established principles of international law'.[7] The author further claimed that 'unusual circumstances' were such that the USA was obliged to intervene. Finally, Davis Robinson, the State Department lawyer, claimed, 'American intervention in Grenada was in no factual way analogous with the "illegal" Soviet occupation of Czechoslovakia or Afghanistan.' Robinson's argument was added as an annex to what was to be called the 'Gordon Report'.

The Armed Forces of the United States attract officers of the highest calibre, and post URGENT FURY, an analysis of the operation was conducted. The multiple flaws in both planning and execution were painfully acknowledged. The official history later concluded: 'The operation succeeded, but flaws in its execution revealed weaknesses in joint operations. Together with the bombing of the Marine Corps barracks in Beirut that same month, the experience of Operation URGENT FURY added impetus to efforts to reform the joint systems which were already under way.'[8]

That rather understates the case. In Grenada, the USA was faced by a third-rate, poorly trained, ill-equipped, unmotivated opposition. Had the Grenadian/Cuban enemy been resolute and skilfully deployed, there is the possibility that the invasion could have been repelled, with considerable loss of life. By happy chance, the invasion met only the most nominal opposition.

URGENT FURY was flawed from day one. Among the multiple contingency plans in the Pentagon, there existed a command structure for an eventuality such as that faced in October 1983. The plan was numbered 2360 and it made provision for an intervention in Grenada (see page 67). However, for no discernible reason, Plan 2360 was not implemented. It continued to gather dust in the Pentagon and an *ad hoc* command organisation was created instead. Many of the deficiencies in the operation can be traced back to this hastily constructed structure that was imposed on Admiral Metcalf and his subordinates. Giving command of a predominantly land/air operation to a naval officer but without an adequate staff to do the job was ill-judged, as was the decision to split the operational cake between every branch of the Armed Forces.

During active operations, Metcalf was nevertheless still subject to orders emanating from the USA. It surely goes without saying that the command and disposition of troops in action must be left to the wisdom and experience of the commander on the ground. History reveals that it was Hitler's interference that was one reason that Germany lost the war. The order to take Camp Calivigny, given by an unidentified, four-star officer in the USA, led to the calamitous debacle.

A facet of the cobbled together chain of command was that neither Admiral Metcalf nor the leaders of the Caribbean Peacekeeping Force were involved in the planning process. Incredibly, Metcalf was unaware of the activities of Major General Richard Scholtes's Special Forces, who conducted a private war entirely to their satisfaction. Similarly, Metcalf was unaware of the need to rescue the Governor General or of the location of the medical students.

The official history commented bleakly that:

> The success of Operation URGENT FURY was *marred* [author's emphasis] by the consequences of inadequate time for planning, lack of tactical intelligence, and problems with joint command and control.[9]

The use of the word 'marred' served to conceal what was high-level military incompetence.

The employment of JSOCS troops was utterly inept. Their attempts to penetrate Grenada failed miserably three times and wasted lives. Their activity was ineffective and is perhaps exemplified by the attack on the Beausejour transmitting station. The attackers had inoperative radios and no maps, and their operation, which was an element of a larger plan involving a rescued governor general, was bereft of even the most basic co-ordination. The fact that this group of SEALs escaped with their lives was due to the quality of their training, the unprofessional performance of the opposition and a generous helping of good fortune.

The SEALs who assaulted Government House were surrounded and dependent upon protective aircraft. There was never the least chance that they would link up with their comrades at Beausejour. The performance of Special Forces during URGENT FURY was well below that expected – not the actions of individual soldiers, but rather the gross ineptitude of their senior commanders. Adkin observed:

> The chaos inside the Black Hawks circling over the Prison was a glimpse of what to expect when tactical principles are ignored. Fortunately, it was a handful of poorly trained, poorly equipped Grenadians, not Vietnamese or Cuban professional soldiers, manning sophisticated weapons.[10]

The operational leadership structure had built into it a deficient communications system. Radios did not always permit the passage of information between ships or between units. This, together with a dearth of maps, poor or non-existent communications and a lack of even the most cursory intelligence, generated especial pressure on the invaders.

If the medical students had been in any danger, then their 'rescue' would presumably have been given a higher priority. The Americans had no idea that the student body was scattered over the south-west corner of the island and 1st/75th, who had been tasked to take the True Blue campus, had not evolved a detailed plan for their liberation. Freeing students was not given any higher priority than airfield clearance.

The employment of Delta Force and Charlie Company in their daylight, unsupported, imprudent helicopter assault on Richmond Hill Prison was an example of how not to use Special Forces. The anticipated freeing of an unknown number of Grenadian citizens from the prison was a very curious priority; even if it had been successful, it would have contributed nothing to the overall mission.

The insertion of the Rangers at Point Salines Airport was blessed with extraordinary good fortune. It took an hour and a half to drop 600 men, in daylight, onto a runway in the face of a passive enemy. The only casualty suffered a broken leg. Adkin, correctly, described this as a 'military miracle' (p. 334). On the occupation of the airport, the Rangers were able to spend time driving Cuban vehicles clearing obstacles. How fortunate that the Rangers faced only lightly armed construction workers who were under specific orders not to initiate any fighting.

The US Marines had an uneventful 'war'. Local conditions prevented them making their assaults on Pearls and Grenville simultaneously. In the event, Echo Company landed one platoon at a time and were unopposed. The taking of Grenville was little more than an excursion. During the brief period of hostilities, the Marines had no casualties in action on the ground; their only losses were three helicopter pilots.

Given the circumstances, the medal awards to USMC personnel seem to be disproportionate. Three officers were killed (Giguere, Scharver and Seagle) and a further eight Bronze Stars were awarded as well as twenty-six Purple Hearts. The records of patrol activity did not make mention of any combat injuries.

The longer-term consequence of URGENT FURY was the protracted exercise to restructure the organisation of the top of the Armed Forces. The retirement of General Vessey in October 1985 and other senior officers of his vintage ushered into office individuals who were prepared to make the significant organisational changes needed. Two reports prepared in the Center for Strategic and International Studies (CSIS) kicked the ball into play and they in turn gave rise to a book entitled *The Pentagon and the Art of War* by Edward W. Luttwak. In his book, Luttwak argued:

> The joint Chiefs system was dysfunctional because no single person was effectively the commander of all uniformed Americans. The president was nominally the commander-in-chief of the military, but he wore that hat only sometimes, in addition to his considerable executive branch and ceremonial responsibilities. The chairman of the Joint Chiefs did not serve as the president's surrogate because by statute the unified commands reported to the secretary of defense.[11]

Luttwak's book hit at the very heart of the matter and a further study by CSIS went far beyond the functioning of the Joint Chiefs in examining the organisation of the Secretary of Defense's office, the manner in which the defence budget was prepared and how weapon systems were acquired. The *New York Times* describe the report as 'the most drastic changes in military management since the Eisenhower Administration'.[12]

The US Department of Defense is the very epitome of bureaucracy, and it was not until April 1986 that President Reagan signed the National Security Decision Directive 219, an executive order to implement the recommendations of the Packard Commission. This was named for its chairman, David R. Packard, who headed the fourteen-member group charged with studying Pentagon-led procurement.

It is beyond the scope of this book to dwell on the post-URGENT FURY restructuring of the US Armed Forces. Nevertheless, it is worth noting that on 5 August 1986, Major General Scholtes, now retired, was called to give evidence to a subcommittee of the Senate Armed Services Committee.

What Scholtes had to say had a significant effect on the ongoing and protracted debate on the reformation of the Armed Forces. The general made it clear that Special Forces in Grenada had been misused. 'Scholtes told the lawmakers how his forces were robbed of their unique capabilities by the conventional planners and chain of command. His forces had suffered relatively significant casualties in Grenada as a result of numerous misunderstandings of their tactics and capabilities.'[13]

It is difficult to reconcile Scholtes's grievance with the multiple serious errors made at unit level in Special Forces. He was the commander on the ground, and it was he who sent SEAL teams into action, unsupported, without maps or functioning radios. It was he, or his immediate staff, who made no arrangement to support these SEALs once they were committed. The implication that, in some way, he was overruled on matters of fundamental military common sense beggars belief.

However, Scholtes was not challenged. Quite the reverse; and Senator William Cohen described Scholtes's testimony as 'vital in the decision of Congress to create the United Stated Special Operations Command'.

It took from 1983 until early 1987 – during which time the machinations of several committees, various interested agencies and innumerable political players who occupied some of American public life – to find consensus, and the long-awaited structural changes to the Armed Forces were put in place.

It could be argued that one of the major benefits of URGENT FURY was the implementation of items of legislation that made alteration to the manner in which the USA would, in future, conduct its military incursions. This new structure's first test was in 1989, and the invasion of Panama under the code name Operation JUST CAUSE.

This mission took two weeks and General Maxwell Thurman commanded a joint task force of 700 sailors, 900 marines and 3,400 airmen. They faced an enemy 12,000 strong. During this invasion, the USA lost 26 killed and 324 wounded.

After the event, the same Pentagon historian who had written the official history of URGENT FURY commented:

> If proportionally lower friendly casualties mark operational success, JUST CAUSE was more successful than URGENT FURY … It showed substantial improvement in joint planning and execution. Part of that stemmed from the Goldwater-Nichols Act, part from the time available and the forces already in place, and part from the close working relationship of top political and military leaders before and during the operation.[14]

Cole's judgement above is a shrewd summation and a final word on URGENT FURY.

Notes

1. Adkin, Major M., *Urgent Fury: The Battle for Grenada* (London, Leo Cooper, 1989), p. 335.
2. Ibid., p. 337.
3. Ibid., p. 333.
4. Kukielski, P., *The US Invasion of Grenada: Legacy of a Flawed Victory* (Jefferson, North Carolina, McFarland & Co., 2019), p. 196.
5. Gordon, E., Bilder, A.W., Rovine. A.W. and Wallace, D., 'International Law and The United States Action in Grenada: A Report' (*The International Lawyer*, Vol. 18, No. 2, spring 1984), pp. 331–80.
6. Kukielski, p. 196.
7. The three 'well-established legal principles' quoted by Robinson were: a) a request by a lawful government authority for military assistance; b) a collective regional action consistent with the UN and OAS charters; and c) the right of States to use force to protect their nationals.
8. Cole, R.H., *Operation Urgent Fury: The Planning and Execution of Joint Operations in Grenada 1983* (US Joint Chiefs of Staff, Washington, DC, Joint History Office, 1997), p. 4.
9. Ibid., p. 5.
10. Adkin, p. 334.
11. Kukielski, p. 207.
12. Keller, B., 'Overhaul is Urged for Top Military' (*New York Times*, 22 January 1985).
13. Boykin, W.G., 'The origins of the Unites States Special Operations Command'. Quoted by Kukielski, p. 217.
14. Cole, R.H., 'Grenada, Panama and Haiti: Joint Operational Reform' *(Joint Forces Quarterly*, Autumn/Winter 1998/9*)*, p. 71.

Annexure A

Timeline

1967

March: Grenada achieves internal self-government. Britain retains responsibility for Defence and Foreign affairs.

25 August: Eric Geary elected for a fourth period in office. He had been dismissed from office previously for financial irregularities in 1962.

1972

Geary re-elected.

1973

11 March: The New Jewel Movement (NJM) established.

Six leading members of the NJM are arrested and beaten by Gairy's police and Mongoose gang.

1974

1 January: Three-week national strike starts.

During a protest march, Bishop's father is shot dead by police.

7 February: Grenada achieves independence from Great Britain.

8–10 April: NJM decides to become a vanguard Marxist-Leninist organisation.

1975

The NJM establishes a Grenada/Cuba Friendship Society.

1976

December: Gairy narrowly wins a sixth term.

Bishop is appointed leader of the opposition People's Alliance in Parliament.

1978

Guns smuggled into Grenada from the USA and delivered to a senior NJM member.

1979

12 March: US agents arrive in Grenada as part of an investigation into gunrunning from the USA to Grenada.

Gairy departs for New York intending to speak at the United Nations. In his absence, the NJM sizes power with minimal resistance.

14–15 March: CARICOM meets to discuss the implications of the coup and what measures to take to restore constitutional government. No decision taken.

20 March: WIAS strongly condemns the coup and refuses to recognise Bishop's government until there is a return to constitutional democracy.

Barbados, Jamaica and Guyana officially recognised the People's Revolutionary Government (PRG).

22 March: Britain, Canada and the USA recognise Bishop's regime.

23 March: US Ambassador to Barbados Frank Ortiz meets Bishop to discuss aid and the holding of elections. British High Commissioner Harry Stanley also meets Bishop to discuss the same issues.

25 March: Bishop suspends the country's constitution and replaces it with a series of People's Laws.

4 April: First consignment of Cuban arms arrives in Grenada. Further arms and personnel arrive on 7th and 14th.

7 April: Bishop requested arms from Britain, USA and CARICOM.

8 April: Bishop reveals that he has asked for arms from Venezuela.

10 April: Ambassador Ortiz advises that USA would 'view with displeasure any tendency on the part of Grenada to develop closer ties with Cuba'.

13 April: Bishops rebukes the USA on Radio Grenada, saying, 'We are not for sale.'

14 April: Grenada establishes diplomatic relations with Cuba.

16 July: Grenada signs the Declaration of St George's with Dominica and St Lucia, where left-wing governments have just been elected.

13 October: Bishop closes the independent *Torchlight* newspaper.

1980

January: Grenada supports the Soviet invasion of Afghanistan at the UN General Assembly.

May: The UK Government establishes a one-man post in Grenada answering to the British High Commissioner in Barbados.

May: US conducts Exercise SOLID SHIELD in the Caribbean.

October: The PRG signs a military agreement with the Soviet Union to provide substantial levels of arms and ammunition.

1981

February: HMG in London decide that 'due to the unsatisfactory political situation', a new loan will not be made under the banana development programme.

March: The USA blocks a Grenadian US$19 million loan request to the IMF.

18 June: The Organisation of Eastern Caribbean States (OECS) is established. Its membership is to be Antigua, Dominica, Grenada, Montserrat, St Kitts and Nevis, St Lucia, and St Vincent.

June: The Caribbean Development Bank rejects a US$4 million US loan because it excludes Grenada on political grounds.

19 June: The independent newspaper *Grenadian Voice* is closed by Bishop.

6 July: The UK underwrites a £6 million Plessey Electronics contract to supply equipment for the new airport project at Point Salines.

1 August: USA mounts three-month Exercise OCEAN VENTURE in the Caribbean.

1982

24 February: President Reagan announces the US$ 350 million Caribbean Basin Initiative to address socio-economic causes of unrest in the region.

9 April: President Reagan visits Barbados and tells regional leaders that 'Grenada' now bears the Soviet and Cuban trademark, which means that it will attempt to spread the virus among its neighbours.

28 April: USA mounts a one-month Exercise OCEAN VENTURE 82.

July: Bernard Coard resigns his membership of the Political Bureau, the Central Committee, and the Organising Committee but retains his role as Deputy Premier and his responsibility for planning and finance. He cites his disappointment over the rate of social and economic transformation and by the difficulties encountered in establishing a Marxist-Leninist party and control system.

21 September: The Soviet Union opens an Embassy in Grenada.

29 October: A Regional Security System established by Antigua, Barbados, Dominica, St Lucia, and St Vincent specifically excludes Grenada.

December: UK Parliamentary Foreign Affairs Committee reports on Central America and the Caribbean and notes 'the considerable degree of success achieved by the economic and social policies of the PRG'.

1983

12 January: Sir John Ure, Assistant Under Secretary Foreign and Commonwealth Office, visits Bishop and they discuss restoring the country's constitution, elections and financial support.

23 March: President Reagan announces his Strategic Defence Initiative (SDI). He says, 'The Soviet-Cuban militarisation of Grenada, in short, can only be seen as a power projection into that region.' US Exercise UNIVERSAL TREK is held in the Caribbean.

7 June: Bishop spends eleven days in Washington, DC, and meets National Security Advisor William Clark and Deputy Secretary of State Kenneth Dam.

13–19 July: PRG Central Committee First Plenary session. Organisational weaknesses are identified and the continued failure of the party to transform itself ideologically and organisationally, is deplored.

14–16 September: At an emergency meeting of the Central Committee, Bishop is subject to wide criticism. The quality of his leadership, and his failure to put the party on a firm Marxist-Leninist footing, are at the heart of the criticism. A joint leadership (with Coard) is suggested and agreed. Bishop asks for time to consider.

25 September: At an NJM Extraordinary General Meeting, Bishop accepts a joint leadership structure but expresses doubts as to its viability.

27 September: Bishop leads a small delegation to Eastern Europe to study economic issues. During this trip, Bishop changes his mind about joint leadership and sees it as a device to undermine him.

12 October: The Political Bureau and Central Committee meet, and Bishop asks that the joint leadership issue be reopened but his request is denied. He is told that he 'was mainly responsible for the crisis in the party'. At this meeting, Bishop's bodyguards say that it is rumoured that the Coards are plotting to kill Bishop.

13 October: At a meeting of NJM members, Bishop is denounced as being 'a disgrace to the party', and 'without redemption'. He is placed under house arrest and the following day expelled from the party he had formed.

John Kelly, the British representative in Grenada, reports to the High Commissioner in Barbados that 'Coard is about to throw Bishop out and declare a Marxist state'.

In Washington, the State Department considers possible unrest in Grenada and the threat this might pose for American citizens.

14 October: UK Deputy High Commissioner in Barbados, David Montgomery, reports to London that Coard has been all but successful in removing Bishop.

Selwyn Strachan, a PRG minister, attempts to announce Bishop's replacement by Bernard Coard at the *Free West Indian* newspaper. But a hostile crowd will have nothing to do with him.

Fidel Castro writes to the Central Committee saying that events were a surprise and disagreeable 'but that Cuba would not get involved Grenada's internal affairs'.

Three days of negotiations between Coard and pro-Bishop ministers in an attempt to find common ground, fail.

17 October: US considers the possibility of a non-permissive evacuation operation.

Barbadian Prime Minister Tom Adams meets with Ambassador Milan Bish and asks for US involvement in Grenadian affairs. Dominican Prime Minister Eugenia Charles discusses the same issue with Charles Gillespie, US Assistant Secretary of State.

18 October: Public demonstrations in St George's in favour of Bishop.

19 October: Tom Adams reiterates his request for US involvement and suggests that Bishop be rescued, and that a coalition of the USA and Eastern Caribbean multi-national force be raised to intercede in Grenada.

Bishop is freed from house arrest by a crowd of his supporters and he moves to Fort Rupert. The Central Committee orders the army to take the fort; 30–40 people are killed in the process. Bishop is recaptured and, along with seven others, executed.

Grenada establishes a seventeen-man Revolutionary Council, headed, nominally, by General Hudson Austin.

20 October: Crisis Planning Group meets in Washington, DC.

St Lucian Prime Minister John Compton speaks with Tom Adams and emphasises the need for a Caribbean initiative to intervene in Grenada on a multi-national basis.

Prime Minister Adams meets Ambassador Bish and suggests intervention under the auspices of OECS. Bish advises that written requests are required.

Fidel Castro condemns RMC and its works.

The Special Situations Group, chaired by Vice President Bush, meet and focus on a large-scale operation and not just an evacuation of American citizens. The Sixth Fleet Carrier Battle Group heading for the Mediterranean is diverted to Grenada.

21 October: The OECS meet in Barbados and agree the need for a military solution. Britain, the USA, France Canada and Venezuela will be approached for assistance. Prime Ministers Adams, Charles and Seaga meet with US diplomats to convey the request 'to depose the outlaw regime in Grenada by any means'.

22 October: British Embassy in Washington reports that after contact with the State Department, it has surmised that no action is currently planned. Robin Renwick, Head of Chancery at the British Embassy, visits the State Department to express British concern over a possible military intervention.

High Commissioner Giles Bullard receives an oral request from Prime Minister Adams, who says that a formal written request will follow.

HMS *Antrim* diverted towards Grenada in case an evacuation of British national is required.

US diplomats Linda Flohr and Ken Kurze with British High Commissioner David Montgomery fly from Barbados.

CARICOM meet in Trinidad seeking a non-military solution and *rule out the use of force or external involvement in a Caribbean problem* (author's emphasis). The OECS members decide to proceed irrespective of CARICOM. Grenada is summarily expelled from CARICOM.

23 October: 241 US Marines killed in Beirut.

President Reagan signs National Security Decision Directive.

David Montgomery and John Kelly meet with Sir Paul Scoon.

British and American diplomats meet Leon Cornwall, a member of RMC. The discussion about evacuating foreign nationals is unproductive. Cornwall insists that order will be restored, and a new government formed.

Montgomery reports that the situation is 'calm, tense and pretty volatile'.

High Commissioner Bullard reports to London that CARICOM offers the best chance of a peaceful solution, but that OECS will go along with a military solution if external assistance is forthcoming.

Derek Thomson, an embassy minister, enquires as to the intentions of the USA and is given no information.

US Ambassador McNeil meets Caribbean leaders in Barbados and tells them that a formal written request will be needed if the USA are to be involved.

Radio Free Grenada announced that the OECS has taken a decision to send military forces to Grenada. The army and militia are mobilised. Cornwall meets US diplomats to plead for talks to avoid bloodshed. RMC inflexibility over evacuation plans and its determination to stay in power make progress impossible.

24 October: US Ambassador McNeil reports to Washington that RMC believes an intervention is imminent and it is not keen to let the students leave. The situation on the island is deteriorating rapidly.

The curfew is lifted. Colonel Pedro Tortolo Comas arrives from Cuba to take charge of the Cuban contingent.

The US Embassy in Barbados receives information that 50 per cent of the students at St George's University want to leave.

British Ambassador in Washington Sir Oliver Wright meets the US Under Secretary of State who confirms that military action is likely.

UK Foreign Secretary Sir Geoffrey Howe informs the House of Commons that London is in close touch with both the USA and Caribbean governments. When asked about the possibility of a US intervention, he replies, 'I know of no such intention.'

President Reagan gives the 'go-ahead' order for Operation URGENT FURY to begin the next morning.

OECS leaders are informed that the USA has acceded to their request.

President Reagan informs the leadership of Congress of his decision to intervene in Grenada.

President Reagan sends a letter to Downing Street stating that he is giving serious consideration to the OECS request and would welcome the Prime Minister's thoughts and advice. A second letter arrives some hours later indicating that President Reagan has decided to 'respond positively' to the OECS request.

Prime Minister Thatcher phones President Reagan and asks him to call off the operation, fearing it will endanger US and British citizens and the Governor General. She says that Britain has not received any written request from OECS. Furthermore, most CARICOM members are opposed to a military solution. President Reagan thanks her but has already decided to proceed with the operation.

25 October: Operation URGENT FURY commences at 0500 hrs local time. Within three days, 6,000 US troops are in Grenada.

Prime Minister Thatcher informs the House of Commons that the government has 'communicated our very considerable doubts' to the USA.

26 October: Governor General Scoon is rescued and flown to USS *Guam* and then on to Point Salines, where he signs a formal, pre-dated, written invitation.

28 October: US forces secure 'all significant military objectives'.

3 November: Hostilities officially end.

9 November: Governor General Sir Paul Scoon named a nine-member interim government to be headed by Nicholas Braithwaite.

Annexure B

Military and Political Interventions by the USA
(This list does not include either of the world wars)

1811
Chile: A US agent arrives in Chile to assess the revolutionary war against the Spanish Empire. This leads to the first of many US interventions in Chilean affairs.

1846–8
Mexico: During the Mexican–American war over disputed territory in what is now the American southwest, Mexico is invaded and partially occupied.

1871
Korea: A punitive expeditionary force arrives in Korea to exact retribution for the attack of an American ship.

1898
Cuba: The island is a Spanish colony. The Spanish–American War is fought for its possession, and when the USA is victorious, Spain also cedes its colonies in Puerto, Guam and the Philippines to the USA.

1899–1902
The Philippines: Following the Spanish–American War, the USA acquires the Philippines from Spain. The Philippine–American war ensues as the Filipinos seek independence.

1899–1901
China: The USA leads the eight-nation China Relief Expedition during the Boxer Rebellion. Initially, the expedition is launched to rescue European and American residents.

1903–25
Honduras: American troops are present in Honduras in 1903, 1907, 1911, 1912, 1919, 1924 and 1925.

1910–19

Mexico: In the Border War, US troops occupy Veracruz for six months.

1912–33

Nicaragua: The formal occupation begins in 1912. The American occupation is designed to stop any other nation except the USA building a Nicaraguan canal.

1915–34

Haiti: US troops take possession of Haiti in 1915 to restore order and maintain political and economic stability in the Caribbean after the assassination of the Haitian President in July 1915. This occupation continues until 1934.

1916–24

Dominican Republic: US troops occupy the Dominican Republic following twenty-eight revolutions in fifty years. The Republic is, for practical purposes, an American colony during this period.

1914–17

The US intervenes in **Mexico** during the revolution, with incidents such as the occupation of Veracruz.

1949

Syria: In 1949, a *coup d'état* overthrows a democratically elected government, which had delayed approving an oil pipeline requested by US international business interests in that region.

The exact role of the CIA in the coup is controversial, but at least one CIA officer communicates with Husni al-Za'im, the leader of the coup, prior to the 30 March coup, and is at least aware that it is being planned. Six weeks later, on 16 May, Za'im approves the pipeline.[1]

1950–2

Egypt: The USA plays an active role in the downfall of King Farouk when he resists taking measures wanted by the USA.[2]

1952

Guatemala: The USA launches Operations PB FORTUNE and PB SUCCESS. The aim of both is the overthrow of the democratically elected president, Jacobo Arbenz. He is replaced by Carlos Armas, one of many US-backed dictators. They plunge the country into chaos, civil war follows and causes the loss of thousands of lives.[3]

1950–3
The US participates in the Korean War in response to the invasion of **South Korea** by its northern neighbour.

1946–55
The USA gives logistic support to the **French** as it endeavours to retain control of its Vietnamese colony.

1953
Iran: The US plays a part in the coup that ousts Prime Minister Mohammad Mossadegh and reinstates the Shah of Iran, Mohammed Reza Pahlavi.

1955–73
Following the defeat of the French, the US commits troops as it seeks to combat **North Vietnam**, to halt the spread of communism and to install its version of democracy.

1958
Indonesia: The USA sponsors a failed revolt against President Sukarno.

1961
Cuba: Bay of Pigs invasion. An operation that is ineptly planned and inevitably fails. It is an attempt to overthrow Fidel Castro, President of Cuba.

1962–73
Chile: the United States has covertly intervened in Chile from as early as 1962, and from 1963 to 1973, covert involvement is 'extensive and continuous'.[4]

1961–6
Guyana: The USA and UK conspire to ensure that Cheddi Jagan does not take control in the colony as it emerges as an independent nation.

1965–6
Dominican Republic: The US intervenes in the civil war, ostensibly to protect American residents in that country. The CIA has assisted in the assassination of Rafael Trujillo, at one-time dictator of Dominica.[5]

1969–98
UK, specifically **Northern Ireland:** The USA acquiesce at fundraising in the USA for IRA terrorist activity in Northern Ireland. The US Government give

tacit support to the IRA and senior representatives of the IRA are entertained in the White House.

This support ends on 11 September 2001, when for the first time, the US come face to face with the effects of terrorism.

The USA interfere in domestic politics in Northern Ireland until 1998, when it participates in the Good Friday Agreement.

1970

Cambodia: Bombing and invasion of Cambodia as an extension of the Vietnam War. Cambodia was a neutral country.

1979

Afghanistan: President Carter began covertly arming Afghan mujahideen in a programme called Operation CYCLONE.

1983

Grenada: The subject of this book!

1986

Libya: The USA launch Operation ATTAIN DOCUMENT in early 1986, in which seventy-two Libyans are killed and multiple boats and SAM sites are destroyed. Later, in April 1986, the US bomb Libya again, this time killing over forty Libyan soldiers.

1989

Panama: US Operation JUST CAUSE is launched to depose the Panamanian leader, Manuel Noriega.

1990–1

Kuwait: The US intervenes in Kuwait to repel Iraqi invaders. This morphs into the Gulf War and involves an international coalition.

1990

Somalia: As part of UNOSOM 1 and UNOSOM 2. US Operation GOTHIC SERPENT fails at the Battle of Mogadishu. President Clinton withdraws US support to UN activity in Somalia.

1991 & 2003

Iraq: The Gulf War in 1991 and the invasion of **Iraq** in 2003 are both major US military interventions.

1995
Bosnia: President Clinton deploys US peacekeepers to Bosnia in late 1995, to uphold the subsequent Dayton Agreement.

1998
President Clinton orders Operation INFINITE REACH. The US Navy attacks al-Qaeda training camps in **Afghanistan** and a pharmaceutical factory in **Sudan.** The factory is suspected of producing chemical weapons. This is the first publicly acknowledged pre-emptive strike against a violent non-state actor to be conducted by the US military.

2001–21
Afghanistan: The US invade Afghanistan in response to the attacks on New York on 11 September 2001.

2011
Libya: The US and NATO allies support those rebelling against Muammar Gaddafi.

2016
UK: President Obama, while visiting the UK, threatens its citizens with commercial sanctions if they support the 'leave' vote in the referendum on membership of the EU. This arrogant and impertinent gesture has the effect of enhancing the 'leave' vote.

Ongoing as at 2024
Syria: The US is participating covertly in this civil war.
Ukraine: The US is the principal supporter of Ukraine in its war with Russia.

A 2016 study by Carnegie Mellon University, Professor Dov Levin, found that the United States intervened in eighty-one foreign elections between 1946 and 2000, with the majority of those being through covert, rather than overt, actions.[6] A 2021 review of the existing literature found that foreign interventions since the Second World War tend overwhelmingly to fail to achieve their purported objectives.[7]

Notes

1. Wilford, H., *America's Great Game: The CIA's Secret Arabists and the Making of the Modern Middle East* (New York, Basic Books, 2013), pp. 94, 101.
2. Holland, M.F., *America and Egypt: From Roosevelt to Eisenhower* (New York, Praeger Publishing, 1996), p. 27.
3. Briggs, B., 'Billy Briggs on the Atrocities of Guatemala's Civil War' (London, *The Guardian*, 2 February 2007).
4. Church Committee, 'Covert Action in Chile 1963–73', 1975.
5. Blanton, W., ed., 'Memorandum for the Executive Secretary, CIA Management Committee: Potentially Embarrassing Agency Activities' (George Washington University, National Security Archives, 8 May 1973).
6. Levin, D.H., 'When the Great Power Gets a Vote: The Effects of Great Power Electoral Interventions on Election Results' (*International Studies Quarterly*, June 2016), 60 (2): 189–20.
7. Malis, M., Querubin, P. and Shanker, S., 'Persistent Failure? International Interventions since World War 1' (*The Handbook of Historical Economics*, January 2021), 641–73.

Annexure C

Whatever happened to old…?
(In alphabetical order)

Abizaid, Captain John P., USA (1951–)
Captain Abizaid served in the army and rose to the rank of general, when he led the United States Central Command. He is pictured in that rank in 2003.

He retired in 2007 and served as US Ambassador to Saudi Arabia from 2019 until 2021. He now serves as senior advisor at Albright Stonebridge Group.

Austin, General Hudson, PRA (1938–2022)
In mitigation pleas made in 2007, Austin sought to be released from prison. He made no attempt to deny his responsibility for what happened in 1983. In the plea, it was said that he 'understands the need to satisfy action for loss and suffering and the trauma of the Grenadian people'.

Austin was released from prison on 18 December 2008, at the same time as Colville McBarnette and John Ventour.

Bernard, Lieutenant Callistus, PRA
It was Bernard who led the executioners and on his release from prison, he expressed the view that 'we cannot change what happened back in October 1983'. He stated that those who were involved should use it positively in terms of never again making hasty decisions.

Boykin, Major William G., USA (1948–)
This officer was badly wounded in Grenada, but he survived and had a very successful military and political career. During his thirty-six years of service, he spent thirteen in the Delta Force and was engaged in several high-profile operations. He retired as a lieutenant general and his photograph shows him

in that rank. He has a very strong Christian faith, which he advertises freely, sometimes ill-advisedly. In February 2014, Boykin said in a speech that he believed that Jesus will return to Earth carrying an AR-15 assault rifle. Alluding to a biblical passage in which Jesus says 'I came not to bring peace but to bring a sword', Boykin said, 'I believe now that the sword he'll be carrying when he comes back is an AR-15.'[1]

Boykin was involved in the attempt to rescue hostages held by Iran (Operation EAGLE CLAW), the hunt for Pablo Escobar, and the Black Hawk incident in Mogadishu, Somalia. He is a published author and a visiting professor at Hampden-Sydney College in Virginia.

Coard, Bernard (1944–) and Coard, Phyllis (1943–2020)

Bernard Coard has published three books. He served his sentence in Richmond Hill Prison, where he was engaged in teaching and instructing fellow inmates in subjects, including economics and sociology. Upon release, he said he did not want to be involved in politics again.

Phyllis was released in 2000 on the basis of her ill-health, having served almost seventeen years. On her death, Lambert Brown, a friend who shared her political views, said, 'She was a powerful presence and was part of the founding of the National Organisation for Women in Grenada, where she had migrated to be with her husband Bernard, who was, at the time, that island's deputy prime minister.'

Cornwall, Major Leon, PRA

Described by *The New Today* as a 'hardline Marxist and senior member of the NJM'. The former major in the People's Revolutionary Army and Grenada's Ambassador to Cuba during the 1979–83 Grenada Revolution is currently employed by the Government as a counsellor at the His Majesty's Prison at Richmond Hill.

Cornwall, who grew up in his formative years as a Methodist in the St Paul's area, stressed that the teaching of the Church is that it is God who calls people as preachers.

The former revolutionary said:

> It's a call of God. People are called by God to be preachers and they are called by God to preach in different churches, different this or that, I am still a Christian, committed to Christianity. I have not in one way drifted or shifted from Christianity. If I am to say anything I am more committed to Christianity because of what I see happening around me in terms of the guys – some of the baddest guys up in the prison here giving their hearts to Jesus Christ.

Erskine, Lieutenant Donald K., USN

Erskine had a successful military career and rose to the rank of commander. He and his family retired to their farm in Maine in September 1996. In the aftermath of the 9/11 attacks, he worked as contractor and Federal employee with the newly formed Department of Homeland Security until 2017.

He currently works for the US Department of Energy's Argonne National Laboratory, where he supports NATO's Energy Planning Group as an Energy Security and Civil-military Relations Expert. He also supports the Department of Homeland Security's Cybersecurity and Infrastructure Security Agency's (DHS/CISA) National Risk Management Centre (NRMC) as a Senior Infrastructure Resilience and Threat Analysis Specialist.

Gairy, Sir Eric, PC (1922–1997)

After URGENT FURY, Gairy returned to Grenada and campaigned in the election of 1984. Cognisant of the public opinion he laid claim to being a changed man. However, his party lost the elections, winning 36 per cent of the popular vote but only a single seat in the House of Representatives. Gairy made further attempts to gain political power in 1990 and again in 1995. He was rejected by the people he had once so robustly abused. He died in Grand Anse, Grenada.

Howe, Richard Edward Geoffrey, Baron Howe of Aberavon, CH, PC, QC (1926–2015)

Howe retired as an MP in 1992 and was made a life peer in June of that year. Following his retirement from the Commons, Howe took on several non-executive directorships in business and advisory posts in law and academia. He retired from the House of Lords in May 2015.

Obituarists noted how Howe was 'warm and well-liked by colleagues', with Nigel Lawson writing that he would be remembered by those who knew him 'as one of the kindest and nicest men in politics'. According to Andrew Rawnsley of *The Observer*, Howe was frequently spoken of by fellow politicians 'as one of the most honest and decent practitioners of their profession'. Howe's devastating resignation speech in the House of Commons was calm and unemotional. However, it was deadly effective and triggered the fall from power of Margaret Thatcher. This photograph was taken in 2011.

McDonald, Admiral Wesley L., USN (1924–2009)

McDonald was the last United States admiral to command all three organisations – Allied Atlantic Command, US Atlantic Command and the US Atlantic Fleet. He relinquished those commands in 1985.

After he retired from the navy in 1985, McDonald played an active role in the aviation community in his leadership positions with the National Aeronautic Association (NAA) and the National Aviation Club (NAC). He helped orchestrate a merger of interests between the NAA and NAC, bringing benefits to both organisations.

Redhead, Lester

When he was released in 2007, Redhead expressed remorse about the events of October 1983. Speaking on behalf of himself and the others who were convicted, Mr Redhead said they were 'very sorry' for those events. 'I don't think it's a situation, an event that can be justified. I mean it was wrong, and it was wrong.' Lester Redhead also says he is making a serious attempt at reconciliation. He has been visiting people who supported efforts to have those convicted of those killings released.

He says since being freed he has contacted a relative of one of the coup victims, a woman who lost her father during the coup events. 'She found it necessary to forgive, and that has touched me in a deep and profound way,' Redhead said.

Other relatives have not been that forgiving, however, suggesting that those responsible for the deaths of Prime Minister Bishop and the others should be 'kept in prison for the rest of their natural lives'.

Metcalf, Vice Admiral Joseph III, USN (1927–2007)

At the conclusion of operations following the invasion of Grenada, Metcalf and several of his senior aides were caught attempting to bring captured Soviet-made AK-47s back to the US as war souvenirs, in violation of both military regulations and US customs law. Twenty-four AK-47s, along with twenty-four magazines, were seized by customs agents from the Vice Admiral's plane at Norfolk Naval Air Station, VA, when Metcalf and his officers were returning from the Grenada theatre.

As a direct result of intervention by President Reagan, Metcalf received only a caution from the navy regarding the incident, and it did not prevent him from later being appointed as Deputy Chief of Staff of Naval Operations for surface warfare. Adverse press accounts at the time noted that in the same conflict, six soldiers and one junior officer, of which two were Marines and five were soldiers from the 82nd Airborne Division, all received reduction in rank, dishonourable discharges and at least one year of prison for the same offence.

The probability is that this lapse of sound judgement cost Metcalf a fourth star and promotion to admiral.

Scholtes, Major General Richard A., USA (1934–)

Served as the first commander of Joint Special Operations Command. Scholtes was a key figure in Operation URGENT FURY, and he played an important role in the reorganisation of the US special operations organisation thereafter.

After his tenure as JSOC commander, Scholtes retired from active service so he could testify candidly in August 1986, before Congress, about the perceived need for a separate, four-star, special operations command.

Schwarzkopf, Major General H., Norman, Jr., KCB, USA (1934–2012)

Schwarzkopf became corps commander in 1986 and had risen to four-star general by 1988. At this point, he was appointed Commander-in-Chief of the US Central Command. In this appointment, he had responsibility for US operations in the Middle East.

After the Iraq invasion and occupation of Kuwait in August 1990, Schwarzkopf directed the assembly of 700,000 US, European and Arab troops to confront the Iraqis. He is pictured here as a general.

From 16 January 1991, allied forces under his command carried out a six-week-long air bombardment of Iraq and its positions in Kuwait. In a ground campaign that and lasted only 100 hours, allied forces speedily retook Kuwait and destroyed or incapacitated most of the Iraqi army, while suffering only minimal casualties themselves. Hailed as a national hero after the war, Schwarzkopf retired from active service later that year.

Scoon, Sir Paul, GCMG, GCVO, OBE (1935–2013)

Scoon published a book entitled *Survival for Service*, which provided a personal account of his experiences as Governor General. In it, he denied writing the 24 October letter, saying it had been delivered to him in draft form on 26 October, after he was rescued. He did, however, confirm that he had asked for US and Caribbean intervention. The accuracy of this book has been questioned.

Smith, Lieutenant Colonel Ray L., USMC (1946–)

Ray L. Smith is a lieutenant general of the USMC. He retired in 1999 after thirty-four years of service, during which he demonstrated that he is an outstanding leader. The award of two Silver Stars and a Navy Cross are testament to his personal courage.

When General Vessey visited Grenada in 1983, Smith told the Chairman of JCS, 'I thought my mission was to liberate Grenada and the [82nd] thought their mission was to attack Grenada.' This exchange was generated by the repeated reports by otherwise friendly Grenadian civilians on the conduct of the airborne soldiers.[2] Smith had twice protested to Metcalf about excessive bombardment of civilian areas by the army, 'but to no avail'.[3]

Smith recalled, 'I told my guys, more than once, that I was a hell of a lot more concerned of the 82nd Airborne than I was of the People's Revolutionary Army.'

For a Marine to comment adversely to the most senior general on the conduct of his army could well have been 'career inhibiting'. But Smith completed his tour in command of 2nd/8th Marine Regiment and moved on from success to success.

He has engaged in a number of community projects, is the co-author, with Bing West, of *The March Up: Taking Baghdad with the 1st Marine Division*. The book is an eyewitness account of the 1st Marine Division's march from Kuwait to Baghdad at the beginning of the Iraq War, published by Bantam in 2003. Smith is a founder and currently serves as Chairman of Sandboxx, a company dedicated to providing communication and lifestyle management tools for military members and their families.

Strachan, Selwyn

In an interview in Amnesty magazine *Wire* (Sept/Oct 2013 edition), Selwyn said:

> Amnesty never wavered in its relentless campaign against the death penalty in my case. Amnesty called for my freedom, and the freedom of my former death row inmates, since we had been incarcerated for years based on a trial which did not meet internationally accepted human rights standards. Amnesty's role in helping to save my life contributed a great deal to my present-day activism against the death penalty.

There is no record of Strachan expressing remorse.

Stroude, Christopher

Stroude is a changed man who now preaches the gospel to prisoners in the same prison that was his home for twenty-four years. In a late-night interview with the *Sunday Sun*, he asserted, 'God is great.' He continued, saying, 'Today I am a child of God. I am no longer an atheist.' The member of the St George's Seventh Day Adventist Church maintains his innocence up to this day. 'I never knew orders were given for Bishop to be killed. Although I was not in the square when he was killed, I was accused of his death.' During his years in prison, Stroude completed a BSc degree in economics, via long-distance education.

Tortolo, CU, Colonel Pedro Comas

The fate of this unfortunate officer, who could not possibly have influenced events in Grenada in October 1983, has been the cause of some speculation. There were reports that Castro wreaked punishment on those he deemed to have failed in Grenada and one of those was Tortolo. The Colonel was tried by court martial and, having been found guilty, was demoted to private. In a videotaped ceremony, the Defence Minister Raúl Castro ripped his rank insignia from his epaulettes. He was sent to fight in the war in Angola, along with twenty-five to forty other Cubans viewed as having surrendered too easily.

In Angola, Tortolo was killed in action – as a private soldier. However, there is another version and *Cuba Confidential*, published on 5 October 2013, claims:

> Although Tortolo was widely reported to have been killed in Angola, Miami Cubans who claim to know him said he returned home, was given a low-profile government job, and, at some point in 1999 or 2000, was selling shoes. They declined to provide his current contact information, saying he wanted to put Grenada behind him.
>
> Miami journalist, Camilo Loret de Mola, said he met Tortolo in 2003 when the former colonel was working as a taxi driver in Havana with his personal LADA, a Soviet vehicle.

Trobaugh, Major General Edward L., USA (1932–2024)

Trobaugh, who was born in 1932, came in for considerable criticism for his overly cautious command of the 82nd Airborne Division in Grenada. The very slow advance, despite minimal and ineffective opposition, was inexplicable. His role in command must have been subject to scrutiny. However, he survived and continued in command of the division until June 1985. Thereafter, he acted as deputy commander of 5th Army until his retirement in 1987, when he went to live in Kokomo, Indiana.

Notes

1. Bleier, E., 'Former US general: When Jesus comes back, he'll be carrying an AR-15' (UPI, 20 February 2014).
2. Kukielski, pp. 148–9.
3. Ibid.

Bibliography

Adkin, Major M., *Urgent Fury: The Battle for Grenada* (London, Leo Cooper, 1989).

Ambursley, F. and James W., 'Maurice Bishop and the New Jewel Revolution in Grenada' (*New Left Review*, Nov/Dec 1983).

Amnesty International Report, AMR 32/001/2003.

Atkinson, R., *The Long Gray Line* (New York, Henry Holt & Company, 2010).

Atkinson, R., *The Long Gray Line* (Boston, Houghton Mifflin, 1989).

'Auditing an invasion' (*Time*, 23 July 1984).

Baker, J.A., Chief of Staff to President Reagan in an interview by Chidester, J., Knott S.F. and Young, J.S., 15–16 June 2004 (Transcript, University of Virginia).

Beck, R.J., *The Grenada Invasion: Politics, Law and Foreign Policy Decision-making* (Boulder, Westview Press, 1993).

Bell, W., 'The American invasion of Grenada: A Note on False Prophecy' (*The Yale Review*, Vol. 75, No. 4, 1986).

Blanton, W., ed., 'Memorandum for the Executive Secretary, CIA Management Committee: Potentially Embarrassing Agency Activities' (George Washington University, National Security Archives, 8 May 1973).

Bohning, D., 'Lots of Story but No way to File it' (*Washington Post*, 28 October 1983).

Bolger, D.P., 'Operation Urgent Fury and its Critics' (*Military Review*, July 1986).

Bolger, D.P., *Special Operations and the Grenada Campaign* (USA, Carlisle, PA., US Army War College, 1988).

Bourne, G.H. 'Revolution, Intervention & Nutrition: What happened in Grenada' (*Nutrition Today*, Jan–Feb 1985).

Briggs, B., 'Billy Briggs on the Atrocities of Guatemala's Civil War' (London, *The Guardian*, 2 February 2007).

Britannica.com

Caribbean Witness Seminar, London, 29 May 2009.

Carney, J.T. and Schemmer, B.F., *No Room for Error: The Covert Operations of America's Special Tactics Units from Iran to Afghanistan* (New York, Ballantine Books, 2002).

Castro, Fidel, speech by, in Havana, 14 November 1983.

Castro, F., Elliot, J.M. and Dymally, M.M., *Nothing can Stop the Course of History* (New York, Pathfinder Press, 1988).

Catto, H.E., 'US Assistant Secretary of Defence' (*Los Angeles Times*, 11 November 1990).

Chalker, D.C. with Dockery, K., *One Perfect Op* (New York, Morrow, 2002).

Clymer, A.C., 'Grenadians Welcomed Invasion Poll Finds' (*New York Times*, 6 November 1983).

Cole, R.H., 'Grenada, Panama and Haiti: Joint Operational Reform' (*Joint Forces Quarterly*, Autumn/Winter 1998–9).

Cole, R.H., *Operation Urgent Fury, Grenada: The Planning and Execution of Joint Operations in Grenada 1983* (US Joint Chiefs of Staff, Washington, DC, Joint History Office, 1997).

Collier, P. and Horowitz, D., 'Another "Low Dishonest Decade" on the Left' (*Commentary*, January 1987).

Commander-in-Chief, US Atlantic Command, Operation URGENT FURY. 25 October–2 November (6 February 1984, Enclosure 2, Chronology).

Confidential memorandum from Dam to Reagan, 'Meeting with Prime Minister Maurice Bishop of Grenada June 7, 1983' (Department of State).

Couvillon, M.J., *Grenada Grinder: The Complete Story of AC-130H Spectre Gunships in Operation Urgent Fury* (Marietta, Georgia, Deeds Publishing, 2011).

Davidson, J.S., *Grenada: A Study in Politics and the Limits of International Law (*Aldershot, Gower Publishing, 1987).

Department of State and Department of Defense Preliminary Report, 16 December 1983.

'Documents on the invasion of Grenada' (*Caribbean Monthly Bulletin*, October 1983), Supplement No. 1.

Durant, M.J., Hartov, S. and Johnson, R.L., *The Night Stalkers: Top Secret Missions of the U.S. Army's Special Operations Aviation Regiment* (New York, G.P. Putnam's Sons).

'Elated Coard: Speaks of Prison' (*Jamaica Gleaner*, 13 September 2009).

'Eric Gairy: Carribean Hall of Fame.tripod.com' (caribbean.halloffame.tripod.com.)

'Excessive Severity: Treason and the Grenadian Rebellion of 1795' (UK National Archives, retrieved 4 August 2023).

Fialka, J.J., 'In Battle for Grenada, Commando Missions Didn't Go as Planned' (*Wall Street Journal*, 15 November 1983).

Fischer, B.B., *A Cold War Conundrum: The 1983 Soviet War Scare-Phase II. A New Sense*, 1997 (CIA Study).

Fraché, Colonel L.D.H., 'Grenada Lessons Learned' (briefing at Fort Leavenworth, KS, 14 February 1984).

Gordon, E., Bilder, A.W., Rovine. A.W. and Wallace, D., 'International Law and the United States Action in Grenada: A Report' (*The International Lawyer*, Vol. 18, No. 2, spring 1984).

Gormly, R.A., *Combat Swimmer: Memoirs of a Navy SEAL* (New York, Penguin Group, 1998).

Grenada: A Preliminary Report (US Department of State and Department of Defense, 16 December 1983).

Hall of Valor Project (*Military Times,* https://valor. militarytimes.com/hero/4094).

Haney, E.L., *Inside Delta Force: The Story of America's Elite Counterforce Unit* (New York, Dell Publishing, 2003).

Hobson, J.L., 'Operation Urgent Fury' (*Air Commando Journal*, spring 2012).

Holland, M.F., *America and Egypt: From Roosevelt to Eisenhower* (New York, Praeger Publishing, 1996).

House, J.M., *The United States Army in Joint Operations 1950–1983* (Washington, DC, US Army Center of Military History, 1992).

Howe, Sir G., restricted telegram, 'Grenada', No. 291, to UK High Commissioner.

Howell, P.A., *The Judicial Committee of the Privy Council, 1833–1876: Its Origins, Structure, and Development* (Cambridge, UK, Cambridge University Press, 1979).

'Hudson Austin, Biography' (www.thegrenadarevolutiononline.com).

'In nobody's back yard' (Bishop speaks, 13 April 1979).

Jenkins, L., 'Search and Destroy Patrols Under Way' (*Washington Post*, 30 October 1983).

Jones, C.V., *Boys of 67: From Vietnam to Iraq. The Extraordinary Story of a Few Good Men* (Mechanicsburg, PA, Stackpole Books, 2006).

Kallander, D.C. and Matthews, J.K., *Urgent Fury: The United States Air Force and the Grenada Operation* (Military Airlift Command, Office of History, Scott AFB, 1988).

Kaplan, F., 'The World came much Closer to Nuclear War than we Ever Realized' (*Slate* magazine, 17 April 2022).

Keller, B., 'Overhaul is Urged for Top Military' (*New York Times*, 22 January 1985).

Kissinger, H., quoted in his book *The White House Years (*Simon & Schuster, 2011).

Kukielski, P., *The US Invasion of Grenada: Legacy of a Flawed Victory* (Jefferson, North Carolina, McFarland & Co., 2019).

Lessons learned as a Result of the U.S. Military Operations in Grenada (US Congress, House Committee on Armed Services, 24 Jan 1984).

Leventhal, M.A., *Entrepreneurship and Nation Building: Proprietary Medical Schools and Development in the Caribbean 1976–1990* (doctoral dissertation, University of Chicago, 1995).

Levin, D.H., 'When the Great Power Gets a vote: The Effects of Great Power Electoral Interventions on Election Results' (*International Studies Quarterly*, June 2016).

Lieutenant Colonel R. Hagler, interviewed by Major C.R. Bishop, 30 October 1983.

Louison, G., *George Louison and Kenrick Radix discuss-: Internal events Leading to the U.S. Invasion of Grenada* (New York, Grenada Foundation, 1984).

Macintyre, B., *The Spy and the Traitor* (London, Penguin Books, 2018).

Malis, M., Querubin, P. and Shanker, S., 'Persistent Failure? International Interventions since World War I' (*The Handbook of Historical Economics*, January 2021).

Maraccini, M.J., 'Task Force 2/325 Operation Urgent Fury' (from a study conducted at Fort Benning, GA, 1988).

Maurice Bishop, Line of March Speech, 13 September 1982.

McDonald, Admiral W., in his 'After-action Report' to JCS, January 1984.

Mendoza, Jorge L., 'Granada, La Nueva Joya del Carib', *Grenada: The New Jewel of the Caribbean* (Havana. Editorial de Ciencias Sociales, 1982).

Metcalf, Admiral J., 'Decision Making and the Grenada Rescue' in *Ambiguity and Command: Organizational Perspectives on Military Decision Making*, ed., Marsh, J.G. (Marshfield Mass, Pitman Publishing, 2006).

Miles, S., 'The War Scare That Wasn't: Able Archer 83, and the Myths of the Second Cold War' (*Journal of Cold War Studies*, 1 August 2020).

Montalbano, W.D., 'Coup Began as a Debate Among Leftists' (*Los Angeles Times*, 21 October 1983).

Montgomery, D., 'Grenada: General Impressions', confidential telegram, No. 344 to UK Foreign and Commonwealth Office, 23 October 1983 (Margaret Thatcher Foundation Archives).

Moore, C., *Margaret Thatcher: The Authorised Biography* (London, Alan Lane, Vol. 2, Chapter 5, 'Reagan Plays her False', 2015).

Murphy, P., *Monarchy and the End of Empire* (Oxford, Oxford University Press, 2013).

O'Shaughnessy, H., *Grenada: Revolution, Invasion and Aftermath* (London, Sphere Books, 1984).

Oberdorfer, D., *From the Cold War to a New Era: The United States and the Soviet Union, 1983–1991* (New York, Grenada Foundation, 1984).

Ortiz, F.V., 'Grenada Before and After' (*Atlantic Monthly*, June 1984).

Paine, S.C.M., *The Wars for Asia 1911–1949* (New York, Cambridge University Press, 2012).

Payne, A., Sutton, P.K. and Thorndike, T, *Grenada Revolution and Invasion* (New York, St Martin's Press, 1984).

Perkins, A.H., 'Operation Urgent Fury: An Engineer's View' (*The Military Engineer*, 1984).

Pirnie, B.R., *Operation Urgent Fury: The United States in Joint Operations* (Washington, DC, US Army Center of Military History).

Powell, C.L., *A Soldier's Way* (London, Hutchinson, 1995).

Radix, K., *George Louison and Kenrick Radix discuss … internal events leading to the US invasion of Grenada*, (New York, Grenada Foundation, 1984).

Raines, E.F., *Rucksack War: US Army Operational Logistics in Grenada 1983* (Washington DC Center of Military History, 2010)

Reagan, R.W., *The Public Papers of President Ronald W. Reagan* (1981–9), (Reagan Presidential Library).

Reagan, President R.W., Speaking in London to the House of Commons on 2 June 1982.

Reagan, President R.W., Remarks on Central America and El Salvador at the Annual Meeting of the National Association of Manufacturers, 23 March 1983.

Reagan, President R.W., Press Conference, Washington, 25 October 1983.

Reagan, President R.W., interviewed by reporters at the White House on 25 October 1983.

Reagan, President R.W., 'Events in Lebanon and Grenada', Presidential Address to the Nation on 27 October 1983.

Reagan, President R.W., *An American Life* (New York, Simon & Schuster, 1990).

Report of the Duffus Commission of Inquiry into Breakdown of Law and Order and Policy Brutality in Grenada (London, FCO 63/1370).

Report of the Mission of the Special Rapporteur to the United Kingdom, Commissioner of Police of Barbados (UN Doc. E/CN.4/1998/39 add. 4, para 47, 5 March 1998).

Russell, L. and Mendez, M.A., *Grenada: Men at Arms, 1983* (London, Osprey, 1985).

Schoenhals, K.P. and Melanson, R.A., *Revolution and Intervention in Grenada: The New Jewel Movement, the United States and the Caribbea*n (New York, Routledge, 1986).

Schudel, M., 'Joseph Metcalf: Led Invasion of Grenada' (*Washington Post*, 11 March 2007).

Schultz, G.P., *Turmoil and Triumph: My Years as Secretary of State* (New York, Scribner, 1993).

Schwarzkopf interview, 21 November 1983.

Schwarzkopf interview, 15 December1987.

Schwarzkopf, H.N. and Petre, P., *It Doesn't Take a Hero: General H. Norman Schwarzkop* (London, Bantam 1992).

Scoon, Sir P., *Survival for Service: My Experiences as Governor General of Grenada* (Macmillan Caribbean, 2003).

Seabury, P. and McDougall, W.A., 'Extraordinary General Meeting, 25 September 1983' (San Francisco, Institute for Contemporary Studies. The Grenada Papers).

Smith, G. (*The Times*, November 1983).

Smith, H., 'US Defending Grenada Action Before OAS' (*New York Times*, 15 November 1983).

Speakes, L. and Pack, R., *Speaking Out: The Reagan Presidency from Inside the White House* (New York, Scribner, 1988).

Spector, R.H., *Marines in Grenada, 1983* (Washington, DC, History and Museums' Division, HQ USMC, 1987).

Steele, B.A., *Grenada: A History of its People* (London, Macmillan, 2003).

Strober, D.H. and Strober, G., *The Reagan Presidency: An Oral History of the Era* (London, Brassey's, 2003).

'Suriname Ousts Envoy and Halts Cuba Pacts' (*New York Times*, 27 October 1983).

Telegram, 'Grenada Revolutionary Council' (British High Commission to HMG Foreign and Commonwealth Office, London, 24 October 1983).

'The Maurice Bishop Murder Trial' (*The Grenadian Newsletter*, 6 December 1986, Vol. 14, No. 19).

'Theodore Roosevelt's Corollary to the Monroe Doctrine (1905)' (archives.gov/milestone-documents/Roosevelt-corollary, accessed 9 April 2021).

Tiwathia, V., *The Grenada War: Anatomy of a Low-intensity Conflict* (New Delhi, Lancer International, 1987).

Treaty of Basseterre, 1981.
United Kingdom (UN Doc. E/CN.4/1998/39 add. 4, para 47, 5 March 1998).
United Nations General Assembly Resolution 38/7, 2 November 1983.
US State Department, Office of the Historian (History.state.gov).
Vessey, in an interview with Ronald Cole, the official historian, 1997.
Walker, G., *At the Hurricane's Eye: US Special Forces from Vietnam to Desert Storm* (New York, Warner Books, 1990).
Washington Post, 24 November 1983.
Weinberger, C., *Fighting for Peace: Seven Critical Years in the Pentagon* (New York, Grand Central Publishing, 1990).
White House, memorandum of telephone conversation Reagan and Thatcher.
Wilder, A.E., 'Maurice Robert Bishop (1944–1983): The Grenada Revolution 2019' (The Grenada Revolution Online).
Wilford, H., *America's Great Game: The CIA's Secret Arabists and the Making of the Modern Middle East* (New York, Basic Books, 2013).

Index

In this context, USA post-nominal letters stand for US Army, USAF for United States Air Force, and USN for US Navy.

BDF is Barbados Defence Force and PRA is People's Revolutionary Army. Cubans are marked CU.